SETTLEMENT AND LOCAL HISTORIES OF THE EARLY DECCAN

This book is a detailed account of the multi-faceted history of the Deccan. Beginning with its historical foundations it goes on to delineate how it is the key to understanding its social, economic, political and ideological evolution.

Containing nine essays, this volume attempts to look at regional history from the perspective of given localities that provides the many facets of early Deccani society and culture. Hitherto, this was mainly articulated in terms of the broad categories of language and religion in the many historical studies of present-day linguistic states. In focussing on local spatial contexts as the primary layer of historical reality, the book has relied on multiple sources of information, largely extant archaeological material while also drawing information from inscriptions, textual material and oral memory. The book also reflects on the important events of various periods by placing them as part of larger social and economic processes emanating from the local.

The essays in this collection have been presented thematically moving from general issues discussed in Part I to the more particular in Part II and finally, to reflect on the multiplicity and simultaneity of different kinds of processes in a constant state of negotiation, in Part III. The historical sensibilities of people in various locations right from Kotalingala and Dhulikatta to Phanigiri, Patancheru, Kondapur and Nanakramguda and from Thotlakonda to Nagarjunakonda, Amaravati, Vaddamanu and Shravan Belgola have been recounted.

Aloka Parasher Sen Ph.D. (London) taught History at the University of Hyderabad. Since 2018, she is Professor Emeritus in the Department of Sanskrit Studies, University of Hyderabad.

Her major publications are in the area of her interest, i.e. social history, namely, early Indian attitudes towards foreigners, tribes and excluded castes and different aspects of the social, economic, cultural and religious history and archaeology of the Deccan.

Settlement and Local Histories of the Early Deccan

ALOKA PARASHER SEN

MANOHAR
2020

First published 2021
by Routledge
2 Park Square, Milton Park, Abingdon, Oxon OX14 4RN

and by Routledge
52 Vanderbilt Avenue, New York, NY 10017

Routledge is an imprint of the Taylor & Francis Group, an informa business

British Library Cataloguing-in-Publication Data
A catalogue record for this book is available from the British Library

Library of Congress Cataloging-in-Publication Data
A catalog record for this book has been requested

ISBN: 978-0-367-72621-8 (hbk)
ISBN: 978-1-003-15560-7 (ebk)

Typeset in Adobe Garamond 11/13
by Kohli Print, Delhi 110 051

MANOHAR

To Hyderabad for all that it gave me

Contents

Illustrations

MAPS

PLATES

Preface

This book has been put together with the earnest intention of presenting at one place my forays into understanding the early history of the Deccan. Apart from my other research, my interest at looking deep into the early history of the Deccan emerged out of my stay in Hyderabad for the most part of my academic life. Having been primarily trained in the use of textual sources for my doctoral work, research on early Deccan, where texts for the ancient period are largely absent, led me on to looking at other sources, like those emanating out of archaeological excavations. My initial interest in looking closely at the local particularity of the Deccan emerged when my professional pre-occupation with teaching history at the newly established University of Hyderabad propelled me to prepare new courses on the region that would have some relevance to students from the region, who were the first primary entrants to the new University. Their varied locations in different modern states that broadly covered what we have designated as the Deccan, then also provided me the immediate impetus to familiarize myself with the history of localities that they hailed from. At the outset therefore, I would like to thank the several batches of students that took courses with me for their attention and interest in taking these courses. Most significantly, my research students followed the cue and took up topics of research on different parts of the Deccan that also educated me on the still unearthed wealth of information that lay buried on the early and early medieval history of the Deccan. These students know well, the pains with which we all worked hard to bring to light this fascinating history. They cannot be thanked enough. Their endeavours became mine and vice versa leading to an energizing dialogic collaboration that benefited all of us.

Though my first individual interactions with the diversity of life around Hyderabad and visits to numerous historical destinations across the Deccan and South India were peripheral, they subsequently led me on to take up serious projects of study that resulted in research writings in the form of articles that are now put together in this book.

Two major projects that supported my research activities in a focused manner are the French Institute Pondicherry collaborative project with colleagues from other Universities of South India, namely, 'The Digital Historical Atlas of South India' funded by the Ford Foundation and, more recently, the interface collaboration on a project entitled: 'From Dargah to Patancheru' funded by the University Grants Commission under its UPE I and II programmes given to the University of Hyderabad. They provided not only financial support but, since they were part of collaborative activity they energized the academic questions posed and provided directions to how my research expanded. I would like to acknowledge this support and thank all concerned, who knowingly and unknowingly, became part of these endeavours.

Having written the articles, now converted into chapters, over a period of time and in different publishing locations, there would inevitably be some overlap of thought and data, which I have tried to minimize while editing them for this volume. By and large these articles had pertained to the early Deccan with only two of them (Chapters 6 and 8) bringing in the early medieval period. The last chapter veers into the contemporary period in order to take a look at the state of heritage and the challenges this poses for its conservation for posterity. Despite the chronological order in which they were published, I have tried to thematically divide them so as to put forward an argument that from our general concerns we should move to particular or individual themes of research and then finally to also suggest that the individual can only survive and flourish in the midst of interactions. Thus, we have three broad parts in which the chapters are organized, namely, Part I entitled 'Establishing the Terrain', Part II 'Standing on the Particular' and Part III 'Accessing the Other'. The rationale for doing so has been detailed in the Introduction to the volume.

While preparing the chapters on the issue of the way each of them had different citation styles, I have made an attempt to use a common footnoting style and have prepared a combined bibliography to address these citations. Diacritical marks have been kept to the minimal and have been made uniform across chapters. I have acknowledged at the beginning of the book, all the editors and publishers who have granted me permission to reprint some of the articles. I would like to now thank them for all the help rendered. Two of the chapters (Chapters 5 and 9) have not been published earlier. For a couple of them (Chapters 1 and 6) some changes in text have been made, while for the majority only marginal changes have been effected.

The long period during which these articles were written has meant that I am indebted to innumerable scholars and colleagues with whom I have shared the ideas incorporated in these articles. Some of the articles initially were presented at national and international seminars and conferences—Chapter 1 is based on my Presidential Address for the Ancient Section to the Andhra Pradesh History Congress held at Guntur, Chapter 2 was first presented at the Centre for Historical Studies, Jawaharlal Nehru University, Chapter 3 was presented at the Centre for Archaeological Studies in Eastern India and later at a conference at the Institute of Asian Studies, Leiden, The Netherlands, Chapter 4 was prepared for a conference organized by the Department of History and Classics at the University of Alberta, Edmonton, Canada and later presented at the Centre for Excellence at the University of Heidelberg, Chapter 7 was prepared for presentation at the Telugu University, Hyderabad and Chapter 9 was first written for oral presentation at a conference organized by the Department of History, University of Hyderabad. It was at all these locations and the meeting with scholars who reacted to my presentation that I was provided by the necessary impetus to proceed further and refine the gestating ideas to ultimately then write and publish the articles that form the core of this book. I sincerely thank all my colleagues and friends for having provided this energetic academic environment which enabled me to complete my research.

Over the years, the late Dr. V.V. Krishnasastry, the late Dr. B. Subramanyam and Dr. E. Siva Nagi Reddy of the former State Department of Archaeology and Museums, Government of Andhra

Pradesh had always been forthcoming with providing me information on the excavations conducted by them. It was their deep knowledge of the region under study that enabled me to grapple with the significance of the local in a meaningful way. I place on record my sincere thanks to them.

Last but not the least this book has taken shape after I occupied my new position as Professor Emeritus at the Department of Sanskrit Studies, University of Hyderabad. Without the congenial atmosphere provided by the Department and the positive interactions that I have had with colleagues and students here, my endeavours would not have been so pleasantly accomplished. I would like to thank all of them and especially the office staff for giving me the much needed infrastructural support.

Long hours of proof-reading were intercepted with talking to Urvi, my grand-daughter who provided the much needed joy and creative impulse for continuing doggedly with the task on hand. In some unknown and enchanting ways she has become a part of this endeavour.

24 April 2019 ALOKA PARASHER SEN

Acknowledgements

The author and the publishers would like to thank the editors and publishers of the journals and books listed below for the permission they have granted for the inclusion in this volume of the material cited:

For: 'Defining the Deccan: The Archaeology of Localities and the Writing of Regional History', *Journal of Deccan Studies*, Centre for Deccan Studies, vol. I, no. 1, 2003, pp. 14-32, the editor and publisher, *Journal of Deccan Studies*, Centre for Deccan Studies, Hyderabad.

For: 'Localities Coins and the Transition to the Early State in the Deccan', *Studies in History*, vol. 23, no. 2, n.s., 2007, pp. 231-69, the editors of *Studies in History* and Sage Publications, New Delhi.

For: 'Urban Centres—Deccan', in Gautam Sengupta and Sharmi Chakraborty (eds.), *Archaeology of Early Historic South Asia*, Pragati Publications, New Delhi in collaboration with Centre for Archaeological Studies and Training, Eastern India, Kolkata, 2008, pp. 313-35, the editors and the Centre for Archaeological Studies and Training, Eastern India, Kolkata.

For: 'Unravelling the Reality of a "City" on the Deccan Plateau', in Adam Kemezis (ed.), *Urban Dreams and Realities: Remains and Representation of the Ancient City*, Brill, Leiden, 2014, pp. 89-107, the editor and Brill, Leiden.

For: 'Understanding Local History: Archaeological Remains at Patancheru' (with R. Himabindu), *Journal of Deccan Studies*, vol. IV, no. 2, July-December 2006, pp. 5-27, the editor and publisher, *Journal of Deccan Studies*, Centre for Deccan Studies, Hyderabad.

For: 'History and Literature: Unravelling Conversations in the Local Context of Buddhist Deccan, in D.N. Jha (ed.), *The Complex Heritage of Early India: Essays in Memory of R.S. Sharma*, Manohar, New Delhi, 2014, pp. 327-46, the editor and Manohar Publishers & Distributors, New Delhi.

For: 'Renunciation and Pilgrimage in the Jaina Tradition: Continuity and Change in the Deccan', *Journal of Deccan Studies*, Special Issue on Jainism (Guest Editor: Aloka Parasher Sen), vol. V, no. 1, January-June 2007, pp. 157-76 (now titled under Chapter 8 as 'Renunciation and Jaina Tīrthas), the editor and publisher of *Journal of Deccan Studies*, Centre for Deccan Studies, Hyderabad.

In addition I would like to acknowledge the financial support from various funding agencies and thank them:

— To the Ford Foundation through the French Institute, Pondicherry co-ordinated project 'Historical Atlas of South India' that helped do field-work and collect data for Chapters II, III and V.

— To the Saroj and Prem Singhmar Chair in Classical Indian Polity and Society at the University of Alberta, Canada for field-work at 'Kondapur' for Chapter IV.

— To University of Hyderabad's UGC for University with Potential for Execellence Phase II programme that granted project 'From Dargah to Patancheru' for Chapters VI and IX.

17 April 2019 ALOKA PARASHER SEN

Abbreviations

APDAM	Andhra Pradesh Department of Archaeology and Museums
ASI	Archaeological Survey of India, New Delhi
EI	*Epigraphica Indica*
IAR	*Indian Archaeology: A Review*
ICRISAT	International Crop Research Institute of Semi-Arid Tropic, Hyderabad
KEAR	'*Kondapur Excavations*', *Annual Report* 1940-1 of Archaeology Department of H.E. the Nizam's Dominions, Hyderabad
HUDA	Hyderabad Urban Development Authority, 1998, 2000

Introduction

As soon as one turns to write a regional history, there is an anxiety to define the region of our study in specific terms. It is our intention in this volume to try and define the Deccan but at the same time, there is a recognition that within this large landmass of the subcontinent there are flexible boundaries and heterogeneous entities that have continually changed to define her character from time to time. The simplistic paradigm of looking at linearity and spatial confinement have been challenged to reflect on the earliest historical foundations of her personality that can provide a basis around which questions can be posed to understand her social, economic, political and ideological evolution.

The objective existence of a 'region' is questionable. In a minimal sense it is a 'bounded space' but the accompanying questions of who/what delimits a region remain. What are its distinguishing characteristics? And how do disciplines define regions? These automatically complicate the nature of that 'bounded space'. Apart from geographic markers that may define a region, one must at the first instance begin with the recognition that the historical conceptualization of regions is accompanied by several factors—political and military activities, technological and economic processes of change and administrative actions by states/kingdoms and so on. Regions, thus, are never given or are self-evident entities of analysis. They are necessarily marked out with human interaction—political, technological, economic, social and religious. These defining facets have to be delineated from extant material remains since it is often the case that all of them may not define the entire region. In some cases they may coincide with each other and make it possible for us to outline certain clear spatial and cultural variables that give a region its temporal identity. Eventually we must begin with the assumption that the notion of a region remains tenuous. Further, that it also interacts with spatial entities beyond its boundaries and therefore, social identities within a given region survive only through their cultural structures and the network of places that hosted them implying of course social and economic functions, which are now no longer visible. Thus, only the extant material remains enable one to embody a region with a semblance of identity while absences of what has not survived can only be imagined and interpreted upon.

It is commonplace to follow rather simplistically an old English adage 'Geography is about Maps and History is about Chaps'. This could not be more off the mark in today's interdisciplinary environment and neither parts of this statement are of course true. The former is now increasingly understood in terms of human intervention with space that changes boundaries in time and the latter is today a discipline that must necessarily be more inclusive. Given the development of both the disciplines in contemporary times, there are a few key issues that have to be highlighted at the outset. Most historians value knowledge of the past in a way, which gives primacy to the dimensions of 'time' rather than 'space' in understanding historical reality.[1] Today this, as the only legitimate view of the past, is under scrutiny by geographers, who wish to identify the spatial context as being far more significant in social science theory than has hitherto been the case. Thus Soja,[2] while introducing his *Post Modern Geographies,* notes that space is immediately viewed in terms of its multiple dimensions but when we begin to describe this space, language imposes linearity. In other words, a sequence is described and therefore, there is a losing out on the simultaneity of what space gives us and this is then taken over by 'time' and, over a longer duration, by History. The multiplicity and simultaneity of historical events and processes has to be kept in mind so that the spatial context can be shown not only to change over time but that at a given point of time, it is inhabited by co-existing historical levels of development.

The relevance of this understanding for looking closely at Deccan's history is that over space and time we can highlight the interconnectedness of heterogeneity and variability that define certain geographical and social compositions that by their very innate nature are complex. The focus on a study of particular sub-regions and localities of the Deccan therefore, became necessary as this enabled an analysis of the inter-dependence of such complex entities, which then showcased diversity and variability but yet, were part of an interconnected pattern of social change. We draw in contemporary theory[3] to make the critical point that complex regions like the Deccan throw up intransient forces that do not collapse all diversity into singular and homogenous models of growth. We argue in these chapters that both the particularity of space and the specificity of time have to be galvanized to discuss this trajectory of change and it is for this reason that for certain elements of this exercise Taylor's use of the terminology 'unruly complexity' comes in useful. It is our submission that environments that lie at the interceses of rich ecological diversity survive only in dependence with each other. It is the co-existence of a variety of landscapes in close proximity to each other that then defines their character of sustenance. This was noticed well into the twentieth century by not only British officials but also ordinary travellers who noted the challenge of traveling across this landscape's diversity.[4]

It was a terrain difficult to travel across as over large parts one was confronted with a landscape that was still marked with huge Archean rock-formations. These are considerably older than any human structural interventions on this landscape. One does not subscribe to the notion that nature alone determines the pace of a civilization's progress but one would concur with Griffith that 'Nature determines the route of development, while Man determines the *rate* and the *stage*'[5] (emphasis added). This plateau is the vast hinterland of both the eastern and western coastline of Peninsular India. Hinterlands in the present understanding are those areas in this region that have limited potentiality for large-scale agrarian production, being dependant on constrained geographical features like the non-availability of large tracts suitable for cultivation, with only monsoon fed water sources, being incessantly interspersed by rocky, shrub infected landscapes that are least conducive for any effective large-scale productive activity and so on. The particular significant feature of this ostensibly 'unruly' hinterland that we wish to highlight is the tenacity with which the ancient settlements that emerged in the midst of these difficult terrains survived. An element of sustained sustenance particular to the nature of resources available led to the accumulation of knowledge about a variety of food production processes that was reflected in different modes of production. Even in the agricultural domain, mixed farming became the norm rather than the exception in these parts. Recent studies into crop diversity patterns in this part of the country has revealed movements by farmers to lead campaigns to protect their seed diversity[6] as that is what is best suited to the terrain rather than bring in cash crops alien to its environment. This knowledge base created a unique basic structure of village life, which according to Paddayya goes back to first farming communities of the Neolithic times. He argues incisively that 'the larger political and socio-religious conditions may have undergone drastic changes across time but these had little or no effect on the basic structure of village-based agropastoral life which had its genesis in the Neolithic period and tied tightly to the region's resource base.'[7] The adaptational strategies point to change but there was a tenacity with which the pattern of subsistence continued to negotiate with the diversity of its landscape. Studies for different periods in its history clearly establish it as home to various habitations and political upheavals that emerged on this particularity of the Deccani landscape.

In the Southern Peninsular as a whole, interspersed as it is by hills and forests, there has been a tendency in some locations for its inhabitants to isolate themselves in what are called *culs de sac* or refuge zones. These have been called 'areas of isolation' and primarily inhabited by tribal populations.[8] The larger domain of the Deccan has a different nomenclature used by Subbarao to describe it, namely, 'areas of relative isolation'. In this differentiation we consciously bring to attention zones that are perhaps 'unruly' and most certainly complex, not because they are isolated or inaccessible but because it is difficult to put them all in similar frame of a uniform cultural or physical landscape. In fact, Subbarao suggests that these are zones which, apart from highlighting diverse ecologies are also those through which 'trans-continental communication' happened. This has historically led it to form certain particularities and peculiarities in the way influences from outside the region impacted it. He writes: 'The areas of relative isolation are characterized by their distance from the main highways for the movement of peoples and cultures. Hence they display a different and complicated culture pattern, since their isolation was frequently broken by fresh movements and we see a curious pattern of survival of the older with the new.'[9] It is thus that mass of land through which, over historical times, peoples, products and ideas have traversed from the plains of the north India that was shielded by the Himalayas, to the far South marking the southernmost tip of the subcontinent. Historical forces of change have converged on this unique landscape highlighting interesting economic trajectories of material change alongside socio-political interactions of confluence while maintaining a distinctness that brought together complex characteristics and traits that are difficult to iron out and homogenize. It is this that the chapters in this volume aim to capture. Clearly, we do not want to depict the Deccan historically as merely acting as a bridge in carrying the highly evolved norms of civilized life from the north Indian plains to the far south. Rather, it is our intention to highlight is own internal dynamics of historical genesis and change and assess the extent to which it incorporated external influences.

The initial motivation for my studies on hinterlands of the Deccan was to focus on relatively marginal localities of Telengana (then located in the linguistically unified state of Andhra Pradesh). These localities had significant historical data, frequently ignored in the meta-historical narratives of the larger regional identity formation since it did not fit into the dominant historical narrative propounded for the newly formed state of Andhra Pradesh in the late 1950s. Much after several of the articles in this collection were first published, I was involved with an interesting project on preparing a *Digital Historical Atlas for South India.*[10] In a broad sense maps are cultural products, which express the beliefs of those who created them, and as such are an index to ideas that are not necessarily found in such a multi-faceted way in other extant more traditional and ancient texts. This endeavour of making a digital historical atlas had to first take into account that historically, imperial designs of states have over time struggled to reshape boundaries and societies and that the boundaries thus created by them are only transitory. Such tendencies continue even today. Many of the articles now forming chapters in this volume were written before the formation of the present-day state of Telangana and therefore the same region was referred to through another nomenclature that formed the composite state of Andhra Pradesh. This reflects a historical point in time in which the superstructure of political control passed on to a new elite. However, space and place in it are in fact relational, constructed, imagined, and often, deeply contested. In looking back to the past, the pinpointing of time is critical in defining boundaries, space and place. However, implicit in the way time and history are written about today, are certain paradigms of theory and interpretation, which lead us to another significant point of recognition, namely, that history cannot lay claim to a pure past devoid of interpretation and representation.

In our contemporary times we also need to recognize that there is before us a broader public discourse about 'history' with popular, even mass, appeal that falls outside the oversight structures of professional historians. Rejecting all the suppositions upon which the discipline of history is built would be too far-fetched but a space for public knowledge about the past that is not encased in theory and complicated jargon has to be allowed for a while, opening up a dialogic approach to retrieving the past. In fact, as opposed to the academic and the intellectual elite in general, a majority of lay people are usually interested in their local past with an immediacy about understanding it in a narrative/visual form that is shorn of accretions of controversy and complex explanations. Mapping these local moments within a larger whole from time to time thus becomes a challenging task and it is a task that we have tried to incorporate in this book. At stake here is the question of how regional identity can eclipse the complexities of local identities that are firmly rooted in the region but have their own particular trajectory of evolution. For local and small communities maintaining the memory of their past in modes of representation that is acceptable to all is of great value rather than merely that which is dictated by formal research methods and sources of the different modern disciplines—geology, geography, archaeology, history and the like.

For the earliest periods of Deccan's history, archaeology seems to have turned into a proof giver to construct a timetable of history in a region that has few literary records for corroboration during the pre-medieval period. For the medieval period the magnitude of the monumental remains overtake other aspects of the historical narrative so much so that all history gets subsumed as the history of important sites. In both cases historiographically not much attention has been given to understanding social processes and the socio-cultural context of artefact complexes or the extant monumental remains.The danger of eulogizing a forgotten past within an essentialized and primordial frame to assert a dogmatic ideology of uniqueness of the sub-region and its people had to be avoided.[11] In my earlier writings I have explained how over time regions and sub-regions developed a tenuous identity that changed in the context of the demands of the economic and political challenges of the times.[12] In other words, all periods did not exhibit similar boundaries for a particular sub-region under discussion, and in some periods the local identity was necessarily more prominent than the total identity.[13] By creating several parameters for the retrieval of the data through the use of multiple sources like tools, coins, writing samples, buildings, burials, and religious edifices, and within each further demarcating several types by using written material and oral memory found in local contexts, it became possible to highlight in greater depth the intricate nature of the way early historic settlements emerged in this hinterland. In straddling the diversity of time, space, and data thus discussed we noted a multiplicity and simultaneity of different kinds of processes in a constant state of negotiation. For those seeking to look for a region's monumental aspects with an element of permanence and certainty, this kind of characterization of the formation of settlements as explicated in some of the chapters in this volume is perhaps inhibiting. This is so because a layering of the small but significant pieces of information has often been ignored by scholars but, in my opinion, these were the ones that we have to use to inscribe the past of these localities in decidedly different but complex ways. The effort was to avoid the pitfall of essentializing and romanticizing the local by simply glorifying the apparently monumental in one area, which in any case, in the earlier historiography was not considered on par with the monumental and classical as found in other sub-regions of the Deccan as a whole.

The 'unruly complex' environments of the Deccan, we argue, were also important to analyse for another reason. They helped us introduce questions and themes that disturbed conceptual boundaries, as for instance, the question of linearity in understanding social change in terms of a universal definition of progression. Thus, for instance, the socio-political and economic units that were focussed upon in Chapter 3 and had been loosely called 'urban' or 'cities' became terms that were difficult to apply across various kinds of settlements in the Deccan that arose during our chosen chronological period for discussion, namely, 300 BCE-400 CE. The so-called early historic urbanization was difficult to envisage in an environment traversed by limited expansive agrarian tracts, perennial water sources and broken into by a rugged landscape of hard rocky foundations. The environment did give rise to settlements but each of a different kind, some that may fit into the definition of an early historic urban centre as available for other regions of the country. However, apart from describing a monument in all its architectural details, the name and achievements of various kings known through their coins and inscriptions, the location of urban settlements in the particular landscape of the hinterland and their socio-economic context was hardly considered as a factor in understanding them in earlier studies on the region.

The specificity of archaeological artefacts found at these hinterland settlements, each telling their own local story were squarely compared to those that had become signs and models of age found in more prosperous sub-regions. Further, the intangibles of how the Buddhist monks interacted and lived off the local inhabitants, the opening up of local spaces to traders of all hues and colour, and the way local artists, craftsmen, technologists coped with all these changes, were hardly considered the themes that scientifically trained archaeologists and scholars discussed or wrote about. In some of the chapters we have brought in sources like stories, oral narratives and recent literature to capture the textures of time in ways the more hard core sources of information like the archaeological artefact, monuments, inscriptions and coins would be able to capture. In fact, as we delineate below, the last of the chapters in this book discusses changes in a local hitherto rural environment in contemporary times to gauge how communities here remember their past. Scholars who use the techniques of doing ethnographic-cum-archaeological work tell us that wherever the archaeologists try using local memory to understand their archaeological monuments and artifacts, they find it deeply rooted in a strong sense of the community, which has its own version of those remains. Thus the newfound interest of historians of memory suggests that 'History is commemorative, not because it resurrects living memory, but because it is constructed out of these ruins of imagination'.[14] These memories naturally reflect on local situations and in no way talk of the region as a whole, least of all, the country as a whole.

No doubt formation of identities have to draw on history but in doing so scholars have to simultaneously look afresh at the question 'whose identity?' are we talking about. As Ian Hodder writes one can suggest that 'some interpretations of the past are not as good as others, that not everything can be said with equal integrity. . . .' But, he goes on 'The contemporary social basis of our reconstructions of the past . . . must understand where our ideas come from, and why we want to reconstruct the past in a particular way.'[15] Diversity in Deccani culture and indeed, Indian culture as a whole, has been much talked about but articulated only in terms of broad categories as those based on language and religion. These tendencies have inhibited our being able to focus on understanding the commemorative leavings of the past enshrined in small artifacts or icons, and even monumental buildings in a local spatial context, which do not fit into totalities of pan-regional or pan-Indian identities. In our opinion they in fact, constitute the primary layer of a reality, which may reflect on larger events of time, but necessarily were not originally constituted to do so. Having survived, often in fragments, it is pertinent for us to analyse the human imagination in these local structures to identify a collective memory of the people at a local level. By only placing them as part of larger social and economic processes, they get subsumed within the broader concerns of the centrality of theory.

This search for the history of 'locatedness' we ultimately argue, must be seen in bringing forth both local and non-local elements so that in order to capture power relations it is possible to show that it operated within the fluid spatio-temporal bounds of the unit. Thus, we break away from existing models of historical interpretation and wish to also emphasize that the historical development at the local level can also unravel the experiences of the local community. In fact, several overlapping territorialities need to be cognized since it is the multiple layers of this complexity that enables an understanding of the negotiating elements that go into making the local community. Local histories dot the pan-regional and pan-Indian landscapes and we have to understand their interactive elements as well since they go into the making of a total system, which is the Indian subcontinental civilizational entity. We conclude with a suggestion from Todorov to remember that it is essential that the 'restricted universality of the past should be opened up as much as possible, until it is able to account for both the diversity of cultures and the differences which exist within one and the same culture'.[16] This type of analysis must then necessarily draw on local situations, within broader regional contexts. For regional constructions, the past, it must be fundamentally recognized, resides locally and not nationally. It is well recognized by social theorists that there is no space for value-free archaeology or history that is being done out there in the field or the archival room. The best solution Ian Hodder suggests is: 'Perhaps our own contexts and past context can be critically evaluated in terms of each other.'[17] An attempt to do so has resulted in the various articles written over the years by me that now form the different chapters of this volume.

The volume is divided into three parts. Part I 'Establishing the Terrain' emphasizes on definitions of the region, locality and urban centre. It delineates the essential direction in which each of these entities is understood by us. The first chapter explains the reasons why this is necessary and Chapters 2 and 3 develop these ideas in the context of understanding the processes of state formation and urbanization respectively. All the three chapters raise theoretical issues that point to the fact that when looking at regional history, models of explanation valid for a pan-Indian situation need not apply. This thus raises the concomitant question of how one should frame the data from these regions into a coherent argument diverging from earlier frames of reference. 'Defining the Deccan' in Chapter 1 sets the tone for this volume in that it articulates a perspective that underlines the importance of understanding her by first delineating the importance of the small and local within her. Since originally these views were presented orally, the first part of the chapter retains the generality of raising key points that need to be addressed in this regard. The latter part of this chapter is an exemplification of two areas of the Deccan, namely, Telangana and coastal Andhra that are strikingly same and yet different. Post-2014 when Telangana was formed, attempts at writing its history began in earnest. These histories must recognize that all regions and localities do emerge with their distinct identity but this is not in isolation but in constant interaction with contiguous areas. It was for this reason why history cannot provide a static identity but one that is constantly changing every time to incorporate different characteristics on the way.

Chapter 2 continues to expand on the issue of the difference between the hinterland sub-region of Telangana with a focus on the mid-Godavari valley locality and contrast it with the Andhra coastal areas, with a focus on the lower Krishna valley locality. It unravels data that can be found in local contexts and how it can be used to elaborate on processes of historical change. It takes the example of the above-mentioned localities in terms of the interconnected sites or places within these two sub-regions of the Deccan to indicate how similarities and differences played out in the rise of the early state in these parts.

Chapter 3 goes on to expand why difference in the making of the various sub-regions of the Deccan have to be highlighted by taking a close look at the way the so-called 'urban centres' and other settlements emerged in these sub-regions. With a focus on the advantages and pitfalls of using archaeological data in a regional context it first raises issues about how labelling is done of the archaeological data, often misleading the direction of research to be undertaken. The fundamental question of comparing the evolution and nature of urban centres with other regions, particularly the Ganges plains is raised to underline the idea that differences in their emergence must also effectively be raised. In a large part this chapter gives a broad overview of how in its different sub-regions the Deccan saw a proliferation of various kinds of settlements that had been brought to light by earlier studies on the region.

Part I having set the background, in Part II entitled 'Standing on the Particular' we see a set of articles that go into details of specific sites. The aim here is to highlight variance and difference in the way settlements historically evolved over time on the Deccan plateau and for which purpose. Chapters 4 and 6 address the question of how primarily trade and economic centres leave behind a religious imagery that is difficult to contain within the parameters of one faith. The evidence on economic and trade activity is emphatic at Kondapur and it is interesting that labelling it as a purely Buddhist centre has become problematic. Patancheru, on the other hand, has been a lived in space, unlike the former and therefore, evidence of its ancient and early medieval economic activity is minimal. However, this chapter addresses how a variety of art historical data left behind in fragments, dislocated from their original context, poses challenges in reconstructing the history of the place. In both cases the particularity of their existence was important to emphasize. Chapter 4 on Kondapur also raises the question of how two different excavations at the site came up with two different interpretations about the nature of the site in terms of its religious affiliation. In Chapter 6 on Patancheru, a substantial part of our efforts were to draw in as much information on the place through its extant art historical remains to carve out a local history that is rapidly disappearing due to the fast-moving economic changes engulfing the place.

In the context of writing about early historic urban centres, it is usually assumed that any site with monumental remains that has survived was a city. We therefore, raise the particularity of *vihāra* settlements in Chapter 5 by taking a close look at two monasteries of the Deccan. At Thotlakonda we focussed on describing several water cisterns that were excavated on the hilltop where this monastery was located to argue that the monks were deeply concerned about conservation of water. The same picture emerges from the descriptions of another monastery located on a hill top called Phanigiri. In this case we focussed on expanding on the layout of its *vihāra* settlement. The structures found clearly indicate that these were habitations for monks and were surrounded by a rural countryside for their sustenance. The question whether these settlements should be called 'urban' is problematic though material remains found during the course of the excavations conducted here do indicate the presence of coined money and other objects indicating economic munificence.

Part III is entitled 'Accessing the Other' and addresses issues around the interface of religious and social history that emerge out of a study of regional history. The chapters in this part have been put in a chronological order beginning in Chapter 7 with a focus on Buddhism and its interactions in the local context of an important zone in which it flourished, namely, Nagarjunakonda. Many facets of the history of Nagarjunakonda are well-known. However, we have chosen to focus on how a modern imaginative literary narrative of the place does help us get a realistic picture of how social and religious interactions took place in this important centre of Buddhism. In the latter half of this chapter we have drawn on inscriptions and art historical material to propose that some of what was written in the above narrative fits in well with historical evidence found at the site.

This is followed in Chapter 8 by taking close look at the Jaina faith and its spread into the Deccan with a particular focus on its pilgrimage network as it had evolved during early medieval times around one of the most important centres, namely Shravana Belgola. This chapter brings out the tensions of the ultimate goal of the Jaina faith in renunciation and how over historical time, Jainism began to become a religion with a strong institutional base. The process of making these important religious centres or pilgrimage places then provided a new interpretation of how the faithful looked at the notion of renunciation by visiting places where the monks and nuns as well as some laity had undertaken the vows of *sallenkana*. Apart from inscriptions and art historical material, we have brought in stories to look at how the faith continued to define its goal in sustaining the ideal of renunciation.

The last chapter in this part on Nanakramguda brings us to contemporary times with the avowed aim at looking at the multiplicity of little traditions that remain intact in a place despite far reaching changes impacting the lives of the inhabitants. This chapter retrieves briefly the key extant historical structures that are still intact at this place. However, the main focus in this chapter has been on the fact that given the fast moving changes engulfing this hitherto village, how did the communities remember their past and relate it to the present. This exercise enabled us to recognize that for these people understanding the past was not to be viewed as an alien land but very much entwined in their present. All the three chapters have at their centre the issue of local populations and the way they interacted with outsiders that inhabited their spaces from time to time. While in chapters 7 and 8 these issues are woven around their religious identities, in chapter 9 the focus is around the social and economic status the various communities had and in that context how they accessed the religious in their environment.

The aim in putting together this collection was to present before readers my research on the Deccan over the last three decades at one place. But more importantly, the chapters in this volume hope to generate more interest in future scholars on the Deccan taking a look at data that is often only available to us in fragments, in particular, in sub-regional and local situations. This may not be amenable for interpretation within simplistic deductive theories that would prompt us to fit it into a larger pan-Indian narrative. Nonetheless, individuality of place and time must necessarily be highlighted to ultimately generate greater debate on how the history of the subcontinent should be more equitably presented.

NOTES

1. A good example is the way historical maps are made as for example Schwartsberg's historical atlas, 1978.
2. Soja, 1989: 21-3.
3. Taylor, 2005: Prologue, xiii.
4. Frere, 1989: Preface to the Third Edition, ix-x.

5. Taylor, 1953: 14-15.
6. Sateesh, 2001.
7. Paddayya, 2019: 133.
8. Subbarao, 2011: 7; 1958: 8-35, identifies these as 'areas of isolation' in contrast to *perennial nuclear regions* identifiable as the chief river basins of the country.
9. Subbarao, 2011: 8.
10. This exercise was part of a project on preparing a Digital Historical Atlas for South India now accessible at the French Institute of Pondicherry Historical Atlas of South India Website: http://www.ifpindia.org/histatalas accessed 2010-01-11.
11. Parasher Sen, 2009: 183-207.
12. Parasher Sen, 2006: 91-8.
13. Parasher Sen, 2007: 231-69.
14. Review Essay on Jacque Le Goff, 1994: 77.
15. Hodder, 1986: 169.
16. Todorov in Gates, 1986: 374.
17. Hodder, 1986: 161.

PART I

ESTABLISHING THE TERRAIN

CHAPTER 1

Defining the Early Deccan: A Re-think*

The Deccan can be characterized as that area of the Indian sub-continent where cultures meet. The roots of this go back to earliest settlements found here. However, at the same time, three major components define the unique individuality: its physical and environmental specificity, its long and continuous history and its cultural heterogeneity. These characteristics entwine with each other in space and time to project textures of cultural plurality that cannot be described in simple compartments of rigid identities in linear capsules. Continuity and integration, thus, mark its social landscape that is also found in its geographical complexity.

The Deccan is a heterogeneous and complex physical locale, being one of the oldest land masses in the world. The physical Deccan (Map 1.1) is broadly understood as the land south of the Vindhyas and up to the Krishna-Tungabhadra basin. Over this broad geographical area, except for the rivers Narmada and Tapti, the others like the Godavari, Krishna and Pennar flow from west to east into the Bay of Bengal, cutting across the Deccan Plateau. The high altitude Ghats and strategic passes on its western part mark its physiographic and ecological heterogeneity. The Konkan coast further to the west is rather narrow. In contrast to the black soil of the Maharashtra areas, moving towards the centre of the

* First published as 'Defining the Deccan: The Archaeology of Localities and the Writing of Regional History', *Journal of Deccan Studies*, vol. I, no. 1, June-December 2003, pp. 14-32. This article was based on an oral Presidential Address 'Small Localities and the Writing of Regional History' for the Ancient Andhra History and Archaeology Section of Andhra Pradesh History Congress at Guntur, 1996.

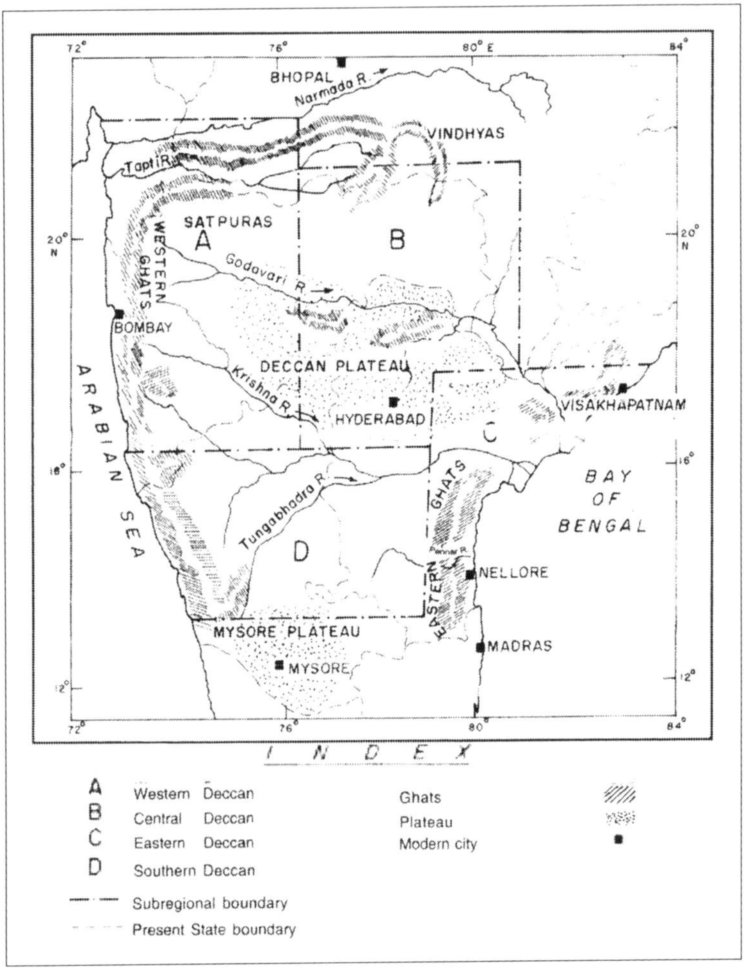

Source: Map prepared by the author.

Map 1.1: The Physical Deccan

Deccan, there is an upland plateau marked by red soil in many parts that does not retain much moisture. This is Telangana territory that has, therefore, been described as the land of tanks and artificial irrigation throughout history. The eastern parts of the Deccan, with the low-lying hills and ranges is, characteristically, home to the land of wide fertile deltas and the plains of the rivers,

Godavari and Krishna. The eastern plains are broader than the western ones and the alluvial soil has helped the sustenance of cultural growth, particularly in the Krishna basin, almost endlessly throughout history. The coastal plains show considerable variations from north to south. Nonetheless, the eastern coastal plains were important for generating an agrarian surplus and they cover the entire area from Mahendragiri hills in the north to the boundaries of the state of Tamil Nadu in the south. In the southern sub-region of the Deccan, the upper reaches of the Krishna-Tungabhadra plains cut across the plateau. The fertile Raichur Doab marks the land between these two rivers.

A major portion of the southern India, has historically been called *Dakshinapatha* or *Dakkhinapatha* in ancient Sanskrit and Pali literature, a geographical notion that literally meant 'path to the south' or 'to set foot in the south'. The Deccan was clearly identifiable as being a part of this description, and one of its greatest early rulers, Satakarni I, styled himself as *Dakshinapathpati* or 'Lord of the South'. He was the member of one of the earliest dynasties in southern India that had the nucleus of their power outside Ganga valley. Ultimately, the Sātavāhanas ruled a major part of the present-day states of Maharashtra, Telangana, Andhra Pradesh and Karnataka which fits in well with the description of the Deccan that is currently popular. Medieval sources in Persian and Urdu commonly use the term *Dakkhan* to describe the territorial as well as cultural parameters of their control that clearly included a major part of these present-day states as well. Madhya Pradesh and Orissa surround it in the north and Tamil Nadu and Kerala do so in the south, though in ancient and medieval times, political boundaries were in a constant state of flux and all major border areas were marked with bilingual populations. The region opens to the Bay of Bengal in the east and is delimited in the west by Arabian Sea, always making it a potential destination for people from across the oceans. Migration from these regions in all directions on the subcontinent as well as overseas was not uncommon in historical times.

Social and cultural evolution in India has passed through various phases—from the Stone Ages to the great civilizations of Harappa and Mohenjo Daro and beyond. However, we have often tended to shy away from looking at these developments from a regional perspective. As part of one of the oldest land masses on the subcontinent, the Deccan Plateau has hitherto commonly been understood to have simply acted as a 'bridge' in carrying the highly evolved norms of civilized life from the north Indian plains to the extreme south; the latter two being considered the prime progenitors of 'civilization' in India though their origins may have initially varied. Our concern here is not with denying that there were dynamic external influences into the Deccan, but at the same time, emphasizing and demarcating its centrality in the larger processes of social and cultural evolution in India. It is both external and internal forces, we argue, as well as their interaction with the diverse physical configurations of the region that enable one to define its regional specificity. As it so happens, a 'bridge,' in our view, was also the stable ground that over the ages allowed for a fluidity of cultural exchanges to produce the uniquely textured but strong multi-cultural ethos of the Deccan without losing its own individual identity. Within the geographical entity of the Deccan, it is interesting to note that clear-cut sub-regional variations emerge and they need to be increasingly highlighted for any complete history of the Deccan to be achieved for all periods of its history.

India, as a civilizational entity has had certain common historical and cultural experiences. But these have been collectively and concertedly been built on layers of cultural profiles of its innumerable regions. Each of these regions, in turn, gets its regional identity from the variegated historical experiences of its equally distinctive localities which reach out to smaller segments that go beyond the spatial dimension we conveniently label as sub-regions. There is a general tendency among historians to look at the history of a region from its broadest definition first and then move to its smaller units. I think it beneficial first to focus on the history of the small entities and then move both horizontally and vertically to etch the historical moorings of society in ancient Deccan as a whole. In this method, a systematic building of a region's history cannot do without the small place or locality which automatically then becomes the foundation on which the edifice of regional history must necessarily stand.

We are here talking of a period when substantial literary records are absent to provide a meaningful source base. It, therefore, becomes all the more significant that the understanding of archaeology to positively enhance and build new outlines of the cultural, economic and social history of early Deccan be under scored in the right direction. This is also of special concern to me since it is only in archaeology that material information on the history of various strata in society, even of those groups outside village or urban-based productive units can be got, provided that the small and unassuming pieces of information are given due attention while interpreting the data.

A dialogical interaction between archaeology and history will not only take us to small localities and places, but I hope, will enable us to fundamentally change our perceptions of how history at the regional level can be written. The multiplicity and richness of data in these contexts poses a challenge for us to understand more fully the diversity of Indian culture as a whole and how this was maintained over millennia, which, in my opinion, is our great strength as a civilizational entity. Therefore, as historians it should be our considered aim to document this diversity, its local manifestations and, most importantly, their transformations in time. We cannot do this if we subsume this diversity into broad models of historical change which, having taken place elsewhere, supposedly reflect an all India phenomena.

II

There has been a tendency among most historians dealing with the ancient period of the subcontinent to focus only on the history of the so-called nuclear or core areas of the major river basins of the Indus, Ganges and Kaveri as the prime progenitors of 'civilization' in India. In itself this is not a historically invalid exercise and has, of course, enriched our understanding of the totality of the Indian past. However, there has been a simultaneous, though unconscious, implication of this in that we have come to view the nature of historical change in the so-called 'minor' cultural regions of India as though they were only derivative from a given model. Further, the written source and the power of its infallibility over generations has tended to lead historians to look for the 'origins' of the diverse parts of the country always in terms of the Vedic, Shastric or the Great Puranic and Epic antecedents. This referential treatment in historical documentation has meant that a considerable weightage is given to even fragmentary pieces of information embedded in the Vedas or Shastras to define regions immediately south of the Vindhyas. Thus, we see that whole historical narratives are structured on these pieces of information, Once again there is no harm in using a source located outside the region of the study but this has to go hand in hand with the recognition that the evidence being given so much weightage is indeed only *one perspective of understanding and, therefore, has to be viewed critically rather than accepted arbitrarily as a foundational truth.* More pertinently, the region being thus defined had a perception of itself which, even though not known to us through the written word, can be found nested in valuable pieces of evidence located in small edifices and locales. These material remains can be given shape to in order to visualize the origins of any society in its myriad forms. The fundamental point I wish to emphasize is that the historical evolution and transformations of such regions must be formulated to emanate from the concrete reality of the location where we stand. Undoubtedly, this stand can then look outwards to see the extent to which other influences and perspectives can help us or, engage our attention so that the texture of historical analysis can be made more complete.

If this change of standpoint is put into effect in, for instance, for history writing of ancient Andhra, we will not have to begin the history of early Andhradeśa as though it was 'lacking' in something or that it was merely a land of 'mixed races' or, still further, only to be remembered as the land where the 'cursed sons of Viśvamitra' found abode.[1] These images have become strongly entrenched in our historical idiom of the earliest phases of Andhra history. In my view, even if these 'events' or 'images' from the cultural memory of the early Brahmanical tradition have to be taken into account, they should merely reflect for us one point of view and be treated as such rather than become arbitrary markers for us to compulsively begin the history of the region with a lack of some sort or the other.

Another entry point conveniently labelled for us to define the early Andhra region is in terms of the boundaries of states which had their epicentre outside the region. These political boundaries continually and repeatedly changed and, therefore, cannot be accepted as viable criteria for defining the historical character of a region. It is often erroneously accepted by historians that in short periods of political unification, a political homogeneity developed in the region. This idea is, in fact, an assumed and contrived one fundamentally ignoring the spatial and cultural variables within it. The latter interact within a region and lie embedded in social identities which only partially get integrated in the political enterprise that is being projected as the most important happening of a particular period. The solidity of the Mauryan and later the Sātavāhana, their political enterprise is strongly entrenched in our mind. However, now it is fairly well accepted by a large number of historians that despite these empires, differential political locations of ruling families, each having its identity in terms of the coins they issued, presaged, co-existed and succeeded them in different sub-regions of the Deccan.

III

Let us now turn to focus more particularly on an exemplification of these ideas from a case study of ancient Andhra history and archaeology. I suggest in this chapter ways of understanding the origins of civilization in early Andhradeśa by emphasizing on the internal processes of change rather than looking at the history of this region only in terms of influences from outside. Simultaneously, within this broad region of inquiry, my recent interest has been to write on those sub-regions and localities of ancient Andhradeśa which have hitherto been considered 'areas of isolation'. I do not in any way want to submit that historical processes of change and development should be understood as autonomous. They certainly interacted, in the long range, with similar processes in other parts of the country, particularly with those contiguous to it in the Deccan but, if one turns to look at the developments from the perspective of the small locality, they appear amazingly solid and well defined in the immediate environment. Further, the parameters of their interaction with the external forces, seen from this perspective, seem much more limited as the local materials do not necessarily reflect them.

The local cultural evolution and its transformation in time has, therefore, to be made central to our research agenda rather than look for support from the outside in an attempt to define it. I firmly believe that a greater strength of the 'Self' namely, the region, can come from standing on the small but solid ground of these localities. This solidity will only strengthen our understandings of regional history since the material evidence got from archaeology is rooted in specific settings. There will naturally emerge multiple such settings which, as I explain below, were interlocked with developments in the larger space of the region. However, the regional developments of the early historic times did not destroy the diversity of the various local situations. In other words, the complexity of social, economic and cultural interaction was integrated into a pan-Deccan identity without destroying the individuality of small localities. The firmness of the latter, in fact, becomes the ground on which the heightened awareness of diversity can be understood in its proper perspective.

In specific terms this raises the question of how best to understand the historicity of different localities in a broader region when they vary so much from each other in terms of basic features like nature and quantum of habitation, access to resources of different kinds and, therefore, to cultural accessories that may seem natural to one sub-region but totally absent in another. The transition from the proto-historic situation known to us from the innumerable megalith remains strewn all over the Deccan, and the elements of their interaction with the beginnings of the historical cultures again, known rather uniformly in the Deccan from the Sātavāhana layers of habitation, i.e. between the late centuries BCE to the early centuries CE is thus, most crucial to highlight in the present context. As mentioned above, the earliest allusions to the Andhras have been understood from mainly Brahmanic and Buddhist sources. This has most obviously meant that those sub-regions of the Deccan, which had failed to yield monumental Buddhist edifices (like those found in the 'western Deccan' or the Krishna-Godavari delta region of the 'eastern Deccan') or, those lacking concrete evidences of Mauryan contact such as the inscriptions of Aśoka (with their concentration in the' southern Deccan') were in advertently not taken up for historical inquiry, or, taken up only when the Mauryan contact first began. Further, the apparently startling 'historical' edifices of these select sub-regions pre-occupied most archaeologists and historians who mainly dwelt on an intrinsic description of these.[2]

The early history of the ancient Andhras cannot be disassociated from the history of the Deccan as a whole particularly in the context of the political unification of the Deccan under the Sātavāhanas. Further, for the first state formation in south India, Deccan interestingly emerges as the nucleus and, from our point of view, this cannot be detached from an integrated study of the economic, social and cultural *variations* of the various sub-regions of the Deccan. Two of those that I propose to focus on in this exemplification, the Telangana plateau and coastal Andhra, form important cultural zones of the present-day states of Telangana and Andhra Pradesh.

IV

As in the case with the other sub-regions of the Deccan, I would like to argue that the nature of historical development in these two sub-regions during the early historical period was embedded in: (a) the particular ecological context, (b) consequently, this sub-regional variation is reflected in the proto-historic diversity, which was essentially related to the agrarian development, or lack of it, in them (c) the rise and then spread of political power in these two sub-regions had its own individual trajectory and, finally, (d) the impact of the Mauryas and of Buddhism as the ideological influence on each particular locality took on its own form and definition while maintaining a commonalty across sub-regions.

We recognize that the heterogeneity of the Deccan in terms of given physiographic and ecological peculiarities provides at least four distinct entities. In a larger background study[3] we divided it (Map 1.1) into the western Deccan (marked A on the map) with its high altitude Ghats and strategic passes, the central Deccan with its upland plateau, (marked B), the eastern Deccan with its fertile plains (marked C) and the southern Deccan with the upper reaches of the Krishna-Tungabhadra plains and the Mysore plateau (marked D). These sub regions of the Deccan were the specific locale for the origin, growth and then expansion of the Sātavāhana power, but at chronologically varied times. In recent decades, new numismatic and archaeological data helps us to stress on these sub-regional variations, ecological differences and their subsequent influence on the material and cultural setting in a more specific manner. This we highlight keeping in focus the comparison and contrast of the Telangana plateau and coastal Andhra cultural settings, wherein we emphasize upon the importance of the existence or co-existence of particular sub-regions as independent or semi-independent entities contributing to the whole region's historical development.

The first settled village communities with some form of an organized but nascent political authority can be traced to the Chalcolithic cultures which have been dated around 2000-1000 BCE. These cultures, as is well known, are clearly identifiable and substantially found in the western and southern Deccan sites. On the other hand, there are few well-documented Chalcolithic sites in Coastal Andhra. Sites like Nagarjunakonda and Kesarapalli suggest a Chalcolithic intrusive phase on an already existing Neolithic culture, which has been dated to around 1500 BCE. This is further in clear contrast to the near total absence of Chalcolithic settlements in the Telangana plateau with the rare exception of the recently excavated sites in the Mahbubnagar district, particularly that of Chagtur. Instead, the Neolithic settlements in this area are immediately followed by the Megalithic iron using cultures at most of the sites.

Interestingly, after the decline of the Chalcolithic cultures, the western Deccan witnesses the apparent sudden emergence of the early historic cultures with a total absence of the proto-historic archaeological cultures based on iron technology known throughout the Deccan with megalith characteristics. Though in the context of the western Deccan there has been some evidence of the disappearance of the Chalcolithic cultures, the same cannot be said for coastal Andhra. Iron age emerges here either in an overlap situation with the Chalcolithic or immediately succeeding it. This is not only at major settlements like Amaravati-Dharanikota, Jaggayyapeta, Kesarapalli, Nagarjunakonda and Yelleswaram but also at lesser known sites such as Agiripalli, Gudimellanka, Kanukollu, and so on. The cultures with megalithic characteristics are, however, found more prolifically in the Telangana plateau area and Vidarbha as well as in the southern Deccan sites of the Mysore plateau, which have been generally dated to between 1100 BCE-100 CE. Bhagmahari, Khapa, Naikund, Paunar, Pauni and Takalghat are significant Iron-age sites in the Vidarbha region of Maharashtra and cannot be ignored as they have significant cultural linkages with the Telangana Iron age megalithic sites. Budigapally, Chagtur, Chinnamarrur, Kadambapur, Kolakonda, Polakonda, Peddabankur and Pochampadu are some of these though it would be no exaggeration to say that the entire Vidarbha and Karimnagar regions are strewn with evidence of Megalith burials. Another point of contrast with the coastal Andhra region is that here, the settlements seem to have emerged out of their antecedent Neolithic and Chalcolithic cultures whereas in Telangana as well as the Vidarbha region, their emergence is apparently sudden and clearly independent of earlier cultures.

Though the Megalithic cultures are generally accepted to have some common features, their heterogeneity must be appreciated as well. Indeed, within these two sub-regions under focus they are not represented in an identical manner. In coastal Andhra, the megalithic cultures form the essential agrarian background to the early historic phase in the fertile belts of the Krishna-Godavari basin. The sites found here show that the megalithic people had mostly chosen to settle on fertile riverine beds. It is important to note that in coastal Andhra, the megalithic cultures have largely been evidenced by the occurrence of ceramic traits like black and red ware, red and black ware, black ware with only an occasional occurrence of iron objects. Thus, the role played by iron in the transformation of the pre-urban society here seems to have been minimal. Megalith related artefacts like horse remains and particularly iron tools and implements are found more prolifically in Telangana than in coastal Andhra. Indeed, by far the most striking aspect of the megalith economy in this sub-region was its ability to generate iron objects on a large scale. This is undoubtedly related to the availability of iron in this region. It has been pointed out that a 'number of ancient iron working spots were located in Karimnagar region at Regonda, Tellakunta, etc.'[4] At the latter site, enormous deposits of iron slags and nodules of calcium carbonate indicate this. Though a large amount of iron slag indicates that level of technology was not very high but that iron was locally and easily available cannot be doubted. In all probability, the people of coastal Andhra and also those of the southern Deccan were in contact with the central Deccan for their supply of iron artefacts.[5]

At a general level, therefore, the economic activities of the megalithic people can be said to be based on either agriculture or pastoral activities with craft specialization depending on the local, sub-regional situations. The impact of iron technology in Telangana was related to an increased craft production whereas in coastal Andhra we can perhaps suggest its greater use for agricultural expansion. In this regard, a point of difference at the Telangana sites of Pochampadu and Peddabankur is that apart from agricultural implements such as flat axes, sickles, spades, hoe-blades and knives we also find the bone remains of such domesticated animals as cattle, sheep, goat, swine, which probably indicate that these formed part of their diet.

V

Next, we turn to take a look at the difference between the two sub-regions in terms of external contacts they had. The strategic location connecting the ports of the south-east coast with the north Indian plains on the one hand and the southern peninsular on the other, afforded it with a unique environment for the development of nodal points of exchange and then trade that finally supported the growth of some of the most important non-religious urban centres in the Deccan as a whole during the early historic period.

In this regard, the coastal Andhra settlements flourished in a big way during the early historic period when compared to the Telangana sites. In fact, when compared with all the other sub-regions, the western Deccan sites show the maximum connections in this regard specially through the display of the maximum occurrence of northern black polished ware sherds, which at Nasik, at least, have been dated to as early as 500 BCE. At some of the sites, early punch-marked coins have also been found whereas coins of the pre-Sātavāhana ruling groups have only been found at Brahmapuri in the western Deccan. Notable Mauryan presence here is documented at Sopara and Kaudinyapura. In coastal Andhra too, interesting evidence of northern black polished ware has been found at sites like Amaravati, Dharnikota, Kesarapalli and Vaddamanu. Further, the spread of Buddhism and trade activities here with the help of the evidence from Amaravati has been dated back to the pre-Aśokan period by I.K. Sarma who also points to the existence of pre-Mauryan punch-marked coins found in coastal Andhra.[6] It is significant that in archaeological terms, the Mauryan phase here is evident in the megalithic context[7] as substantiated by the megalithic phase being found just below the Stūpa complex at Amaravati. Further, other indicators of Mauryan contact in coastal Andhra are the black and red ware found at Amaravati which is said to have graffiti marks in Aśokan Brahmi and Mauryan punch-marked coins, which have been found in Amaravati and Dharnikota.[8] Interestingly, Mauryan inscriptional and other evidence is amply found in all the sub-regions of the Deccan except for the Telangana area. It has been suggested that the conspicuous concentration of the Aśokan edicts in mineral rich areas of the southern Deccan and important port towns in the coastal Andhra is indicative of the fact that the interests of the Mauryan state were of an economic nature, namely, in the exploitation of the local resources and not in territorial annexation and control.[9] The lack of a significant Mauryan presence in the case of the Telangana area did not inhibit this sub region to lag behind in the development of urban centres during the early historical period though, both the nature of their economic growth and institutional support they got was different.

Two aspects of the pre-Sātavāhana situation need to be emphasized in the development of the early historical sites in Telangana. Both these are related to the dynamics of internal changes and transformations in the pre-Sātavāhana society. One was the particular nature of the economy which rested on the small-scale production of iron related artefacts and the other to the substantial existence of pre-Sātavāhana levels of habitation not necessarily related with the Megalithic material remains. We suggest this primarily on the basis of archaeological and numismatic data found at Kotalingala. Indeed, the stratigraphy of the excavation independently suggests a clear pre-Sātavāhana level.[10] At Peddabankur, Dhulikatta and Kondapur considerable amount of iron objects were present and at the former two sites Megaliths and all black ware pottery was also found. Whereas the availability of iron objects is equally prolific in the Vidarbha sites, what adds a significant dimension to defining this phase is that it sees the mobilization of resources at a local level wherein the political elites had the ability to issue their own coins.

In terms of pre-Sātavāhana chiefs who issued their own coins, evidence is available from all sub-regions but it is most striking again from Telangana. A significant point to be recognized here is that the dates of these vary from sub-region to sub-region. In this context, it has been pertinently pointed out by B.D. Chattopadhyaya that punch-marked coins of the Deccan, which began with the Mauryan period and continued to be manufactured in the early centuries of the Christian era can, in fact, be associated with specific 'localities'. These were followed by uninscribed cast coins and uninscribed die struck coins and they all provide a necessary background to the emergence of 'local' inscribed coins series of the Deccan.[11] P.L. Gupta has made an attempt at analysing these coins series from the numismatic and archaeological point of view to conclude on some of the major issues of their dates and distribution. First and foremost, he has rightly classified the big lead coins with inscriptions issued by local dynasties in the Deccan, sub-region-wise. They are listed as 'Kuras in the Panchganga basin (Kolhapur); Sadakanas in and around Chitaldurg district; Hastin in the Krishna valley; an unknown dynasty in the Tungabhadra basin and Sadas in the Mahishaka country' which he says, 'existed continuously till they were uprooted by the later Sātavāhanas in the time of Sri Yajna Satakarni or a little earlier in circa second-third centuries CE.'[12] Veerapuram, Yerragudi, Rajulamandagiri and Chandravalli have been identified as important centres which provide numismatic evidence of the local rulers like Maharathis and Sadakana rulers.[13] Kura and Hastin coins are important from the perspective of the western and southern Deccan and the Sada coins reveal the political profile of coastal Andhra after the Mauryan period and before the rise of the Sātavāhanas.

The situation in Telangana is different and substantially significant from our point of view because of the discovery of several pre-Sātavāhana coins along with early Sātavāhana coins, some of them in a stratified context, at Kotalingala.[14] Unlike the others, numismatic evidence of the Kotalingala finds are outstanding because a number of coins of a certain Chimukha (25) 'founder of the Sātavāhana dynasty' have been collected. Several others of the early rulers of this dynasty like Sātavāhana (234) and Satakarni (47) have also been found. Apart from these, those of Samagopa (68), Mahatalavara (3), Gobadha (7) and Narana (9), open up a new vista of the pre-Sātavāhana history of this region.[15] From our point of view, these clearly highlight the fact that some form of specific political authority had become a force continuously from pre-Sātavāhana times in Telangana where the Mauryan presence cannot be archaeologically located.

It would, however, be appropriate to emphasize at this juncture that power relations were rooted in old kin ties in post-Mauryan Deccan as a whole. Epigraphic sources from the Andhra region also give us similar evidence as for instance, the mention of Kubiraka *raja* of the relic casket inscription found at Bhattiprolu of the third century BCE, Somaka *raja* of an inscription of the second century BCE, found on the outskirts of Vaddamanu, Aira Mana Sada of the Velpuru epigraph, and so on.[16] Here coins from Amaravati also attest to the existence of local rulers in this sub-region. Even in Sātavāhana times, the Naneghat inscriptions show the existence of local chieftains.[17] On the basis of this kind of information on the local power groups in Deccan, it has been postulated by scholars that the socio-economic changes within these 'localities' during the Mauryan period made it possible for them to acquire a certain level of political authority.

The agricultural surplus generated in the preceding megalithic societies was also one of the chief factors for generating forces of expansion during the early historic period. In the fertile lower Krishna valley in the Andhra region, several urban centres have been found, associated with Buddhism. Prominent among these were Amaravati, Bhattiprolu, Chandavaram, Jaggayyapeta, Nagarjunakonda, Salihundam, Vaddamanu and Yelleshwaram. Inscriptions from Amaravati give evidence of powerful individuals and rulers who had made religious donations to the Buddhist monastic establishments. Further, the mention of chiefs associated with *gosthi* or merchant guilds indicates that they must have benefitted from the expanding trade activities. In fact, trade and commerce was flourishing in this sub-region even in the pre-Sātavāhana period as is indicated by the existence of early levels of habitation at commercial centres like Guntupalli and Kesarapalli. The association and spread of the Buddhist order in the western Deccan is well known, but we shall not dwell on it for the present. On the other hand, it is significant to point out that in comparison, in Telangana and also in the southern Deccan, the number of sites associated with Buddhism are few though at all the sites in Telangana at many of the large settlements like Dhulikatta, Pashigaon, Phanigiri and Kondapur, there is evidence of early Buddhism. In this connection it is also no coincidence that the early Sātavāhana coins have mainly been reported from Telangana and the western Deccan at sites like Kondapur, Hyderabad, Kotilingala, Nevasa, Nasik, Bhokardan, Paithan and Pauni signifying that these must have been the prominent seats of early Sātavāhana rule. The concentration of the Sātavāhana rule might have shifted to coastal Andhra later, as has been suggested by I.K. Sarma on the basis of an important mint centre located at Nagarjunakonda.[18]

VI

In any case, to conclude, the Sātavāhana rule at its climax was associated with all the sub-regions of the Deccan, but its beginning in each sub-region was at chronologically different times. King Satakarni I of the Sātavāhana dynasty was styled as *Daksinapathpati.* The Nasik cave inscription of Queen Balasri has mentioned the component parts of Gautamiputra Satakarni's empire as Asika, Asaka, Mulaka, Suratha, Kukura, Aparantha, Anupa, Vidarbha and Akara Avanthi.[19] Sātavāhana rule represents in the Deccan, for the first time, the beginning of an organized set up in which certain features like a bureaucracy, an organized military and a well-defined administrative ideology of the state, often represented through religious patronage. *Dakshinapatha* has been used to denote the Sātavāhana empire as a whole.[20] It has been observed that the economy of the Sātavāhana period in the Deccan as a whole was dependent on three main features, viz., plough agriculture, commodity production and trade. While the practice of land grants promoted agriculture, Buddhism seems to have encouraged important trade and commercial activities. Whereas the western Deccan and coastal Andhra as two important sub-regions were active for trade and religious activities, they were evidently reliant on each other and also on other sub-regions.[21] In Telangana and the southern Deccan, we have observed that though sites with Buddhist remains and monasteries were comparatively fewer, they were crucial areas for development of long distance trade and, thus, it is noticed that urban centres here grew in the vicinity of important trade routes.

The important feature of the Sātavāhana economy was the ability of the rulers to support areas of prominence for external trade and commerce. These areas interestingly also emerge as important administrative centres. Commercially important palaces like Broach, Bhokardan, Kaundinyapura, Nasik and Sopara in the western Deccan, Adam, Paunar and Pauni in the Vidharbha area, Dhullikatta, Peddabankur, Kondapur and Ter in Telangana, the Amaravati-Dharanikota complex, Jaggayyapeta, Bhattiprolu, Ghantasala, Kesarapalli, Nagarjunakonda, Salihundam, Vaddamanu, Yelleshwaram in coastal Andhra, Banavasi, Brahmagiri, Chandravalli, Sannati, Satanikota and Vadgaon-Madhavpur in the southern Deccan all indicate the prosperous nature of urban settlements in all the sub-regions of the Deccan. The form that these took and their distribution pattern in relation to the Buddhist monastic settlements[22] (Map 2.1) however, differed from sub-region to sub-region.

The ecologically varied zones provided different kinds of surpluses and revenues to support them. It is interesting to note that under the over-arching power of the Sātavāhanas, various geographically different zones of the Deccan could be united together while maintaining their particular regional characteristics. Further, it needs to be emphasized that any understanding of the rise of the Sātavāhana state without appreciating the material and socio-economic background to it would lead to an erroneous impression that it had an apparently sudden emergence. It is only by taking into account the antecedent cultural phases of habitation which in the various cultural sub-regions were often very different from each other in material and cultural development that we can appreciate the extent to which the Sātavāhanas played an essentially integrative role in a society which was otherwise still rooted in particular sub-regional economic and material moorings.

That there was a continuous habitation at these sites is generally accepted by scholars. But what is unconsciously ignored in the historical analysis is that these existing complex cultural traits were not obliterated during the succeeding historical stage of habitation despite the multiplicity of habitation areas or the non-uniform nature of the 'overlap' situations at the particular excavated sites. The element of continuity has hitherto tended to be underplayed as often the use of the term 'tribal' or 'tribe' to indiscriminately describe and club together all pre-state groups creates not only a discontinuity between the pre-civilization and civilization stages, but also pejoratively dismisses the importance that these well-entrenched communities played in the formation of the civilized society. On the contrary, in my opinion, when new elements were subsequently added due to inter-regional trade and contact as a consequence of the Mauryan intrusion or later with the Indo-Roman contact, it was done on a solid foundation of economically differentiated communities. The complexity of the co-existence of archaeological cultures and their interaction with each other and then, their sequencing in the particular local situations, reflects upon the overlapping time scales of the historical transformation.

This is intrinsic to the character of the early social formation in the Deccan which leads us to summarize that the transition from Neolithic to the Chalcolithic and their interaction with the Megalithic and early historic occurred independently and variably in select parts of the Deccan and evolved gradually under different local environments.

VII

In contrasting the two important cultural zones of ancient Andhradeśa, I have only tried to highlight how if the archaeology of small localities is given its due importance we can change the interpretations of early Deccan history in a positive direction recognizing the importance and contribution of all its sub-regions to the formation of the most ancient cultural traditions of the region. During the early years of independence the concern had been with identifying the Buddhist sites, particularly in coastal Andhra.[23] This predominant activity had sidelined the question of under taking problem-oriented excavation in the so-called 'regions of isolation' as they were considered of little importance because no monumental remains had been found there. Sir Mortimer Wheeler's Maps,[24] published in 1948 of the different sites from the pre- to the early historic phase show a total blank for the Telangana region. This had, in turn, unconsciously undermined our understanding of the Telangana region and, therefore, it had emerged in negative light. I have stated elsewhere that the importance of this region got prominence in the context of excavations conducted by the State Department of Archaeology and Museums, Government of Andhra Pradesh since the 1960s.[25] This has also brought to the forefront the major issue of the Sātavāhana origin and early rule being located here raising legitimate questions about the region's crucial role in the transition from pre-state to state society. Further, the many settlements that developed urban features in this region represented the mechanisms through which local groups participated in the spheres of economic, social and cultural activity and their interaction with other sub-regions of the Deccan.[26] Political power in pre Sātavāhana times was necessarily segmented, but under the new forces of social change these groups interacted with each other to ultimately establish the larger network of the Sātavāhana empire, which covered other sub-regions of the Deccan as well. Thus, the two areas of Telangana and coastal Andhra provide data, which when taken together highlight the salient features of the formation of the early society that due to the geo-cultural and techno-economic as well as institutional constraints and possibilities developed an individual character, different in content and style from other sub-regions of the Deccan and also from other parts of India.

It is legitimate, of course, to state that archaeology has played a valuable role in recovering data on a regional scale that cannot be labelled in terms of Harappan or Vedic indicators of cultural development. However, as suggested by us above, it has been difficult to evolve an independent criteria of labelling them, or even, taking into account that their distribution was across present-day linguistic boundaries. This has been so because regional history writing is still intrinsically embedded in nineteenth century historiographical issues of wanting to locate all this rich archaeological data only in terms of who were ruling or how it is related to a dominant religious force sweeping region from time to time. Underlying these attempts has been the unconscious but real effect of excluding local and small identities in assessing archaeological remains that did not fit into the given paradigm of history writing. In fact, these have been consistently marginalized thereby excluding any discussion on how small local groups and tribes in regions could be studied from the archaeological remains.

Diversity in Indian culture has been much talked about but articulated only in terms of broad categories as those based on language or region. These tendencies have inhibited our being able to focus on understanding the commemorative leavings of the past enshrined in small artefacts or icons and even monumental buildings in a local spatial context, which do not fit into totalities of pan regional or pan-Indian identities. In our opinion they, in fact, constitute the primary layer of a reality which may reflect on larger events of time, but necessarily were not originally constituted to do so. Their constitution is best suggested to be embedded in the subjective meanings that are reflected in the objects as part of human and cultural sensitivities attached to them. Having survived, often in fragments, it is pertinent for us to analyse the human imagination in these local structures to identify a collective memory of the people at a local level. These memories cannot be detached from the particularities of cultural meanings that are inherent in them. This type of history must then necessarily draw on local situations within broader regional contexts. For regional constructions the past, it must be fundamentally recognized, resides locally and not nationally and, therefore, archaeological remains of those small traditions must inspire the passion of historians rather than those based on political considerations.

NOTES

1. References such as those from the *Aitareya Brāhmaṇa,* VII, 18; *Bhāgavata Purāna,* 11.4.18; *Brāhmaṇda Purāṇa,* II.16.59; III.14-80; *Mahābhārata,* III.188.35; *Mānavadharmaśāstra,* X. 36; 38; 48 and also from the Buddhist and Jaina texts like the *Samantapasādika* (Commentary on the *Vinaya Piṭaka,* 1.8.4), vol. I, p. 255; *Bhagavatī Sūtra,* 380, 143; *Prajñapana,* I. 36-7 which are most often cited to define the beginnings of Ancient Andhra are usually negative in content and description and interpretations of what they in fact meant to convey are often given in a complicated way and this varies from historian to historian.
2. Sarkar in Pande and Chattopadhyaya (1987: 631-2) has significantly raised questions about this pre-occupation of archaeologists and historians and has suggested a new direction for forthcoming studies on this region.
3. The original references on which Sections IV, V, VI are based can be found in Parasher Sen (1992: 437-77). All this data in a tabulated form is available in Parasher (1999: 153-91).
4. Krishnasastry (1983: 107).
5. This is true of the Vidarbha sites as well. Deo in Deo and Paddayya (1985: 90).
6. Sarma (1975a: 16); Sarma (1985: 15-16).
7. Begley (1986: 303-4).
8. Sarma (1994: I); Sarma (1971: 12); Sarma (1975a: 17).
9. Thapar (1987: 13).
10. Krishnasastry (1978: 74). Pre-Sātavāhana levels from excavations have also been reported in this region from Vadluru in Nizamabad district and Polakonda from Warangal district—Krishnasastry (1983: 129-30).

11. Chattopadhyaya in Pande and Chattopadhyaya (1987: 727-9).
12. Gupta (1990: 237-310) with emphasis on pp. 305-6
13. Sastry et al. (1984: 98); Gupta (1990: 271)—Maharathi coins have been found at Kotalingala as well according to Gupta.
14. Singh (1995: 1-37).
15. Sastry (1979a: 136-7); Singh (1995: 1-37).
16. Sastry in Handa (1989: 71-2).
17. Burgess (1883: 84); Sarma (1975a: 18-21).
18. Sarma (1980: 33; 38); Sarma (1971: 9).
19. Senart (1905-6: 61).
20. Some scholars suggest it to be a feudal polity, e.g., Gairola (1955: 42; 46).
21. Parasher in Banga (1991: 19-47).
22. Heitzman in Kennedy and Possehl (1984: 132-3). He has shown this interconnection for the whole of India since the Mauryan times.
23. Clearly visible in the reporting of the *IAR* from 1954-5 to 1959-60; 1973-4; 1974-5.
24. 'Brahmagiri and Chandravalli 1947: Megalithic and Other Cultures in Chitaldurg district, Mysore State', *Ancient India,* no. 4, 1947-8. See maps of Microliths, Megalith and Indo-Roman Sites.
25. No systematic report of any or the sites in this region has yet been published by the Department of Archaeology though the material remains found at some of these sites have been discussed by Krishnasastry (1983), which has been reviewed by me in *Indian Historical Review,* vol. XIII, nos. i-ii, 1986-7, pp. 183-5.
26. Parasher in Banga (1991: 40-6).

CHAPTER 2

Local Polities and State Formation*

Looking from the perspective of different localities while making the numismatic data central to our analysis, this chapter not only raises critical questions about the transition to early state, but also interrogates the nature of this state in the Deccan. Localities cannot be understood as isolated historical entities, but in the context of region-based studies they cannot be treated as mere peripheries either. Since this task necessarily entails a minute and an in-depth study of the sources, we shall take two illustrative examples of localities in what are today the states of Telangana and Andhra Pradesh with their nodal points that spread around the sites of Kotalingala-Dhullikatta-Peddabankur and Amaravati-Bhattiprolu-Vaddamanu respectively. The coins under discussion that will be used as the primary sources shall necessarily be related to the broader archaeological and material profile of these two localities. There is a general tendency among historians to first look at the history of a region from its broadest definition and then move to its smaller units. Here we prefer to first focus on the history of small entities or localities, and then move both vertically and horizontally to etch out the historical moorings of early society and state in the region as a whole—the Deccan in this case study.

The main thrust of this chapter is to understand the transition to the state in the early Deccan by emphasizing internal processes of change rather than looking at it only in terms of external influences. I focus on localities situated within certain geographical sub-regions of the Deccan, which have hitherto been studied either in

*This is a slightly shortened version of what was earlier published as 'Localities, Coins and the Transition to the Early State in the Deccan', *Studies in History*, vol. 23, no. 2, n.s., 2007, pp. 231-69.

a cursory manner or with thick descriptions, but without particularly highlighting the variations in their material and socio-political characteristics during the transition to the early state.

The underlying premise that has so far been implicitly accepted by historians who emphasize processes of historical change is that 'civilization' as a progressive, development was diffused, concomitantly followed by the processes of secondary state formation[1] that initiated the rise of the state in the Deccan.[2] This view is built on the theoretical notion of contrasting the 'civilized' with 'barbarian' societies, the former being technologically superior[3] and, therefore, able to impose a 'high' culture on to a 'low' level of cultural evolution. A binary distinction between the two evolutionary stages tends to ignore the continuity of the earlier elements and their co-existence with the stage of 'civilization'. The popularity of this generalization of the diffusion of civilization from certain core regions of the Indian sub-subcontinent to the rest of the country stems from inherent value judgements in favour of the connotation of 'progress' attached to the term 'civilization'.

Tringham[4] has discussed the unfair comparison made in identifying stages of civilization in temperate Europe with those in the Mediterranean. For later periods of history, models of the state particular to given European (in this case Greek) experience are sought to be applied to states of the East,[5] erroneously leading to an assumption that they lacked in effective cultural traits that should to be associated with 'development' and, by extension, civilization and state. At another level, in quantitative terms, many regions and sub-regions have received little or no attention or only recent interest simply because the origin and foundation of 'civilization' as the mainstream development was not found located in them.

Broadly, three types of historical research have been done for the Deccan. Innumerable coins of the Sātavāhana kings, the flourishing state of Buddhism under the rule of the Sātavāhanas, and the great proliferation of archaeological sites associated with the material culture of the Sātavāhana levels of habitation have been studied by scholars initially concerned with establishing a cohesive history of events, monuments and the like. Therefore, these are primarily done within the gamut of: (a) numismatic studies;

(b) studies on Buddhism; and (c) documentation and description of monuments and archaeological remains.[6]

Often, these studies have been carried out in the context of regional history as understood within with boundaries of the present-day linguistic states of Maharashtra, Telangana, Andhra Pradesh and Karnataka, which constitute the landscape of what geologists and geographers prefer to call the Deccan.[7] Scholars writing on the early history of the Deccan give undue emphasis to describing its political features[8] and dwell on details of dynasties and the political events of the period without any relevant discussion of the social base that made the Sātavāhana state possible.[9] Thus, numerically the largest number of studies have been by those preoccupied with writing what can be called event-based histories of the Deccan and, even till relatively recent times, despite the use of numismatic material from excavations, the preoccupation has been with determining the chronology of kings that ruled these parts.[10] The region under study has also seen the benign impact of the work of archaeologists and epigraphists. Their efforts have thrown up vast data but the enigma of the Megalithic material remains[11] and an obsession with documenting the overarching monumentality of Buddhist structures continues, which has not enabled them to move beyond their primary concern with documentation.[12]

It is the Deccan as a geographical and historical entity that became the locus for the first centre of political power in south India that did not have its original moorings in north India. In moving beyond event-based history and marking material cultural phases of change, there is a growing group of historians and archaeologists who now see the potential of reinvestigating different types of sources, permitting them to see history as a process, so as to conceptualize the nature of historical change in the Deccan.[13] In fact, at a broader level, this is essential because, as we shall argue later, the rise of the state was intrinsically linked to the antecedent stages of social evolution, which is marginalized in the dominant narrative of political history. It is usually confined to the often ritualistic mention of prehistoric remains or to fragmentary allusions to this region in literary sources from outside of the Deccan. Elsewhere[14] we have argued that in establishing the historical structures of the

Deccan, periods of overall change did not necessarily coincide with political change. And further, even before the origin of the state in these parts, we find differential systems of political and economic organization that ultimately enable a characterization of the specific socio-political evolution of some of the earliest societies in these parts.

Worldwide methodological studies on understanding the origin of the early state have been many, but scholars have had 'considerable difficulty in drawing the dividing-line between the state and the non-state'.[15] It is, however, agreed that to pinpoint a precise moment for the birth of the early state is impossible. Instead, efforts have to be made to emphasize the process of the transformation of one to the other. Broadly, two important suggested views can be stated here to provide a working hypothesis for our present endeavour. Are the origins of early state to be found in what Service characterizes as 'chiefdoms' or, what Claessen and Skalnik describe as '*inchoate* early state'? The former are socio-political organizations with an aristocratic ethos of hereditary and hierarchical structures of power, but without the legal apparatus and institutions to enforce forceful repression.[16] Service does concede that difference between what he calls chieftaincies and states is difficult to explain, and it is often arbitrarily given so that the matter remains unresolved. The latter is 'where kinship, family, and community ties still dominate relations in the political field; where full-time specialists are rare; where taxation systems are only primitive . . . and where social differences are offset by reciprocity and close contacts between the rulers and the ruled'.[17] Both characterizations are different from what these scholars define as the '*typical* early state' where territorial ties balance kinship and the '*transitional* early state' in which administrative officers appointed are primarily non-kin persons. To this there are other scholars who add that certain 'environmental factors . . . depending on local conditions' could ensure 'minimum surplus . . . within different systems of production and technological development'.[18] The emphasis in all of these views is that in the stage, before the rise of the early state, the local community dominates along with the emergence of centralizing tendencies, social inequality and a complex social structure.

We find it worthwhile to accept Cohen's analytical perspective that 'the state emerges from a number of differing sources and relations between groups and that *once the process is set into motion the political sector becomes more and more a major determinant of the structure of society and its correlated culture*'[19] (emphasis added). He insists in maintaining a dichotomy between state and non-state because in his argument the latter 'fission' and the former do not. This fission/anti-fission criterion enables him to categorically suggest that even if fissioning societies have some characteristics of centralization, they are not states. Following Braudel, Cohen has also put forth the view that one of the factors that state formation is dependent on is geographical location, but also hastily adds that it is not 'physical conditions of the environment', but 'pure location' that provide the impetus for changes leading up to the processes of state formation.[20]

In the introduction and the preceding chapter we have outlined the physical particularity of the Deccan in terms of broadly four sub-regional variations. Below we draw on parts of the two sub-regions of the central and eastern Deccan to focus more minutely on the kind of historical data that can be culled that would enable us to see connections between different phases of the evolution of small localities to throw light on early state formation in its setting of the Deccan. Elsewhere,[21] following this idea, in our elaboration on the rise of urban settlements in the Deccan, we had stressed on the heterogeneity of the Deccan as this is visible in the earliest evidence of human habitation in these parts. This discussion on the nature of settlements that arose in each of the sub-regions of the Deccan is elaborated upon in Chapter 3. In a similar way it is of some relevance to argue that in the transition to early state in the Deccan, a number of traits were inherited from the preceding pre-state phase as defined by their location, especially in the way locally conditioned continuity was observable in the coins that were issued and used by the local elite. Localities[22] have been understood them in the sense that they depict the formation of a kind of 'centralized polity' at the local level reflecting an accumulation of socio-economic and political power to control local resources. In using the term 'localities' we concur with the particular context of its application by B.D. Chattopadhyaya to what he calls '*janapada-*

like localities'[23] that presaged the rise of the Sātavāhanas in the Deccan and are known to us primarily from numismatic data.

It is against this background that we shall highlight the numismatic data found in multiple contexts. Since heterogeneity was apparent both in terms of the locational imperatives and physiographic/ecological peculiarities, as well as in terms of the nature of sources available for these sub-regions, we begin our descriptions in each case with defining the archaeological profiles of the two localities. This is followed by a descriptive account of the coin finds with special reference to two excavated sites-Kotalingala in the mid-Godavari locality (Map 2.1) and Vaddamanu in the lower Krishna valley locality (Map 2.2). Part of our scholarly endeavour

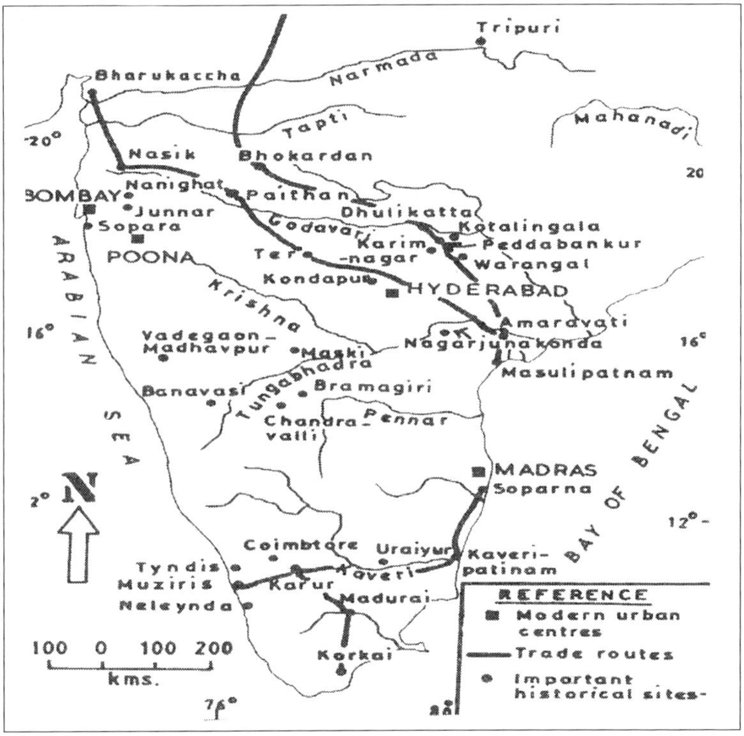

Source: Map prepared by the author.

Map 2.1: Major Early Historic Urban Centres in South India with focus on Mid-Godavari Valley

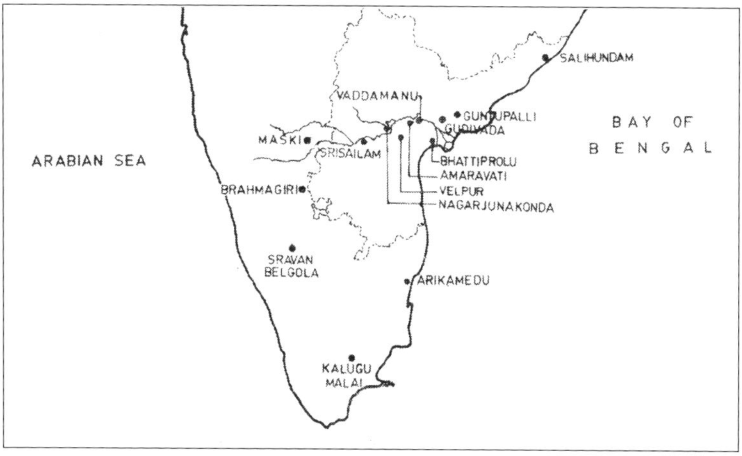

Source: Reproduced from T.V.G. Sastry (1992: 2).

Map 2.2: Major Sites under study: The Lower Krishna Valley in Peninsular India

in the recent past[24] has been to recover, document and understand historical pasts of sites, places and locales that provide us with new data at the micro level and bring out the distinct profile of different localities. Coins have rarely exclusively been taken into account to define the earliest historicity of a locality. Primarily, this material evidence has been used by us to highlight the nature of emerging polities before, and those that were coterminous, with rise of the early and late Sātavāhanas, also known to us from a variety of coins.

I

In central Deccan our first case study is the mid-Godavari valley where the sites of Dhulikatta, Peddabankur and Kotalingala are located (Map 2.1). The first two are in the Peddapalli *taluk* of Karinmagar district[25] and the last is in the Kotalingala *taluk*. In ancient literary texts this would be part of what was described as Asmaka or Assaka, located on the river Godavari with its own geo-cultural identity.[26] The earliest Stone Age cultures were found in abundance at places like Vempalli, Narsapur (Lower Paleolithic),

Kazipalli (Middle Paleolithic), Manikgudem (Upper Paleolithic), and at Medipalli, Alluru, Jangaon, Devunipalli, Godavarikhani, Malkapur, Narashallpalli, Rachapalli, Takkellapalli and Ramagundam (Mesolithic). In the contiguous district of Warangal we also have sites typifying these cultures.

Unlike in the other parts of the Deccan, here the Neolithic is found independent of the Chalcolithic. Several sites have been identified with these remains, again, especially in Karimnagar district at places like Peddabankur, Gunjapadige, Koheda, Molanguru, Vemulavada, Kadambapur, Budigepalli, Parlapalli, Sanigaram and Togarrai. In the Warangal district too, important Neolithic sites have been brought to light in the last couple of decades. It is significant to note that a separate Chalcolithic cultural phase is absent in this locality; a feature characteristic of this entire sub-region, though the occasional find of copper objects is noted at some sites.

Further, excavators have clearly pointed out that historical sites, with what are called Sātavāhana material remains, have been found in almost every alternate village in the various *taluks* of the Karimnagar and Warangal districts.[27] Even more significantly, the locality and the sub-region as a whole are rich in material remains identified with Megalithic funerary monuments. In a recent enumeration of sites with Megalith-related artefacts in these districts, based on published material, it is noted that for the period roughly between 1000 BCE and 100 CE,[28] thirty-seven sites with Megalith remains can be identified—fifteen can be located in Karimnagar district[29] and twenty-two in Warangal district. Further, in north Telangana as a whole, forty-two sites have been identified and a majority of them, that is, thirty-six, were only burial sites and only six had some evidence of habitation. These occur either alongside Neolithic material remains or immediately succeeding them. Kadambapur in Karimnagar district, in close proximity to the locality under discussion, and Polkonda in Warangal district have both yielded impressive Neolithic and Megalithic evidence. In fact, Peddabankur, one of the sites in the locality under scrutiny, has Megalith burials, as well as indications of being a Neolithic site of considerable dimension.[30]

On the other hand, all the three sites in the locality, namely,

Peddabankur, Kotilingala and Dhulikatta, contain an archaeological sequence of Megaliths followed by early historic remains. Other sites with a similar pattern include Kadambapur in Karimnagar district, Polakonda in Warangal district and Kondapur in Medak district. Though it is difficult to clearly identify these two cultural phases, for the central Deccan as a whole a significant pre-Sātavāhana phase is envisaged by scholars and, therefore, as we describe later, they refer to the Megalithic phase as a time period and end it around 100 BCE, when numismatic evidence begins to emerge, especially from the excavations at Kotalingala.

Closer look at the material evidence alongside the structures excavated from Kotalingala, Dhullikatta and Peddabankur in this locality would further demonstrate their specificity. The structural remains at each of these sites are far from uniform. They may be divided into three broad categories: (a) those of a political nature including remnants of fortification walls, ramparts, moats and palace-like buildings; (b) structures of clearly religious character such as *stūpa* and *vihāra* complexes; and (c) heterogeneous structures such as dwellings, shops, storage areas, industrial working areas, irrigation-related structures, burial areas and so on.

At Kotalingala (long. 79', 47° E; lat. 18', 41° N) situated on the confluence of the Peddavagu and Godavari rivers, the largest mound (about 50 ha) 6 to 9 metres (m) above the plain and encompassed by a mud fort was excavated (Figure 2.1). The mud fort was enclosed by the river Godavari on the north and by the Kapparaopetvagu *nullah* on the east, which took a turn to the south and thus fortified the town at this end also. It is postulated that there were bastions, which now appear as a mound that sat on all the corners of the fortification (Figure 2.2). There was evidence of several gates opening towards the cardinal points; the main gate to the fort was noticed towards the south connecting a highway. Towards the riverside on the north and west the fort wall ran to a distance of more than 300 m. The bricks used were 50 to 59 cm long. The brick structure adjacent to the water course, it is said, indicated the presence of a wharf.[31]

Cultural data were found on the mound in several habitational floors going to a depth of between 2 and 2.5 m. Four such floors

Source: State Department of Archaeology and Museums, Government of Andhra Pradesh (before 2014).

Figure 2.1: Kotilingala: Structures under Excavation

Source: State Department of Archaeology and Museums, Government of Andhra Pradesh (before 2014).

Figure 2.2: Kotilingala Brick Fortification

were dug, divided into two phases. Phase one representing floors three and four, were said to be clearly pre-Sātavāhana, as the fourth floor showed only the use of mud-mortared walls and rubble, and no brick. It was only from phase two, that is, floor levels one and two, that bricks came into vogue, and this is identified as representing Sātavāhana times. No radiocarbon dates are available for this site, but a very significant discovery of pre-Sātavāhana and early Sātavāhana coins were found, some of them in a stratigraphic context, discussed below.[32] If one has to broadly date the structural developments at this site, one could follow the general pattern suggested by Margabandhu[33] in putting material remains from early historic settlements for the western and central parts of the subcontinent into three periods. His Period II *c*. 300 BCE to 200 CE could be taken as coterminous with the phase of structural activities at Kotalingala.

Though Kotalingala is the largest mound so far discovered in this locality, it is at Dhulikatta that the details of a fortified town emerge more clearly. Dhulikatta (long. 79', 2° E; lat. 18', 12° N) is situated amidst fertile black soil on the right bank of the Hussainivagu. The historical mound was about 18 ha in extent, about 6 m above the plains, and enclosed by mud ramparts with a present height of 3 to 5 m. This rampart was constructed with earth dug from trenches outside the fort and this area must have served as a moat.[34] The rampart consisted of hard yellowish *morrum* overlayered with black soil. Traces of a rubble foundation were found, which must have been the base of a brick fort wall of which no evidence remains.

Four gateways have, however, been traced at the cardinal points. At the southern gateway it is suggested that the plans of what were possibly guard rooms appear, but these are difficult to describe as only the foundations have survived. These comprised two rectangular halls, the flooring of which was paved with bricks measuring 56 × 27 × 7 cm. In the front of these was a gatehouse. According to Krishnasastry, the fortification followed the specification given in literary texts.[35] The mud fortifications have been traced to pre-Sātavāhana times by the excavators, while the brick-built gateway and the rows of guardrooms and pathways of *c*. 300 BCE to 200 CE have been dated to the Sātavāhana period.[36] The dating once again has been primarily done on the basis of the coins found here. Radiocarbon dates for Dhulikatta are, however, available as '(a) 2210 +/- 100 years Before Present, (b) 2965 +/- 90 years BP'[37] and these are used to date constructional activity at the fortified mound to as early as 320 BCE or so.[38]

At the centre of the fortified mound at Dhulikatta was exposed a palace complex, residential quarters and granaries, which were in inverted pyramidal form (Figure 2.3). As at Kotalingala, here too several phases of construction were available as occupational levels. In the first two phases a huge enclosure of 26 × 30.50 m was identified with a single coarse rubble foundation. The buildings here were not clear because of successive phases of occupation. In the second phase a little evidence of lime concrete flooring was available. In the third phase, however, 'spacious halls with floors paved with brick, granaries, wells and multi-storeyed buildings provided with sewage [facilities], signifying a period of prosperity' were found.[39]

Source: State Department of Archaeology and Museums, Government of Andhra Pradesh (before 2014).

Figure 2.3: Dhulikatta: Structures under Excavation

The main structure in this phase was what has been called a *chatussala* with four rectangular halls on four sides and a central courtyard. At the south-west corner inside the enclosure wall was found a brick well almost square in plan. To its north two granaries, partitioned into compartments, were located (Figure 2.4). During the fourth phase of construction all the buildings were plastered with lime and burnished to a smooth surface, and lime concrete was used for paving the floors. Construction of granaries is said to have continued in this phase and along with it a soakage pit, with a partition in the middle, was noticed to the north-east corner. There was also a fifth phase identified, which was probably raised on the ruins of the earlier. Finally, during the last and sixth phase the complexion of the habitation was supposed to have completely changed. Brick ceased to be used and small hutment-like structures appear on the ruins of the palace, probably, as Krishna-

Source: State Department of Archaeology and Museums, Government of Andhra Pradesh (before 2014).

Figure 2.4: Dhulikatta: Brick Granary

sastry concludes, as the habitat of artisans.[40] Thus much of the main constructional activity during the climactic period at Dhulikatta was done with bricks of 55 × 27 or 50 × 25 cm, though wood and tiles may also have been used for pillars and roofing.

The most outstanding structural monument (Figure 2.5) discovered near the historical mound of Dhulikatta was a Buddhist *stūpa*—the best representative of the beginnings of Buddhism in the mid-Godavari locality. It is said to be pre-Sātavāhana in its origins because no anthropomorphic representation of the Buddha was found there.[41] Its construction is, thus, dated to the last quarter of the third century BCE and its further development with embellished carved *āyaka* slabs, to the first quarter of the second century BCE. Evidence of a monastery (*vihāra*) was found to the north-west of the *stūpa*. A striking feature of the Dhulikatta *stūpa* was that though it was quite large with a solid drum of bricks capped by an *aṇḍa*, fragments of limestone carvings were fairly simple in theme and included only such engravings in relief form of *stūpas*, Muchalin-

Source: State Department of Archaeology and Museums, Government of Andhra Pradesh (before 2014).

Figure 2.5: Dhulikatta: Stūpa

danāga, Dharmachakra, Buddhapāda and the like—all indicating a symbolic representation of the Enlightened One and signifying its affiliation to the Theravada doctrine. Its discovery was considered significant because after Kondapur in the Medak district, this was the next important Buddhist site then discovered in the Telangana areas of the former state of Andhra Pradesh.

Little work has been done to explicate the Buddhist remains at Kotalingala though a *stūpa* was excavated at Pashigaon, near the site. Subsequently, the well-established Buddhist settlement at Phanigiri in Nalgonda district has been brought to light yielding exquisite sculptural wealth that can be compared with that found at Nagarjunakonda. No evidence at all of any Brahmanical temple or sculptures was found in the locality under discussion, though several terracotta figurines of the mother goddess and *yakshas* have been discovered.[42] Other evidence such as the worship of serpent (Nāga cult)[43] hardly proves that elements of Brahmanical cults were prevalent here, as Krishnasastry tends to indicate. These perhaps indicate, rather, that the indigenous community-based forms of belief were common.

In fact, it is interesting that the Dhulikatta *stūpa* is located 1 km away from the historical mound here, at a place called Venkatapur, and further, the Buddhist iconography and other elements of worship were not found integrated with the structural remains of the fort at Dhulikatta. The same is true for the other two sites in this locality. Thus, despite considerable excavation work, neither Kotalingala nor Peddabankur have yielded any major evidence of religious structures; the former at least was an important political centre and this absence in its case becomes conspicuous.

Structures of a totally different kind were excavated at Peddabankur (79', 20° E; 18', 35° N) in this locality. It is just 10 km away from Dhulikatta and can be contrasted with it since no signs of fortifications were found here. The historical site had an extent of about 30 ha, which was bound in the south and the west by a *nullah* called the Hussianivagu. The site lies amidst alluvial black soil and the surrounding hills were supposed to be good sources of secondary minerals. Krishnasastry has characterized this site as a 'village' and discussed it under the sub-heading of 'Folk Architecture'.[44]

What has been excavated here in terms of the many residential buildings constructed of brick and mud over rubble foundations, cisterns, wells (Figure 2.6), soakage pits, and drainage systems and so on, in quantum and in variety, far exceeds what we have for the fortified townships of Kotalingala and Dhulikatta. There have been many seasons of excavation conducted at Peddabankur, as is evident from the early brief reporting by the Archaeological Survey of India.[45] Following these reports, Margabandhu has noted that there were two phases of structural development at this site: the early period dated from *c.* 100 to 25 BCE and that which continued to the Sātavāhana period *c.* 50 BCE to 200 CE.[46]

There are three main enclosures identified and described by Krishnasastry as I, II and III (Figure 2.7). They were constructed of well-burnt bricks, were squarish in plan, with walls of a breadth of nearly 2 m. Enclosure I (measuring 16.80 × 15.80 m) had a small entrance in the middle of its southern wall and outside it; on its south-western corner, a brick well with terracotta rings connected to a soakage pit was located. Enclosure II (measuring 30 × 40 m) has been identified by Krishnasastry as a mint because several thou-

Source: State Department of Archaeology and Museums, Government of Andhra Pradesh (before 2014).

Figure 2.6: Peddabankur: Wedged Shaped Brick Wells

Source: State Department of Archaeology and Museums, Government of Andhra Pradesh (before 2014).

Figure 2.7: Peddabankur: Brick Square Hall

sand Sātavāhana coins came from here.[47] This had an entrance on the north-eastern corner. In Enclosure III two elliptical houses of mud walls were also found, one earlier and the other later to the date of the enclosure itself.

Outside these enclosures and contemporary with them were found houses of mostly mud walls, which had originally probably been covered with thatch or tiles. It has been suggested that these may have been the habitation dwellings of the common people. On the other hand, the purpose of the enclosure is not very clear, though it has been suggested that single families or groups of families may have lived here.[48]

There is no doubt that Peddabankur was a substantial and well-inhabited site. Being situated away from the river course, water must have been an absolute necessity for the people, and we find that during the course of excavation about twenty-two wells of varying sizes and shapes were exposed. A brick drain of about 12 cm, with its floor paved with brick has also been brought to light.

By far the most significant structures excavated at Peddabankur are the cisterns. These too were constructed with well-burnt bricks and some had brick-laid floors to avoid percolation. One cistern was found in the middle of Enclosure III and measured 80 × 75 cm. Adjoining it was a sort of unpaved washing floor bordered with bricks. In the south-west direction of Enclosure II three brick cisterns at varying distances were noticed. Of the several such cisterns found, one was discovered with fragments of iron slag, which has been taken as an indication of a blacksmith's workshop[49] (Figure 2.8).

Against this background of remnants of structures that have survived in the fort areas at Dhulikatta and Kotalingala, such as residential quarters, some kind of palace complex, and the granaries, one can deduce that a sort of ruling or dominant elite inhabited this locality. At Dhulikatta particularly, the innumerable granary structures must have been used to store the surplus generated in the adjoining countryside and kept under the control of the elite, pointing to some form of stratification. At both these places entrances on the riverside indicate the presence of wharf-like structures as transportation along the river must have been cheaper and easier.

Source: State Department of Archaeology and Museums, Government of Andhra Pradesh (before 2014).

Figure 2.8: Peddabankur: Smithery Workshop

The exact nature of the ruling elite is difficult to discern. We have a solitary inscriptional find dated on paleographic grounds to the second century CE from the *chatussala* area at Dhulikatta. This is an ivory sealing shaped as a cup on a pedestal with the words *ajanisiriya game kumariya* (Figure 2.9). This has been interpreted in one case as the mother goddess Kumari from the Grama Ajani Siriya, which is identified as Dhulikatta itself.[50] Elsewhere, it has been interpreted as a 'royal lady' from the village of Ajani Siriya.[51] The location of Dhulikatta amidst fertile black soil and the considerable number of granaries in the fort area may indicate that the ruling clans or chiefs here were from powerful landowning agricultural communities. Also apparent are the massive fortification walls built by them.

Of great historical significance is the valuable data on coins recovered in a stratified context from Kotalingala.[52] This gives us, for the first time, a variety of numismatic data that can definitely be located in a habitational phase that we cannot simplistically call Megalithic or Sātavāhana. These include punch-marked coins, the bull and flower uninscribed coins and inscribed pre-Sātavāhana coins at Kotalingala. Based on Raja Reddy and Suryanarayana Reddy's descriptions[53] of the evidence from the Kotalingala excavations, we are told that a total of 800 coins were reported from this site. Some thirty-five were reported from excavated layers and 450 were collected from the surface. The following stratigraphic levels yielded coins:

Source: State Department of Archaeology and Museums, Government of Andhra Pradesh (before 2014).

Figure 2.9: Dhulikatta: Ivory Seal

1. The bottom most fourth layer[54] yielded ceramic evidence along with punch marked and bull and flower type uninscribed coins along with gold beads. This level probably begins from the sixth century BCE or, from pre-Aśokan times and ends at the second century BCE.
2. The third layer, we are informed, was the thickest in terms of material remains and had both pre-Sātavāhana and early Sātavāhana remains including coins with legends of chiefs/kings. This material may begin with the second century BCE and end around 100 BCE.
3. The second layer has been identified as one where the evidence of destroyed brick is a feature and there is interestingly an absence of later Sātavāhana coins—a phase that probably begins with 100 BCE to the end of the first century CE.
4. The topmost layer, it is noted, had rammed the earth with silt and humus. It is this level that reveals evidence of later Sātavāhana coins—those of Vasishthiputra Pulumavi and Vasishthiputra Satakarni along with a silver Roman coin.

Findings of punch-marked coins in hoards are fairly common in the Deccan and also at excavated sites like Amaravati and Peddabankur. However, their occurrence at Kotalingala in the form of hoards, one of 400 and the other of thirty-seven during excavations,[55] adds a new dimension to the numismatic history of the locality. Not only is their number large, but they are found in a stratified context. Though these hoards still await analysis, Parabrahma Sastry refers specifically to twenty-one silver punch-marked coins in square, rectangular and round shapes. The punch-marked coins found on the surface appeared to be very fresh, indicating that they were not used for wide circulation and were probably minted locally.[56]

It is the uninscribed coins (the flower and bull type), however, that clearly appear to have been the earliest coins issued from Kotalingala.[57] These types have also been found in the Vidarbha region.[58] There are two unique symbols that appear on the Kotalingala uninscribed coins. One is the *nandipada* or *triratna* symbol[59] that, as is well-known, later came to be used over a long period of time by different rulers. The other is particularly significant as it depicts a human figure holding hunting weapons,[60] reminiscent of similar figures seen on rock paintings and of the occurrence of such weapons in Megalith burials. Scholars studying these coins point to other types—elephant, horse, lion, wheel—and note that a majority of them were of copper, with only a couple in lead. They were of different shapes and occurred from the earliest levels of the trenches excavated and coexisted with the early historical levels.[61] In other words, they coexisted with the punch-marked coins and also with the inscribed ones.

This brings us to the inscribed coins found at Kotalingala in level three. It is possible to decipher the names of kings, but not the family that they were affiliated to and, therefore, a large number of them have been referred to as the pre-Sātavāhana coins, alluding to many small local rulers. It is opined that 'these local rulers issued uninscribed coins to start with and later inscribed ones'.[62] The first of those who issued inscribed coins at Kotalingala has been identified as Gobhada (fifteen coins)[63] followed by those of Narana (three coins), Kamvayasa (four coins) and Samagopa (thirty-nine coins) (Figure 2.10).

There are certain significant features about these coins. First, the layer in which the Gobhada (Raño Gobhadasa) coins[64] were found also had gold beads, punch-marked coins and the flower

Coin of Samagopa Obverse — Coin of Samagopa Reverse

Source: Reproduced Photo Collection of D. Raja Reddy, Hyderabad.

Figure 2.10: Kotalingala: Coin of Raño Samagopa

Source: Reproduced Photo Collection of D. Raja Reddy, Hyderabad.

Figure 2.11: Kotalingala: Coin of Raño Siri Chhimuka Satavahana

type uninscribed coins. The reverse of some of his coins is blank. This may indicate that they predated the coins that have symbols on both sides.[65] Kamvayasa was the first of these rulers to adopt the Ujjain symbol. A few coins have unclear legends and this makes it difficult to identify specific names, but it seems that they all belonged to the same family.

By far the most important of them was Samagopa whose coins are found in plenty and, further, they were issued in various denominations with multiple symbols on the obverse, but the reverse invariably has the composite *nandipāda*. Most of his coins were in copper with a few in lead and potin, invariably square in shape.[66] His coins have also been found at Peddabankur and Dhulikatta. These coins are succeeded by those of Chhimuka (Figure 2.11), who scholars suggest could have been an official under Samagopa, as both their coins share a close resemblance.[67]

All these coins of the local rulers have been identified and analysed by scholars in a variety of ways. Parabrahma Sastry identifies the Gobhada and Samagopa coins with the Sunga dynasty of Vidisha that ruled over these parts.[68] Thakur Raja Ram Singh in his analysis identifies them with the descendants of the Andhakarattas referred to by Budhagosha who ruled from Kotalingala as pre-Sātavāhana Andhra kings.[69] In a broader context, Ajayamitra Sastri points out that coins of two kings (Satyabhadra and Damabhadra) along with some others were also found in the Vidharbha region and attributes them to some 'ruling chiefs' whose 'family affiliations and exact date' one cannot be sure of.[70] It must be mentioned that the close contact between the Vidharbha region and the mid-Godavari valley sites is also evident in a similarity of the Megalith burial furniture.[71]

The Kotalingala finds are outstanding because the inscribed coins were succeeded by a number of coins of a certain Chhimuka (eight coins),[72] the so-called 'founder of the Sātavāhana dynasty' in a stratified context, while others were collected on the surface.[73] Some scholars suggest that he is the same as Simuka/Sisuka, the first king in the list of Andhrabhrityas of the *purāṇas* and Simuka of the Sātavāhana *kula* mentioned in the Naneghat inscription.[74] Others question whether he should be considered the founder or only a member of the middle group of the Sātavāhanas.[75] In another context Sarma writes: 'He [Chhimuka] can at best be regarded as a collateral who ruled as a local chief because of family identity, like many chiefs bearing Sada- and Sata-ending family names'.[76] Parabrahma Sastry makes a major argument in the context of the stratigraphical placement of these coins in the Kotalingala excavation to place Chhimuka after Siri Sātavāhana and Satakarni I since both their coins occur in layer five, while those of Chhimuka are found only in the upper layers: three, two and one.[77]

For the present purpose it is important to emphasize that coins of Chhimuka have not been found in any other part of Andhra, not even in the contiguous sites of Dhulikatta and Peddbankur; he seems to be a ruler of Kotalingala at the first instance. Later, it is suggested that when he conquered other territories he issued coins as 'Rano Siri Chhimuka Sātavāhana'. In this view of Reddy and Reddy, coins of Chhimuka and Sātavāhana refer to the same king, as 'Rano Siri Sātavāhana' and 'Rano Siri Sadavahana' were found not only at Kotalingala, but also at Dhulikatta, Peddabankur, Kondapur and Warangal, and even in Vidarbha and other parts of Maharashtra.[78] In fact several coins of early rulers of the Sātavāhana family such as those of Sātavāhana (234 coins) and Satakarni (forty-seven coins) along with those of Mahatalavara (thirteen coins) have been found, which open up a new vista of the history of this locality.[79]

As is well-known, fixing the succession sequence of the Sātavāhana rulers has been a point of animated discussion: suffice here to say that after Satakarni II,[80] Sātavāhana kings seem to have left Kotalingala, Dhulikatta and Peddabankur. Instead, it is suggested that since this locality was not under the effective control of the Sātavāhanas, the Mahatalavaras, whose coins have been found here, became the effective rulers. They were followed by the Mahasenapatis. The latter were overthrown by Gautamiputra Satakarni in the Kondapur area. It was his son Vasistiputra Pulumavi who overthrew these rulers in the Kotalingala locality, as his coins have been found here during excavations. Thus: 'He seemed to have destroyed Kotalingala with its population shifted to Peddabankur, Dhulikatta and made Amaravati or Dharanikota his capital. This is corroborated by evidence of destruction and abandonment at Kotalingala and the find of his and his successor's coins at Peddabankur and Dhulikatta'.[81]

An examination of these coins enables us to make the critical point that politically powerful groups in this locality had become a force to reckon with from pre-Sātavāhana times. One may not agree with Singh's view that there existed in this sub-region as a whole a 'confederation of Petty and Tribal rulers and other kingdoms controlled by Andhra Kings'.[82] These Andhra kings, according to him, were located at Kotalingala, which he thinks is an older site than Dhulikatta.[83] From the perspective of our argument, it seems more likely that power relations were still rooted in old kin ties. The prefix *go* in the names of chiefs like Gobhada and Sama Gopa, who are said to have ruled from Kotalingala, is suggestive of the fact that their origin may have been from pastoral communities. A stone pillar, now lying in a paddy field 1 km away from the Kotalingala fortress, bears a label inscription *nāgagopinikāya*,[84] meaning an assemblage or group of 'Naga Gopi', which may have also referred to a kin group living outside the fortified township. It is pertinent to point out that both Kotalingala and Dhulikatta were surrounded by early historical sites.[85] Kotalingala was surrounded by two such small sites on both the right and left banks of the river Godavari. On the right bank was Vemnurru, a site of 3 to 4 ha, and here 'the presence of iron slag and iron ore may indicate the existence on an indigenous iron industry'.[86] On the other bank was Karnamamidi, which has yielded typical early historical pottery and bricks.[87] Similarly, Peddabankur was just 10 km away from Dhulikatta, and another early historical mound of Chinnabankur was about 4 km north of Peddabankur.[88]

Of all these, it may be suggested that Peddabankur probably had an independent political and economic existence. Here, as at Kondapur, the major early historical site of the central Deccan sub-region, a large number of coins, punch-marked and also early Sātavāhana types, were found. I.K. Sarma has suggested that Peddabankur was a mint centre;[89] Krishnasastry located this mint in Enclosure II where scores of coins were found during excavations.[90] Sarma deduces this particularly on the basis of a large number of terracotta moulds found in stratified deposits and the existence of hundreds of small die-struck pieces in pots. Two hoards of punch-marked coins have also been found here.[91] A variety of coins of different types were reported also from Kondapur and this had led its excavator Yazdani to designate it as 'an important Andhra town where coins were minted'.[92] Here too thousands of punch-marked and early Sātavāhana coins were found along with a discovery of coin moulds to which the punch-marked coins fitted[93] (Figure 2.12).

Though we have focused on three major sites in the locality, it is pertinent to point out that there existed other major centres that have yielded evidence of Sātavāhana and Roman coins, or have substantial Buddhist remains dotting the landscape of north Telangana. We have discussed below in Chapter 4 the data available from Kondapur that made it an archaeological site with immense historical significance. Similarly, Buddhist remains at Pashigaon, not far from Kotalingala, Vakatapur near Dhulikatta, at Peddabankur, Gajulabanda, Phanigiri and so on cannot be ignored. However, the integrative role played by Buddhism seems to have been limited, since after the early Sātavāhanas many of the chiefs in this locality lost their control to the Mahatalavaras and Mahasenapatis who came from outside of this locality.

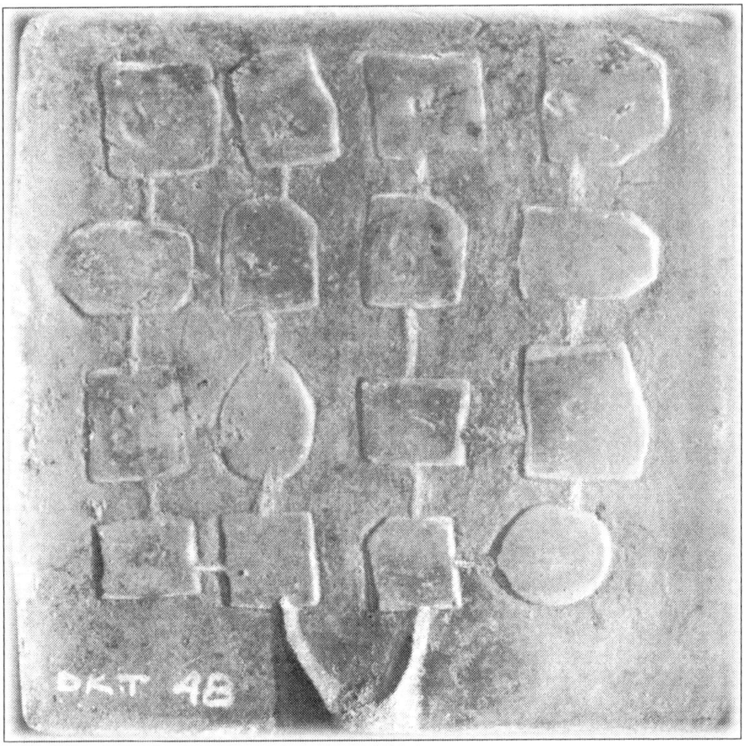

Source: State Department of Archaeology and Museums, Government of Andhra Pradesh (before 2014).

Figure 2.12: Dhulikatta: Coin Moulds

II

In giving a brief archaeological profile of the lower Krishna valley, (Map 2.2) the other locality that we take up for illustration, it is noted that its prehistoric remains are confined to only some parts of the Guntur district and mainly to areas around the Eastern Ghats. Generally, early Stone Age remains occur prolifically in the Mahboobnagar and Nalgonda districts lying to the west of the locality under discussion. That the Krishna district has substantial prehistoric remains has been elaborated upon by C.L.N. Sastry[94] and a wider study of the Krishna-Tungabhadra valley plotting sites of the earliest evolutionary patterns in the eastern Deccan has been done by B. Subramanyam and J. Varaprasad Rao in two independent monographs.[95] There is evidence of the Neolithic from excavations at Nagarjunakonda where an intrusion of the Chalcolithic is also visible in an overlap with the Neolithic, dating around 1500 BCE.[96]

In the Krishna district evidence of the Neolithic, but without certain dates, has been found at such sites as Agiripalli, Kondapeta, Puslapadu and so on, though without a transition into the Chalcolithic.[97] The same is true of the evidence of Neolithic found at Amaravati, now located in the Guntur district.[98] The Chalcolithic as a cultural phase is found only at a few sites, prominent among them being Kesarapalli and Pusalapadu in the Krishna district.[99] Based on the pottery traits, scholars have suggested a possible cultural contact between the western Deccan Neolithic-Chalcolithic cultures and those found in eastern Deccan.[100]

Most of the aforementioned sites, except Kondapeta, give evidence of the use of iron and Megalith burials. This is not only at the major settlements such as Amaravati, Dharanikota, Kesarapalli and Nagarjunakonda, but also at lesser known sites such as Agiripalli and Padidigutta in the Mahaboobnagar district where the Chalcolithic is followed by the evidence of iron.[101] At some of the sites, such as Peddamarrur in the Mahboobnagar district, Gudimellanka in the East Godavari district, and Jaggayyapeta, Konukollu and Kesarapalli in Krishna district, evidence of habitation areas near Megaliths has been reported.[102] Sites with Megalith habitation are not as prolific here as they are in the north Telangana sites discussed earlier. Nonetheless, it seems that iron-using settlements had emerged out of their antecedent Neolithic and Chalcolithic cultural phases in some cases. The extent to which they form the essential background to the early historic phase in eastern Deccan is difficult to generalize. Suffice to say that at sites such as Amaravati, Dharanikota, Vaddamanu, Gudimellanka, Jaggayyapeta, Kesarapalli, Nagarjunakonda, Pagidigutta and Peddamarrur, we find early historic material succeeding the layers yielding evidence of Megaliths. There are other places that yield early historical material, but without any reference to an iron-using Megalithic culture. These include Chintalapadu, Eturu and Kondapeta in

Krishna district, and Kudavelli in Mahboobnagar district. Further, there are other sites such as Kanukollu that only yield Megaliths.

In the midst of a society that can archaeologically be defined only in terms of its Megalith remains, we have some important material evidence that emerges on the horizon in the lower Krishna valley through contacts with Buddhism and the Mauryas. This is in the form of northern black polished ware (NBPW), punch-marked coins and the Brahmi script on some of the earliest inscriptions in eastern Deccan. It is important to reiterate that this kind of evidence is absent in central Deccan, but is found in good measure at many sites in western Deccan—Bahal, Bharuch, Bhokardan, Kaundinyapura, Nasik, Nevasa, Paithan and Prakash all yield evidence of NBPW, which at Nasik at least has been dated to as early as 500 BCE. Some of these sites—Bhokardan Kaundinyapura, Nasik and Nevasa—have also yielded early punch-marked coins. Coins of a pre-Sātavāhana ruling group in western Deccan have been found at Brahmapuri.[103]

In this regard, there is considerable similarity with eastern Deccan. Here, NBPW has been found at sites such as Amaravati, Dharanikota, Kesarapalli and Vaddamanu. With help of this data I.K. Sarma has dated the spread of Buddhism and the accompanying trade activity to pre-Aśokan times[104] since, as he points out there is evidence of pre-Mauryan punch-marked coins in coastal Andhra.[105] Mauryan contact in these parts is thus introduced in the Megalith context. This has been substantiated by a Megalith burial being found just below the *stūpa* complex at Amaravati.[106] It has been pointed out that in southern Deccan at Brahmagiri too material remains of the Iron Age have been used to measure the relationship of the so-called Megalith phase with the Mauryan contact.[107] At Amaravati and Dharanikota the pre-Mauryan punch-marked coins were followed by those that have been characterized as Mauryan punch-marked coins.[108] In the context of the influence of the Brahmi script on local inscriptions it is pointed out that several small Brahmi inscriptions have been found at Malakonda in Prakasham district[109] and the black and red potsherds at Amaravati are said to have graffiti marks in Aśokan Brahmi.[110] This is not unusual, since Aśokan inscriptions have been found in all sub-regions of the Deccan, except, as is well-known, in central Deccan. We will discuss the implication of this influence towards the end of this chapter.

In terms of the political profile of the lower Krishna valley, it needs to be emphasized that in the light of new numismatic evidence and a reinterpretation of the old, scholars have thought it fit to elaborate on the pre-Sātavāhana ruling elite. In this locality what we call pre-Sātavāhana has to be qualified, as it indicates the emergence of later Sātavāhana kings and, therefore, it needs to be further emphasized that the dates of these developments vary considerably in the different localities of the Deccan. In this context a pertinent point made by B.D. Chattopadhyaya with reference to the punch-marked coins has important bearing on the existence of other coins. He informs us that these coins that began with the Mauryan period (I.K. Sarma points to pre-Mauryan punch-marked coins) and continued to be manufactured during the early centuries of the Christian era should in fact be associated with specific 'localities'.[111] Thus, as indicated earlier in our descriptions of the mid-Godavari valley coin profile, the uninscribed cast coins and uninscribed die-struck coins[112] also need to be studied in the given localities as they set the stage for the emergence of what can best be called 'local' inscribed coin series of the Deccan.

As mentioned in Chapter 1 earlier, P.L. Gupta had analysed these coins series on a broader level to classify the big lead coins with inscriptions issued by local rulers as follows: 'Kuras in the Panchaganga basin [Kolhapur]; Sadakanas in and around Chitaldurg district; Hastin in the Krishna valley; an unknown dynasty in the Tungabhadra basin and Sadas in the Mahishaka country', which, he says, 'existed continuously till they were uprooted by the later Sātavāhanas in the time of Sri Yajna Satakarni or a little earlier in *circa* second-third centuries AD'.[113] Further, particular sites like Veerapuram, Yerragudi, Rajulamandagiri and Chandravalli have provided significant numismatic evidence of the local elite such as the Maharathi and Sadakana rulers.[114] Thus, the Kura, Sadakana and Hastin coins reveal the political profile of the western, eastern and southern Deccan after the Mauryan period and before the rise of the Sātavāhanas.

It is against this general background of numismatic evidence that we highlight the epigraphic evidence from the lower Krishna valley; a locality that we focus on to illustrate our larger argument. Here, we have quite early evidence of the existence of local chiefs in the form of the mention of Kuberaka *rāja* of the relic casket inscription found at Bhattiprolu of the third century BCE, Somaka *rāja* of an inscription of the second century BCE found on the outskirts of Vaddamanu, Aira Mana Sada of the Velpuru epigraph, and other examples of a similar kind. Parabhrama Sastry, who had put together this information in an article, laments that regarding: 'the political activity in Andhra Pradesh during the pre-Sātavāhana period . . . the information is too meagre to reconstruct any dynastic history.'[115] Though from the traditional practice of writing dynastic history, this may be true, from the point of view of our present concern this is valuable data as it throws light on the transition from the preliterate to the literate early historical stage emphasizing both the internal and external (the Brahmi script having been a cultural influence brought to the locality by the Mauryan contact) dynamics of the assertion of political-economic power.

In fact, the so-called fragmentary inscriptions have to be read alongside the coins of local rulers that have been found at Amaravati,[116] whose import till recently has not been fully discussed. We turn to take a closer look at this numismatic data in the context of the larger archaeological profile of the lower Krishna valley especially that documented in the Vaddamanu excavation report.

Bhattiprolu (long. 80' 47' E; lat. 16' 6' N) located in Guntur district was brought to light in 1892 by Alexander Rea with his excavation of a ruined mound here. Thus, was exposed the remains of a solid brick *stūpa.* Its plan was clearly traced and Rea also pointed to a portion of the dome still standing at a height of about 5 ft. As is the case with many such *stūpa* sites in coastal Andhra, this too was disturbed as bricks and stones, and even carved slabs had been removed by the local people for construction of roads, etc.

Bhattiprolu is of critical importance as it is this site that has given us some of the earliest inscriptions of individuals from different families and guilds who may have contributed to the construction of the *stūpa.* These inscriptions have been dated by some to about between 300 to 200 BCE,[117] though Sircar dates them to 100 BCE.[118] The most important of these individuals was Kuberaka *rāja,* perhaps a chief of the locality who, writes Debala Mitra, 'earned merit by sharing in the donation of the contents of the receptacles',[119] the receptacles being a 'crystal reliquary' containing some ashes and a few bits of gold leaf and a pearl (Figure 2.13). These were said to be the corporeal relics of the Buddha and in this sense, like Amaravati, Bhattiprolu[120] emerged as one of the most sacred spots of early Buddhism in the lower Krishna valley.

Apart from its sanctity, this site is located just 20 km away from Amaravati and, therefore, they must have shared ideological influences and social networks of interaction. Both witnessed some of the earliest Buddhist activity in the region. Unfortunately, apart from the *stūpa* site, no other excavations were conducted here and this, therefore, makes it difficult to generalize on its antecedent cultural layers of habitation and its importance as an economic centre.

Source: State Department of Archaeology and Museums, Government of Andhra Pradesh (before 2014).

Figure 2.13: Bhattiprolu: Relic Casket Inscription

The same, of course, cannot be said about Amaravati as a religious centre since we have the contiguous fort site of Dharanikota and both have to be treated together. The ancient name of Amaravati (long. 80' 21° E; lat. 16' 34° E), as is well known, was Dhanyakataka. The present Dharanikota is about half a mile to the west of the main *stūpa* site called Mahāchaitya. Excavations at both the *stūpa* site (Figure 2.14) as well as at the high mounds containing the ruins of an ancient city/fort at Dharanikota have been conducted by several archaeologists. It first came to the notice of Colin Mackenzie in 1797. In 1816 when Mackenzie returned to Amaravati to survey the site, he made its first maps. Three areas were put on these maps '(1) the mound of Deepaladinne, which house the Buddhist *stūpa;* (2) the ancient fortified town of Dharanikota; and (3) the spot containing a group of about 20 circles of the Iron Age'.[121] It is reported that Mackenzie also found some coins and noticed inscriptions on stone slabs, and today all these aspects of this famed and much studied site of Amaravati-Dharanikota have been repeatedly opened for discussion and interpretation.

Source: State Department of Archaeology and Museums, Government of Andhra Pradesh (before 2014).

Figure 2.14: Amaravati: Mahāstūpa

Though Amaravati had been inherited by subsequent archaeologists as a disturbed site[122] yet a number of excavations were conducted here since the nineteenth century to primarily establish the stratigraphy and chronology of its innumerable sites. This was not an easy task. In fact, much of the study done for Amaravati has been from an art historical point of view.[123] Further, another element of research that was prolifically done on this site was the documentation the short votive inscriptions found on the structural parts and sculptural slabs of the *mahāchaitya*.[124] These have been dated to between the second century BCE and third century CE. Apart from some of these inscriptions, it is the material evidence from Amaravati-Dharanikota, particularly in the form of coins[125] that indicate the internal forces of change and continuity in this locality.

During the latter half of the twentieth century it was H. Sarkar[126] and I.K. Sarma who emphasized that: (a) we need to look beyond the main *stūpa* and other religious monuments to capture a holist archaeological profile of Amaravati and its environs; (b) we need to look at the archaeological and epigraphic material found at Amaravati and Dharanikota together; and, finally, (c) to relook at the *pre-mahāstūpa* phase of habitation at the site. To look beyond the *stūpa* area one has to first and foremost address the question of the Megalithic association of this site. Some scholars are of the opinion that the Megalithic people acculturated the coastal areas of Andhra at a later date when compared to the interior plateau areas of Telangana,[127] and this period of transition from 'Megalithic to the early historical in the eastern Deccan' has been dated based on the 'appreciable quantity' of 'material remains' found at Amaravati to the fourth to third centuries BCE.[128]

The significance of Megalith finds at Amaravati is, as mentioned earlier, that Megalithic burials occur in a layer just below the main *stūpa*[129] (Figure 2.15) also, some are found in close proximity to the *stūpa*, which at the point of their initial discovery were paid little attention to.[130] In recent years scholars have raised two pertinent issues about these finds well within the Buddhist complex that housed the *mahāchaitya* and several other small *stūpas*. The first is the relationship of the early Buddhist monks who came to

Source: State Department of Archaeology and Museums, Government of Andhra Pradesh (before 2014).

Figure 2.15: Amaravati: Megaliths

inhabit this locality and the existing cultic practices of the Megalith builders. Gregory Schopen has aptly summarized:

> Their choice of such sites would have placed the Buddhist complex at an already established focal point in the local landscape and in the local community. It would have established the Buddhist monastic community as the keepers, the guardians of the native dead, and claim thereby an important function for the newly arrived monks. It also would have assimilated the newcomers own central focus—the *stūpa*—to local, pre-existing structures.[131]

The second is the broader socio-economic context in which the networks established by these Megalithic people were maintained or transformed with the coming of new elements into these localities. Earlier scholarship, based mainly on data from coastal Andhra, has already tried to explain this relationship. That there was some form of exchange in the Megalithic context has been emphasized.[132] However, it is articulated that its pastoral economy in a symbiotic relationship with a semi-agrarian society could best be defined in terms of complex kinship network of a chiefdom gradually transforming itself into a state society with increasing acculturation of the locality under external stimuli.[133] In the midst of these interpretations, we wish to complicate the nature of the transition to the early historic state by highlighting the political patronage networks at Amaravati and the surrounding areas in the context of recent studies on the coins of local chiefs in this area.

As in the case of our discussions on the mid-Godavari locality, here too the main line of argument is based on the identification and study of local coins; in the lower Krishna valley those that have been attributed to the Sada family of kings. Coins and inscriptions bearing the name *sada* have been known to scholars earlier, but because there was no systematic initial discovery, they were studied case by case, with little attempt to understand the significant political role that they may have played in this area. The earliest report of a coin bearing the inscription *sadasa*, which was found in the lower Krishna valley, was made by Rapson.[134] Such coins were found in particular at Amaravati and Dharanikota, but were attributed to a Sātavāhana king by Rama Rao.[135] Subsequently, I.K. Sarma re-examined the earliest find by Rapson and categorically rejected its identification as a Sātavāhana coin and, instead, attributed it to a different dynasty that ruled over coastal Andhra during the first century CE.[136] Sarma elaborates that in fact the beginning of the Sada connection with coastal Andhra should go back to the Guntupalli pillar inscription dated to the first century BCE, which mentions a Siri Sada in the following lines: '*mahārājasa kaliga [ma] hisakadhipatisa mahāmekhavāhanasa sirisadasī*' (Srī Sada the *mahārāja* of the Kalinga-Mahisaka [country] of the Mahāmekhāvahana [family])[137] (Figure 2.16). Though the Mahisaka territory is difficult to clearly establish, most scholars agree that it was some part of the coastal region of Andhra. Based on the evidence of the Hathigumpha inscription, the Kalinga connection is understood as Kharavela's campaign and victory over this region.

Most of the Sada coins have a lion with a tree in railing on the obverse and a six-arched hill and a legend on the reverse, indicat-

Source: State Department of Archaeology and Museums, Government of Andhra Pradesh (before 2014).

Figure 2.16: Guntupalli: King Siri Sada Inscription

ing the possible name of the king. One such coin has been read by Raja Reddy and P.S.N. Reddy with the legend reconstructed as 'Asaka Sadasa' suggesting that this belonged to a king of the Meghavahana dynasty of Kalinga.[138] Reddy and Reddy have done a detailed study of about fifteen such coins from Dharanikota and Amaravati in the collection of the State Museum at Hyderabad bearing the names Raño Siri Maha Sadasa, Siva Sadasa, Sadasa and so on, and have attributed all of them to this dynasty.[139] Thus, they write: 'The kings' names ending as Sadasa probably represent the Kalinga rulers of coastal Andhra belonging to this Meghavahana dynasty in the same way as the Satakarni coins are said to have been issued by Sātavāhana dynasty'.[140]

Many scholars do not concur with this view and suggest that the Sadas had a local indigenous origin. On the other hand, it is suggested by others that Siri Sada of Guntupalli inscription succeeded Kharavela in coastal Andhra.[141] This conclusion is significant from the perspective of the present discussion since so far the largest number of Sada coins have been found in Amaravati and its surroundings of Dharanikota and Vaddamanu.[142] T.V.G. Sastry also suggests that the Sadas succeeded Kharavela in the coastal Andhra regions. In fact, it is the excavations conducted at Vaddamanu that revealed the magnitude of the Sada influence in the lower Krishna valley as here at least thirty-three of their coins were recovered in a stratigraphical context corresponding to 50 BCE to CE 50.[143]

We next turn to examine some of the excavated material brought to light by archaeologists of the Birla Archaeological Research and Cultural Institute of Hyderabad at Vaddamanu[144] against which the numismatic data on the Sadas can be evaluated. Vaddamanu (long. 80', 25.30° E; lat. 16', 32° N) lies 10 km away from Amaravati and, therefore, its links with the material remains there are of some significance. It is surrounded by two hillocks: Chinnakonda (Chinnamadduru) and Peddakonda (Peddamadduru). It is on the latter that four areas of ancient remains were identified and excavated as VDM I, VDM II, VDM III and VDM IV. Ancient remains were also found in the environs of Vaddamanu at Vaikuntapuram, Harischandrapur and Donapadu to its north-east, Anantavaram to its north, and Chavapadu to its immediate west. Archaeological material found in these environs goes back to the Middle Paleolithic and Neolithic assemblages, with mircrolith blades found to the west and north-east of Peddakonda.[145] Besides, the village of Anantavaram, conspicuous by its hills, has revealed Megalithic burials in the form of cairn circles, slabs of orthostats, etc., alongside the usual Megalith pottery of red ware, black and red ware, and black ware.[146] A large part of the report is devoted to a detailed discussion of what the excavators call 'early historic cultures'. These are divided into four cultural sequences based on the evidence provided by pottery, inscribed potsherds, structures, stone inscriptions and coins. The chronology[147] and cultural sequence is described as follows:

1. Period I dated to *c.* 300 to 100 BCE has black and red ware, black ware alongside NBP ware and polished black ware at the earliest levels at Vaddamanu. It is noted that in fabric and form the black and red ware resembles that found at Anantavaram

village where three complete Megalithic pots were found. This is followed by a stage of inscribed potsherds. The most important find is the rock-cut inscription of King Samaka dated 300 to 200 BCE and the script in both has been paleographically dated 300 to 200 BCE as well. In terms of structures, a boulder *stūpa,* some balconies and part of a *vihāra* are identified to belong to this period. It is important to note that no coins were found in this period.

2. Period II dated *c.* 100 BCE to CE 200 has been characterized by the appearance of Rouletted ware, which is considered coeval with similar ware found at Amaravati and dated *c.* 100 BCE. NBPW continues, but exists only at the early levels. Coins of the lion type, known commonly as Sada coins, both with and without legends, emerge only in this period. No other coin of any other dynasty is found in this period. Several structures of *stūpas, vihāras,* etc., are dated to this period (Figure 2.17).
3. Period III dated to *c.* CE 200 to 350 sees the continuation of the Sada coins, those of Sivamaka Sada, in the early levels. Both

Source: Reproduced from T.V.G. Sastry (1992: Pl. XVI).

Figure 2.17: Vaddamanu: Excavation Structures of Periods I and II from East

Sātavāhana and Ikshvaku coins occur together around the third century CE. Ceramics in the form of red ware with evolved rims emerge, and Rouletted ware as a survival of the earlier period continues. In fact, limestone fragments of pillars, coping stones, etc. form the foundation material for structures during this period (Figure 2.18).

4. Period IV is dated *c.* 350 to 450 CE and identified as Vishnukundin.

Our concern here is with Periods I and II. The excavators pertinently note that Megalithic black and red ware[148] is 'associated with the occurrence of NBP ware' and the latter 'belongs to the mature phase of the ware dateable to the end of the fourth century BC'. It is this, they write, which provides the 'chronological peg for fixing the beginning of Period I to *c.* 300 BC'.[149] They also point to one sherd of NBPW found in the upper levels of the Megalithic occupation, which they date to the third century BCE. This dating is comparable to the one given for the occurrence of NBPW found in Period IB at Amaravati[150] and that found at Kesarapalli.[151] Significant coin finds of *rana sirimahasada, rana sirisivamakasada* and

Source: Reproduced from T.V.G. Sastry (1992: Pl. XVI).

Figure 2.18: Vaddamanu: General view of Boulder Stūpa

(*rano*) *asakasada* appear in Period II and they are specifically put in the time bracket *c.* 100 BCE to *c.* 100 CE (Figure 2.19). A total of forty-seven inscribed and forty uninscribed lion type coins were found during the course of these excavations.[152] Prasad attempts to provide a chronological order for these kings, and mentions in addition two more kings, namely, Siri Sada and Siva Sada. He concludes that Sivamaka Sada can be seen as the last of the major Sada rulers in this locality because of the similarity in design of his coins and the ones issued by Vasisthiputra Pulumavi, the first Sātavāhana ruler in this region. Further, both he and his successor Vasisthiputra Satakarni counter struck the Sada coins with the *nandigrama* symbol, suggesting their conquest over them.[153]

70. VDM II. D_5 3. No. 1407. P. II. lead, size 2.77 cms. Wt. 15.08 gms.

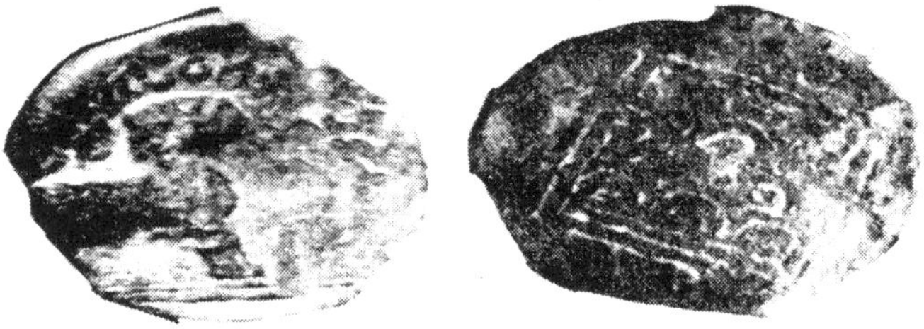

Obv : Lion to the right, two horizontal lines below the animal, legend along the flan reads as *[Siri] Siva Maka Sada sa.*

Rev : Six arched hill surmounted by a crescent, each arch in double lines; below the arched hill a wavy line, enclosed in a double lined square frame.

R : The right side portion in front of the animal is hammered and the last three letters *'Sadasa'* are blurredd.

Source: Reproduced from T.V.G. Sastry (1992: 164).

Figure 2.19: Vaddamanu: Coins attributed to Sivamaka Sada

As mentioned earlier, both from the evidence of punch-marked coins and early inscriptions written in Aśokan Brahmi, the Mauryan contact with this locality is well-established. However, hitherto the *mahāstūpa* chronology has generally been associated with the Sātavāhanas, with little scrutiny given to the history and material remains of the intervening period. Did indeed the early Buddhist monastic organizations only get their legitimacy from major political players (Mauryas and Sātavāhanas) in the area? Akira Shimada has taken up a detailed analysis on this subject to propose a different political setting and, thus, a new chronology against which the Amaravati *stūpa* must have been constructed.[154] Based on this evidence found in the locality as a whole[155] and not merely from Amaravati, Shimada suggests that it must be accepted that a Sada dynasty ruled over the Amaravati region before it came under the influence of the later Sātavāhanas, and that new numismatic evidence on the later Sātavāhanas has to be taken into account to rework the dates when they ruled over this area.

Accordingly, after reviewing the entire gambit of numismatic and epigraphic evidence for Amaravati, Shimada proposes the following chronology: (a) The Sadas: *c.* from 40-30 BCE to *c.* 90-100 CE; (b) the later Sātavāhanas: from 90-100 CE to 224-45 CE; and (c) the Sātavāhanas having risen to power in western Deccan around 50-60 CE.[156] The coins of Sivamaka Sada were found in Period III described in the Vaddamanu excavation report and dated to 100 BCE to 150 CE, and he is the same king whose name is found on a label inscription from Amaravati. Shimada notes that earlier scholars have erroneously tried to identify him with a Sātavāhana king.[157] In fact, he suggests that the inscription[158] on which Sivamaka Sada's name occurs is a rail coping with accompanying sculptures, which have been designated as the 'high' style of Amaravati, leading to an important conclusion, namely, 'that the construction and embellishment work of the *stūpa was highly developed under this local dynasty*'[159] [emphasis added].

A further implication is that the period of the construction of the *stūpa* now must be considered longer and its flowering cannot simply be attributed to the 'great' Sātavāhanas. The magnitude of the discovery of Sada coins in the Vaddamanu excavations, and also at Amaravati and Dharanikota has thus thrown up significant lines of interpretation about the relationship of the later Sātavāhanas with the pre-existing chiefs of the areas. Further, it is not simply giving a so-called 'dynastic' status to pre-Sātavāhana kings that concerns us here, but, rather, the larger question of the critical role they played in the transition to early state in the lower Krishna valley. We would argue that the Sātavāhanas inherited some of the institutional structures and ideological linkages that these local communities had established.

The discussion emanating from the material discussed above in this chapter has to necessarily begin with the following three recognitions:

1. Local polities known to us through their coins emerged in the midst of Megaliths (not as a time period) with their infinite variety of funerary structures and associated material remains and artefacts.
2. The numismatic evidence discussed has helped fill the gap between the end of the so-called Mauryan contact with the Deccan and the rise of the Sātavāhanas, and political history can now be projected in relatively clearer terms, suggesting that the Sātavāhanas as the harbingers of the first State with the Deccan as their nucleus, built their authority on initially establishing a close network with existing local chiefs and the way they did this differed from locality to locality.
3. Finally, the criteria to mark the beginning of what we all understand in general terms as the early historic phase, namely, the emergence of writing, the rise of urban centres, monuments and the like, does not coincide with the rise of Sātavāhana power, but preceded it in terms of their incipient forms.

Is it possible for us to come to some agreement on the nature of these polities and the nomenclature we should use to define this transition to early state? This question harbours one certainty: that the phase of transition being addressed does not warrant the designation of a 'typical state' as defined by Classaen and Skalnik. The groups who issued these coins, nonetheless, did develop certain powers, reflecting some sort of centralization. The broader socio-economic context in which this emerged varied in each locality.

In the mid-Godavari locality details of individual buildings and the layout of the buildings at each of the sites discussed do not enable us to come to any firm conclusion about the residential pattern of the community/communities. In fact, it must also be stated that at each of these sites the pattern is distinct and, therefore, one cannot suggest that there was an overall supervising authority to enforce common layout plans and architectural forms. What is certain, however, is that there emerged an essential interdependence between the fortified and non-fortified settlements.

A more fundamental point is that there was a coexistence of a variety of coin types. What was their link to the economic activity of the locality? Evidence suggests that in pre-Sātavāhana times some social groups were engaged in the minting of coins in what the excavators had designated as 'mint centres'. The mechanism through which the ruling groups and those involved in this activity interacted needs to be established. Elsewhere,[160] we have elaborated upon this locality's ability to generate iron objects on a large scale, which transformed its economy—a process that began with the occurrence of Megaliths in the area. This would suggest the existence of what Rouse calls 'professional co-people', but, as he observes, 'the professional and sustaining co-peoples [both] share civilization' and, further, that they 'may both be urban, both rural, or one may be urban and the other rural'.[161] Drawing on this insight is important in the present context since the 'sustaining co-peoples' he refers to suggests that there was a complex interdependence on different modes of production.

This locality has thrown up considerable evidence of the occurrence of Microliths and Neolithic tools at historical levels of habitation and, as is well known based on anthropological case studies, groups divided on kin lines are involved in the smelting and foraging of iron. We contend that exchange and trade in these parts was stimulated not so much by the production of an agrarian surplus, but by the supply of iron objects and other related commodities. A concomitant effect of this was the working in precious metals like gold and semiprecious stones, bead making, and pottery and terracotta making. It is pertinent to note here, however, that evidence of short fragmentary references to *gahapatis, goshtis*, etc., as found in the lower Krishna valley, is very meagre.[162] A large chunk of the 'sustaining co-people' in the mid-Godavari locality were, thus, artisan groups with strong ties of kinship persisting in the organization of their work. This may explain the existence of a variety of coin types found at these sites.

Political power was necessarily segmented in pre-Sātavāhana times and always, to use Cohen's term, under the threat of 'fission'. In essential terms then it would not be an exaggeration to state that it was the capacity of the dominant social groups in the locality to supervise this production and maintain networks of exchange and trade, which resulted in the growing strength of certain local elite. They were, indeed, able to concentrate and organize themselves in settlements which, due to the geo-cultural and techno-economic, as well as institutional constraints and possibilities, developed an individual character, different in content and style from similar processes of rulers issuing their own coins in pre-Sātavāhana times in the lower Krishna valley.

Hitherto, the rise of the Sātavāhana power in the Deccan has been generally viewed as an overarching and monolithic structure that stood like an imperial edifice, having washed away earlier forms of social and political control. The historiographical thrust in the writing of early Andhra history has been on highlighting the epigraphic evidence that reflects on the power, wealth and spread of *gahapatis, goshtis, nigamas* and the like. What has, however, been unconsciously ignored in the analysis is that there were several complex cultural traits that underlay this apparent uniformity that is projected primarily because the 'hardcore' evidence of the inscription fits in well with providing a historical narrative in a region devoid of textual material for this early period. The pre-Sātavāhana is, thus, projected as this ambiguous, unknown territory described in bleak terms or in the negativity of being on the periphery of civilization. As mentioned at the outset, the term 'tribal' or 'tribe' is used indiscriminately to describe and club together all pre-state groups. This not only creates a discontinuity between the pre-civilization and civilization stages, but also pejoratively dismisses the importance that these well-entrenched communities played in the formation of state society and civilization.

It is well-known that the first settled village communities with some form of an organized but nascent political authority can be traced to the Chalcolithic cultures, which have been dated to around 2000 to 1000 BCE in what has been identified as western Deccan, and this is reflected at a few sites in eastern Deccan or coastal Andhra as well. In the context of the latter, the spread of primarily Megalith funerary structures, and occasionally the habitation areas associated with them, mark the archaeological landscape. In fact, the discovery of Megalith-related artefacts, pottery and structures continues, and, therefore, their documentation remains an ongoing process. Our survey of prominent sites in the lower Krishna valley has revealed that there were signs of an emergent urban economy in these parts much before evidence of late Sātavāhana coins and other material evidence related to them occurred on the archaeological horizon. The early contact with north and central India vide the occurrence of NBPW and structures reflecting well-established monastic communities highlight the dynamic nature of this contact.

It must, however, be emphatically stated when new elements were subsequently added due to interregional trade and contact as a consequence of the Mauryan intrusion or with the Indo-Roman contact, it was done on a solid foundation of economically differentiated communities.[163] The archaeological record for southern and eastern Deccan is particularly telling in this regard.[164] These communities, nonetheless, continued to be organized on the basis of kinship ties. In *The Mauryas Revisited*[165] Romila Thapar rightly postulates that since the political nucleus of the Mauryan empire was so far away from this region, their mechanisms for appropriating the wealth available in these parts must have been dependent to a large extent on the pre-state groups and their network of lineage and kin. It has been suggested that the conspicuous concentration of Aśokan edicts in mineral-rich areas or around important port towns was indicative of the fact that the interests of the Mauryan state were of an economic nature, namely, in the exploitation of the local resources, and not in territorial annexation and control.[166] The Mauryan penetration into this locality of the Deccan was thus based on its interaction with the already existing kin-based organizations through its links with the political power of the indigenous chiefs. This was not uniform and only small localities, as in the case of the lower Krishna valley in the present case study, which had the specific economic potential of being used, were affected. On the other hand, the mid-Godavari valley, which also had a powerful local ruling elite but with little economic resource for exploitation, was devoid of any direct Mauryan influence.

On the basis of the kind of information discussed earlier on the local elite who issued their own coins—the Sadas in this locality—it needs to be clearly stressed that this would not have been possible had it not meant some amount of socio-economic change generated both by an expansion of the technology associated with Megaliths and its impact on society, as well as some amount of contact with Mauryan trade and exchange in certain select areas. In the lower Krishna valley all the three sites discussed—Amaravati/Dharanikota, Bhattiprolu and Vaddamanu—were closely associated with social groups that had much to do with the spread of Shramanic sects. The architectural and artistic wealth of the locality is evidence enough to substantiate this. Further, it has already been pointed out that the inscriptional data from Amaravati tells us about powerful individuals and rulers who made donations to the Buddhist establishment. Those that benefited from the expanding trade prolifically document their names at these monastic sites and, in fact, at Guntupalli and Kesarapalli[167] we find the existence of early levels of habitations as part of commercial complexes. Since much of the analysis on the structure of the Sātavāhana polity has hitherto been built on the data that comes from the lower Krishna valley, it is our submission that the Sātavāhana state cannot be understood without a deep reading of the material and in this case the numismatic evidence of the preceding stages. Otherwise, we will continue to contemplate on a sudden emergence of the 'early historic'. It is our submission that it is only by taking into account the antecedent cultural phases of habitation, emphasizing on continuities rather than disjunctions, which in the two localities exemplified were very different from each other, that we can appreciate the extent to which the Sātavāhanas played an integrative role in a society that was still rooted in particular economic and material moorings. Overall, what we do see when the 'typical state' is clearly visible is the legitimizing role of Buddhism both at the local and pan-regional level so that monastic organizations supported by urban settlements co-existed with those located in farflung zones of relative isolation,which had to be necessarily supported by the local communities that came into contact with the monks.

In re-examining the question of 'transition' to the early state in the Deccan, we reject the hypothesis that the processes of political evolution should simply been seen in terms of a compartmentalized tribal/non-stratified and state/stratified stage. Other binaries projected to differentiate the early history of this region like the juxtaposition of 'pre-history/'proto-history' with 'early history', 'tribal' with 'civilization', 'Megalithic' with 'Andhra' as in classifying pottery types, 'uninscribed' with 'inscribed' coins to signify two separate and unrelated historical processes has to be reworked into our analysis of understanding transition from the regional perspective. We underline that for understanding the processes of early state formation in these parts one needs to highlight the particular ecological and material diversity in the antecedent phases in these localities. This has to be linked to the assertion of political and economic power as evidenced in the variety and nature of coins found in these localities. It remains significant that it was the spread of Buddhism and its various transformations in the Deccan that was able to play an integrative role in a society still rooted in local moorings. In this kind of scenario relationships of power before the rise of state in different regions and localities do not have to be typecast into given definitions of civilization. On the contrary, such case studies throw up a different and alternative way of understanding these processes. These were societies, to use Springborg's words, 'more transactional' than the ones we use as models to discuss the human evolutionary process. In these societies 'power is created by interactions, exchanges and those structures of social life that provide a multiplicity of forums for negotiation, transaction and exchange'.[168] The coins we have discussed above are the outward signs that imply a complex network of sustained interaction: even though power changed hands, they left the networks intact.

NOTES

1. Based on Morton Fried's theorization, Khazanov distinguishes between pristine and secondary types of early state. For details, see Khazanov (1978). The editors concur with his view Claessen and Skalnik (1978: 620).
2. For the Deccan this argument has been coherently put forward by Sudarshan Seneviratne (1980-1) that points to both external and internal processes of changes, but with greater emphasis on the former.
3. Childe (1955; 1978).
4. Tringham (1980: 470-84).
5. Springborg (1992: 7-18).
6. In terms of the documentation of archaeological and monumental remains *in situ* to restore visibility to its past in terms of the extant heritage of a given place, a good example is Sarma (1972). There is proliferation of such studies from the early medieval period onwards.
7. Gupta et al. (2000: pts. I and II).
8. Gopalachari (1941); Murthy (1981); Sudhakar Chattopadhyaya (1974); Yazdani (1982); Sastri (1987).
9. A theoretical discussion of the same can be found in Service (1975: 10-20). The characterization of this social base as concomitant with the rise of urbanization was first formulated by Childe (1957: 36).
10. A case in point is publication of Sastry (1994), The main aim of this small monograph is to provide a new chronological sequence for the rule of the early Sātavāhana kings based on the excavated material found at Kotalingala, leading him to a re-examination of the epigraphic and literary source material.
11. Considerable new data on the subject has been published as in Krishnasastry (1983), but with little analysis on the nature of society that these material remains implied.
12. A cursory glance at the collection of articles in Shastri (1999) exemplifies this type of research.
13. We shall be reflecting on these studies during the course of this paper.
14. Parasher Sen (1992: 437-77).
15. Claessen and Skalnik (1978: 21).
16. Service (1975: 16).
17. Claessen and Skalnik (1978: 23).
18. A.M. Khazanov in Claessen and Skalnik (1978: 80-1).
19. Cohen (1981: 87).
20. Cohen (1978: 37).
21. Parasher-Sen in Shastri (1999: 153-91).

22. Local history studies have hitherto been encapsulated in what is commonly and conventionally called 'Place Names Studies'. A classic example for former state of Andhra Pradesh is Murthy (1985). However, this is not the approach we intend to follow. On the contrary, it is intended to link details of the local with a larger whole for identifying processes of historical change.
23. Chattopadhyaya in Pande and Chattopadhyaya (1987: 728).
24. This has reference to our work done under the Ford Foundation/French Institute of Pondicherry-sponsored *Digital Historical Atlas of South India* published in Parasher Sen (2006).
25. Reference to districts and taluks in this chapter are to those that were formed in the former State of Andhra Pradesh. Since the bifurcation of the state in 2014, district boundaries and names have been changed.
26. This was supposed to be contiguous to Mulaka, identified with the present-day districts of Nasik-Poona, Aurangabad, Osmanabad and Ahamadnagar, and Assika, which has been identified as between the rivers Godavari and Krishna.
27. Krishnasastry in Sitapati (1981: 1).
28. The date assigned for the Megaliths at Arepalli in Warangal district by the State Department of Archaeology and Museums is 800 to 300 BCE. For the rest of what was the former state of Andhra Pradesh the upper limit of Megalith-related material is extended up to 400 CE, being coeval with the historical period as evidenced by the excavations of Nagarjunakonda as summarized in *History and Culture of the Andhras* (1995), a Potti Sriramnla, Telugu University publication.
29. Reference to districts in this chapter are to those that were formed in the former State of Andhra Pradesh. Since the bifurcation of the state in 2014, district boundaries and names have been changed.
30. Krishnasastry (1983: 115)
31. Even three decades after these excavations were conducted by the former State Department of Archaeology and Museums, Government of Andhra Pradesh, no excavation report has been published for this important site. These descriptions are summarized from the annual reports of the department and from Krishnasastry (1983: 125, 132).
32. Singh (1979: 1-12) (1987: 6-8).
33. This scheme is based on the stratigraphy of the datable finds like coins and pottery, and for this reason cannot be considered absolute. The other two periods are: Period I *c.* 600-300 BCE and Period III *c.* 200-400 CE (cf. Margabandhu 1985: 18).
34. The excavation report for this site too has still not been published. The

information cited here has been collated from *Indian Archaeology: A Review* (1974-5: 3; 1975-6: 2-3; 1976-7: 4-5 and Krishnasastry (1983: 124-5, 130-3).

35. Krishnasastry (1983; 124-5, 130-3).
36. Margabandhu (1985: 34).
37. Krishnasastry (1983; 232-3).
38. Singh (1987: 7).
39. Krishnasastry (1983: 136-7).
40. Krishnasastry (1983: 138-9).
41. Krishnasastry (1983: 125; 144-5).
42. Krishnasastry (1983: 186-8).
43. Krishnasastry (1983: 224).
44. Krishnasastry (1983: 138-9).
45. *Indian Archaeology: A Review*, 1967-8: 2; 1968-9: 1-2; 1970-1: 2; 1971-2: 2 and 1974-5: 5.
46. Margabandhu (1985: 25).
47. In the earlier article, Krishnasastry (1978: 60) refers to Enclosure I as having been a mint.
48. Krishnasastry (1983: 139-40).
49. Margabandhu (1985: 25).
50. Krishnasastry (1983: 183).
51. Krishnasastry (1978: 65).
52. Singh (1987: 8)
53. Reddy and Reddy (1993a: 5).
54. Sastry (1994: 3-5) refers to the existence of six layers depending on the trench in which the coins were found. Since a detailed excavation report is not available for Kotalingala, one will have to accept this difference of opinion.
55. Reddy and Reddy (1993a: 58).
56. Sastry (1994: 25).
57. Reddy and Reddy (1984: 22-62).
58. Tiwari (1998: 6).
59. Reddy and Reddy (1993a: 23).
60. Reddy and Reddy (1993a: 18).
61. Sastry (1994: 26-7) thus points out that 'it is difficult to arrange these coins in a strict chronological sequence', and in fact suggests that those with the Ujjain symbol may have been issued by chiefs serving under Samagopa or his successor Siri Sātavāhana.
62. Reddy and Reddy (1993a: 58).
63. These numbers refer to those coins of the kings that were first studied and

analysed by Sastry (1978, 1979b). Singh (1987: 8) who also studied these coins gives the following number of coins of each ruler—Gobadha (seventeen) and Narana (nine) and Samagopa (sixty-eight).

64. Thirty coins of this ruler were recovered from the surface, and only four have been reported from stratified layers. Nonetheless, they are considered the earliest based on the paleography and the fact that some of the letters have been punched in (cf. Sastry 1994: 27).
65. Reddy and Reddy (1993a: 59).
66. Sastry (1994: 29-31).
67. Sastry (1978: 14); I.K. Sarma (1980: 36).
68. Sastry (1979a: 136-7).
69. Singh (1987: 14).
70. Sastry (1978: 963-7); (1982: 4).
71. Krishnasastry (1983: 115).
72. This number refers to those coins of this king that were studied and analysed by Sastry (1978, 1979) in two of his earliest articles on the subject.
73. Krishnasastry (1983: 126, 132).
74. Reddy and Reddy (1993a: 59).
75. Sarma (1980: 92).
76. Sarma in Shastri (1999: 344).
77. Sastry (1994: 7-11).
78. They in fact write: 'Hence it may be concluded that the coins of King Sātavāhana belong to Chimuka'.
79. Singh (1987: 8).
80. Sastry (1994: 40) notes that apart from Satakarni II, coins of Pulumavi I are found on the topmost layers at Kotalingala, but coins of their predecessor Krishna or Kanna as per Purāna lists are conspicuous by their absence here.
81. Reddy and Reddy (1993a: 62).
82. Singh (1987: 3).
83. Singh (1987: 8).
84. Krishnasastry (1983: 148).
85. Krishnasastry (1983: 125-30).
86. Krishnasastry (1983: 125).
87. Krishnasastry (1983: 128).
88. Krishnasastry (1983: 125).
89. Sarma (1980: 35).
90. Krishnasastry (1983: 139).
91. Krishnasastry (1983: 200).
92. Yazdani (1941: 180).
93. Yazdani (1940-1: 20).

94. *Indian Archaeology: A Review* 1978.
95. Subramanyam (1997); Rao (2001).
96. Subrahmanyam, *Nagarjunakonda,* 1954-60, vol. I, New Delhi, 1965: 81, 101, 105, 130, 165, 195, *Ancient India,* 1960: 65. *Indian Archaeology: A Review* 1959-60.
97. *Indian Archaeology: A Review* (1962-3: 67); (1969-70:1); (1976-7: 5); Sastry et al. (1992: 28-35).
98. *Indian Archaeology: A Review* (1973-74: 4); Ramaswamy (174: 2).
99. *Indian Archaeology: A Review* (1961-2: 1-2); (1962-3: 67).
100. Subbarao (1958: 115).
101. *Indian Archaeology: A Review* (1978-79: 65).
102. *Indian Archaeology: A Review* (1962-3: 65, 66-7); (1977-8: 12); *Annual Reports, State Department of Archaeology and Museums, Government of Andhra Pradesh* (1974-5: 3, 56).
103. Parasher Sen in Shastri (1999: 166) for detailed citations.
104. Sarma (1975a: 16); (1985: 15-24).
105. Sarma (1975b: 15-16).
106. Sarma (1985: 23-4).
107. Begley (1986: 301, 304, 306).
108. Sarma (1975a: 17).
109. Sarma (1994: 1).
110. Sarma (1971: 12).
111. Chattopadhyaya (1987: 729).
112. Nasik and Nevasa have yielded these coins datable from the third century BCE up to the second century BCE, and further, even in Sātavāhana times, the Naneghat inscription refers to the existence of local chiefs (Sarma 1980: 9-10).
113. Gupta (1990: 305-6).
114. Sastry et al. (1984: 98); Gupta (1990: 271).
115. Sastry (1989: 71-2).
116. First reported in Burgess (1883: 84).
117. *Epigraphia Indica* (1973: 323-4).
118. Sircar (1970: 224-5).
119. Mitra (1980: 214).
120. As at Bhattiprolu but for a later date such a receptacle containing bone, bead, pearls, gold pieces, etc. was found at Ghantasala, another famed early Buddhist site in coastal Andhra (Mitra 1980: 216).
121. Paddayya (2005: 30-1).
122. See Singh (2001: 19-40).
123. For a short survey of the same, see Roy (1994: 3-6).

124. Texts of these inscriptions first compiled in Luders (1973). Their relationship to the chronology of the *mahā stupa* has been attempted by scholars like Sarma (1975b: 60-74).
125. Both from excavations (Sarma 1980: 253-5) and in hoards (Gupta 1963).
126. Sarkar in Pande and Chattopadhyaya (1987: 630ff.); Sarma (1985: 15-23).
127. For an overview, Krishnasastry (1983: 52-110).
128. Francis (2005: 50).
129. Sarma (1975b: 23-4).
130. *Annual Report,* Archaeological Survey of India (1908-9: 90).
131. Quoted in Francis (2005: 68) from [Gregory Schopen, 'Immigrant Monks and the Proto-historic Dead: The Buddhist Occupation of Early Burial Sites in India', *Festschrift Dieter Schlingloff* (*Reinbeck* 1995), p. 276].
132. Chatterjee (1976: 40ff).
133. Seneviratne (1981: 55ff).
134. Rapson (1908 : 10-11).
135. Rao (1961: 39).
136. Sarma (1980: 225, 256).
137. Sarma (1988: 68).
138. Reddy and Reddy (1993: 6).
139. Reddy and Reddy (1993: 8-14).
140. Reddy and Reddy (1993: 5).
141. Prasad (1993: 58); (1999: 333).
142. Prasad (1993: 53), however, does indicate that their use had spread all along the Andhra coast from Mukhalingam, near Srikakulam in the north, to Padugupadu, near Nellore in the south.
143. Sastry (2003: 232).
144. The summary to follow is based on the excavation report published for this site (Sastry et al. 1992).
145. Sastry et al. (1992: 5).
146. Sastry et al. (1992: 7-9).
147. Sastry et al. (1992: 26).
148. Sastry et al. (1992: 22). The authors note that these are similar to those found at Amaravati, Dharanikota, Maski, Brahmagiri and Salihundam.
149. Sastry et al. (1992: 22).
150. Sarma (1988: 8).
151. Sarkar (1966: 37-74).
152. Sastry et al. (1992: 156-73). A grand total of 350 coins—punch-marked, lion type uninscribed, Sada, Sātavāhana, Ishkavaku (largest in number), Sebaka, Vijayanagar (233 from trenches and 117 from surface) were found

along with two coin moulds, three seals, five sealings and one copper die, catalogued from-catalogued Sastry et al. (1992: 141ff).

153. Prasad (1993: 58); Prasad (1999: 333).
154. This article is part of his Ph.D. thesis work, now accepted by the School of Oriental and African Studies, University of London.
155. Much of his argument on the Sada coinage is built on their availability from the Vaddantanu excavations (Shimada 2005: 34), which we have discussed previously.
156. Shimada (2005: 42).
157. Shimada (2005: 44, fn. 8).
158. Luder's list, *Epigraphia Indica,* vol. X, 1912, no. 1279.
159. Shimada (2005: 34).
160. Parasher Sen (1991: 36-44).
161. Rouse (1972: 103, 105).
162. One such reference that can be cited is from the Dhulikatta *stūpa-gahapatino pathalasa mathuya dānam* (Krishnasastry 1983: 226).
163. That there were economically differentiated communities in the pre-state society for this part of the country was first theoretically formulated and discussed by Sudarshan Seneviratne (1981: 54, 57-8) and elaborated for the ancient Tamil country by Rajan Gurukkal (1989: 159-60).
164. It has been pointed out that there was often a special construction of certain types of burials that probably commemorated the chiefs or leaders of these communities, Also, in such burials value oriented grave goods were found (Rao 1972: 184; Wheeler 1947-8: 197).
165. Thapar (1987: 13-16).
166. Thapar (1987: 13).
167. Ray (1983: 9-14).
168. Springborg (1992: 6).

CHAPTER 3

Sub-Regions and Urban Centres*

In the context of the early Deccan, the way 'early historic' and 'urban centres' have hitherto been defined, needs interrogation. The former, in terms of the labels that have been commonly used to describe it and the latter, in terms of the power of theoretical models applicable for one part of the country and used indiscriminately to define, without questioning, those found in other regional contexts.

This chapter is thus divided into three broad sections. In the first section we shall highlight the question of labelling the early historic in the context of the Deccan. In a regional context that was marked by a conspicuous absence of literary sources, the paramount use of archaeology to discuss the early history of this region led to categorizations and the nomenclature that came to be defined by either, political monumentality of dynastic rule or, monumentality defined in terms of an overarching religious identity. The former marked by a prolific generation of the history of the Sātavāhanas and the latter, with an earnestness to unravel the so-called 'Buddhist Period' of early Deccan history. These preoccupations have blurred the issues of demarcating the beginning of the 'early historic' both in terms of 'historical' and 'archaeological' markers.

In the second section, as an essential but brief background to the main theme of this chapter, one would concur with Ian Hodder's concerns[1] that when one is given the task of disseminating the

*First published as 'Urban Centres—Deccan' in Gautam Sengupta and Sharmi Chakraborty (eds.), *Archaeology of Early Historic South Asia*, Pragati Publications, New Delhi in collaboration with Centre for Archaeological Studies and Training, Eastern India, Kolkata, 2008, pp. 313-35. It has been edited to remove matter that has already been addressed in the earlier chapters.

past, the power of theory and method necessarily control and determine the way we depict, interpret and represent the past. Thus, a wide variety of existing explanations on what are urban centres, how they rose and fell, etc., are, we argue, rarely sensitive to regional contextual situations, which in turn, are dependant on local configurations that have hardly become part of the discourses on the critical relationship between history and archaeology. It is thus argued that the data thrown up from empirical studies of urban centres in various sub-regions of the Deccan does not fit into given models that explain their rise and growth during early historic times in regions immediately south of the Vindhyas. The criteria by which we define an urban centre has thus to be located in context.

It follows from the above that in detailing and describing urban centres in the Deccan during the early historic period, in the third section, we hope to emphasize on: (a) looking at issues of their continuity from the pre-urban stages of their evolution and (b) discussing their spread and nature in terms of sub-regional variations across the Deccan. The regional and sub-regional differences thus, it will be argued, get reflected in the context of the proto-historic changes that defined the region beginning with the earliest agricultural societies whereas, archaeological data as presented on the so-called 'urban centres', unconsciously lead us on to assume that there was a uniformity all over the Deccan.

I

After Independence most issues in 'Indian' archaeology came to be related to the *practice of archaeology* at a regional level. The regional states took up this challenge because in the newly independent Indian nation, they had to also gear themselves to a distinct administratively bounded identity that had, in the past, been culturally far more expansive. Archaeology's agenda in this domain thus necessarily got linked up with the writing of the history of the individual States that had linguistically got formalized in the mid-1950s. In many cases the earliest periods of history writing were heavily dependant on archaeological evidence, as many of the regions especially of the Deccan did not have indigenous literary tradition unique to them for the early historic period.

The common trend in history writing that emerged during the early 1950s and 1960s revolved around those aspects of tradition that were considered most appropriate to events surrounding prominent individuals whose images in the consciousness of the Indian society were deep-rooted. Practicing archaeologists too commonly understood the term 'history' as a description of a series of events leading to a particular moment in time. Most commonly, this time was political time and consequently, the people on the stage were the great ruling elites. This focus on 'writing history' had many ramifications of which the most central was building up a State's past into the master narrative of the newly formed nation. We can best exemplify the relationship of archaeology to the construction of regional identities by looking closely at some of the issues centering around, what is called early historical archaeology, as this is where the 'origins' for such an identity were sought. In contrast, the community basis of pre-historic or proto-historic archaeology in given local situations or still further, as found in particular ecological zones that cut across present-day administrative boundaries of linguistic States was projected in a far more integrative manner pointing out cultural contacts, movements and influences from outside the State's limits.

The question of regional 'origins' and its subsequent 'glorious periods' thus preoccupied much of early historic archaeology. Every year, for the past several years, Indian historians get an opportunity to learn of the latest discoveries in archaeology, epigraphy and numismatics at the annual meeting of the Indian History Congress. Prominent archaeologists in the field usually review the developments in their discipline in the form of Presidential Addresses, which take stock of the situation. In the last decade of the twentieth century these have pertinently focused on significant achievements from the point of view of various state perspectives. Two of them from the broad region of the Deccan are a case in point—those of A. Sundara at the 1984 Session and V.V. Krishnasastry at the 1990 Session.

Sundara's Presidential Address was entitled: 'Archaeology and

National Integration' where he valiantly argued: 'our study of Archaeology should not be merely to satisfy our intellectual curiosity', but our aim should be to inquire into 'what role Historical Archaeology has in promoting right and healthy understanding and integrity among the people of our nation'.[2] This, he argued, could best be done by resorting to an understanding of the archaeological cultures and heritage, which he illustrated in the regional context of the present-day state of Karnataka. Thus, while the pre- and protohistoric cultures are shown to have been considerably in contact with the ones in Andhra Pradesh and Maharashtra and also Tamil Nadu, for the early historical period efforts were made to show that art traditions of the Andhra Pradesh regions affected those in Karnataka.[3] On the other hand, Krishnasastry clearly articulates a more official standpoint when he says: 'During the post-Independence era archaeological excavations in Andhra Pradesh[4] have been taken up at various places to throw light on the dark corners of Andhra history'.[5] This approach neatly presented before scholars an inventory of all the work done in Andhra Pradesh for the last decade or so prior to 1990 to unconsciously frame it as Andhra data. Given the fact that this data was collected as part of the administrative duties of the Director of Archaeology, no questions were raised in the address about the similarities and cultural connections between sites and monuments located in Andhra Pradesh and regions contiguous to it. It is of course well known that there were corridors of cultural interaction[6] that existed in historical time, which were now unconsciously blocked out only to highlight the archaeological personality of a newly constructed administrative entity.

In methodological terms of using archaeology for such constructions there are several similarities in the way these two scholars approach their subject matter. For instance, one of the most striking is their preoccupation with art historical, epigraphic and religious subjects, which has resulted in little emphasis being paid to the study of subsistence and settlement patterns or the material cultural development. Though they both do begin with the prehistoric period, there is a heavy leaning on historical archaeology. This tendency is not unique to them since, as has been rightly pointed out, the circumstance in which archaeology developed in

India 'was influenced by proponents of the British Historical School as Wheeler and Marshall. . . . The ancient and abundant texts and mythologies both written and oral provided a ready made and seductive history, perfect ground for British methodology'.[7] And, it is this mould, which is difficult to break out of for most archaeologists working in India. We take one example of this tendency, pre-determined as it was, with the historical narrative, to illustrate how this had impacted our understanding of the emerging picture of the early historical society in the Deccan.

One of the basic tasks that an archaeologist is faced with after he/she has chosen a particular site for excavation and conducted the excavations is to construct an overall chronology and cultural sequence. This, in turn, is intimately connected to the labelling of the various cultural sequences. Despite extensive excavation of archaeological sites in the early historic period in the Deccan there have been divergent views on how this phase should be labelled in the regional contexts of south India as a whole. The most significant reason why this has not been possible to do is that archaeology has been over burdened with an outline of the early history of the region given to us based primarily on epigraphic and numismatic data, as literary sources that talk of this Deccan are those located outside the region. This has had a two pronged effect: (1) that archaeology has been caught in the throes of solving the existing problems thrown up by these sources of information rather than examining an objective context within a said deductive methodology and (2) in the process of finding these solutions the historical framework given, in this case the age of the Sātavāhanas, itself becomes contestable in terms of their origin, homeland, dates of rule and so on.

A.V. Narasimhamurthy in an interesting article written a couple of years ago took up the case of archaeological excavations in the context of Karnataka for the early historical phase and pointed out how this phase had been labelled by scholars in varied ways. It is pertinent to note that the first nomenclature to do so emerged as 'Andhra' in relationship to the coins of the kings belonging to this dynasty prominently occurring in the archaeological record. However, Narasimhamurthy immediately points out that when M.H.

Krishna first recognized the early historical culture at Chandravalli he did not use the above term but instead called it 'Sātavāhana culture'. The term, it was felt, was better to identify the coins of the early and later kings of a dynasty that had called themselves Sātavāhana in their inscriptions, and not Andhra. Next, he points out how Wheeler when he excavated at the above site and at Brahmagiri had called it the 'Andhra Cultural Stage', not on the basis of the coins but on the basis of the pottery found at these sites. Thus, for instance, Wheeler divided this phase on the basis of what he called 'Andhra pottery', into Early, Middle and late Andhra. Coins were considered a secondary material trait because coins of the Maharathis and Romans had also been found and, therefore, it was not suitable to use this as the exclusive criteria for defining an Andhra cultural phase. Lastly, Narasimhamurthy goes on to point out how Wheeler's nomenclature was rejected by Thapar after his excavations at Maski and he was the first to coin the term 'early historic' for this phase. Thapar cautions other archaeologists on the use of such terms as 'Sātavāhana' or 'Andhra' to describe the material cultural traits of this phase in the words: 'The qualifying epithet Andhra for a ceramic industry which is known to have been in vogue during the first and second centuries AD, is contentious and would be confusing the students of history since it presupposes a relationship between this ware and the Andhra'.[8]

Material traits in cultural layers of habitation can be identified after places (e.g. Jorwe) as in the case of the Western Deccan Chalcolithic cultures, which were prolifically excavated after independence by the Deccan College, Pune or, on the basis of the particular characteristics of the ceramic wares themselves as has been done in the context of the Ganga valley material cultures (e.g. OCP, PGW, NBPW). With the so-called early historical sites of the Deccan this has not been possible to do because even the outline of the history of the region based on the chronology of the rule of different Sātavāhana kings is still riddled with questions and chasing these elusive answers has kept the archaeologists busy to the detriment of research on the 'how' and 'why' of the archaeological record. This largely historical approach to archaeology is thus deeply entrenched in the construction of the political identity of particular regional states. A relatively recent publication[9] on the subject clearly illustrates that this subject of the origin and chronology of the Sātavāhanas is still contentious. Interestingly, Parabrahma Sastry in this presentation has heavily relied on the still unpublished Kotalingala excavation report to counter the earlier views based primarily on the literary Puranic, epigraphic and numismatic data to even change the order of the succession of the early members of the Sātavāhana dynasty as 'Siri Sātavāhana, his son Satakarni I, and the latter's son Simuka'. Hitherto, Simuka had been accepted as the first of the Sātavāhana kings. The numismatic data from Kotalingala is vividly used to arrive at these new deductions. Why such research continues to be sustained is because it ideologically supports the important question that enables a celebration of linguistically defined States, and that this identity is, first and foremost, to be seen in terms of who ruled the ancient kingdoms seems central to the researchers of modern times. This harks back to Collingwood's discussions[10] in the 1940s, which cogently highlights that 'pre-history' and 'history' are the past relived in the present and, therefore, all archaeological and historical investigations are inherently subjective. What gets ignored under the present circumstance is the other material from Kotalingala excavations that does not fit into this dominant concern.

II

In the particular context of the above examples, Archaeology thus seems to have been turned into a proof giver to construct a timetable of history in a region that has few literary records for corroboration. This then most clearly sidelines the broader concern of understanding social processes and the socio-cultural context of artefact complexes, which would address questions of smaller than regional identities. These would necessarily have to begin with a locality to then merge into the supra local or sub-regional and finally, to the regional. However, the growth of this trajectory cannot be determined by already defined boundaries. At the local level of cultural analysis the pertinent question of whose or, what cultural remains are being neglected or left out can be raised and addressed. However, this cannot be done if the agenda is only to find out the archaeological data that fits into some picture that has provided by an epigraph, text or coin. Indeed, it has been pointed out even for the much discussed an analytically interpreted Ganga valley material cultures that the description of urban centres from Buddhist and Jaina sources has been uncritically accepted so that, as Anna King points out, 'the material remains and their chronologies have often been adapted to fit these descriptions', impeding our understanding 'of the archaeological and cultural materials' themselves.[11]

Theoretically, in writing about the history of urban centres one is confronted by a sea of definitions about what is 'urban' or the 'city' in ancient times. In certain quarters a city is understood as primarily a socio-economic structure presupposing an agrarian base of surplus production which was revolutionized because of the use of a metal technology and ultimately, this economy comes to be based on specialized manufacture and trade.[12] Childe propounded these views largely on the basis of the empirical context of West Asia and highlighted dramatically the technological variable. In certain other quarters, it is felt that cities ultimately emerge as complex socially stratified units and therefore, details of not only economic structures but also of the political and social systems that control and manoeuvre these, need to be emphasized upon.[13] Studies on Pre-Hispanic Mexico greatly helped to challenge the theories of economic determinism.[14] These views have been continually debated sometimes, to question the applicability of their use in different regional contexts.[15] In the context of South Asia as a whole, the growth of towns has been often fitted into views emanating from the above definitions.[16] The critical role that the spread of iron technology played in the economic transformation of society in the Deccan has hitherto been much debated by earlier scholarship. It has been pointed out that iron was more profusely used in the Deccan than in the north[17] though its technological variations, scholars argued, revealed a lack of prosperity.[18] Nonetheless, it was pointed out that the diffusion of this technology was associated with the distinctive Black and Red Ware pottery and Megaliths, which were found uniformly distributed all over Peninsula India[19] that, in turn, led to the formation of a complex economic and social pattern[20] different from the one based on the earlier agricultural life dependent on dry farming.[21] However, none of these views raises or takes into account the chronological dimensions of how this spread of iron technology can be demarcated. It was Dilip K. Chakravarti who first pointed out that 'the early historic period . . . did not begin till the third century BC. The period between *c.* 1100-1200 BC and *c.* third century BC is a long one and suggests a substantial Iron Age occupation of the region,' only to raise a fundamental methodological question, 'have we really got beyond the enumeration of megalithic burial types and related assemblages?'[22]

Indeed, the Iron Age base of its early historic period has been only partially and imperfectly understood. Today, even in writings on the north Indian Ganges valley early historic urbanization there has developed a critical view of the apparently 'revolutionary' role that iron may have played in the formation of urban centres.[23] In fact, in this context Erdosy instead posits that we take the crucial indicator for the rise of urban centres to be 'in the development of a hierarchy of settlement types on a regional scale' and therefore, regard the 'sociocultural transformations accompanying the rise of cities as the central issue'.[24] Hitherto, little attention has been paid to analyse the involvement of particular towns in the overall economic and socio-political processes of the different regions of the subcontinent and thereby, enhance the role of internal vis-à-vis external forces in bringing about these changes. For the Deccan in particular its heterogeneity has been ignored and scholars have tended to impose a uniform pattern of economic transition from one mode of production to the other when in fact, not only did the economic structures, but also the political and social systems that controlled and manoeuvred these, diverged conspicuously in each of the sub-regions. Thus, regional specificity for the study of urbanization throws up questions that do not enable us to fit the study of urban centres in the Deccan and indeed, in Peninsular India, into given typologies of towns as rigid constructs for other parts of the country. It is these variations, we argue, that were as much dependant on the physical configurations of the region as on the nature of the antecedent cultures available at these places. These cultures persist, as 'non-urban' forms into the early historical phase, which is when urbanization is supposed to have reached a high watermark on the subcontinent as a whole. The chronological marker for these changes can be placed roughly between 200 BCE to 400 CE. Unlike the plains of the Indus (third millennium BCE) and the Ganges valley (mid-first millennium BCE), that saw the growth of urban phenomena during earlier periods, the first urbanization in Peninsular India as a whole was comparatively late. Thus, it was only during the early centuries CE that 'visible manifestations of this urbanism' begin to emerge in Peninsular India.[25]

In terms of political configuration of the Deccan the peak period of early historic urbanization coincides with the rule of the Sātavāhana dynasty (Map 2.1). However, changes in this direction began with the influence of the Mauryan rule in the Deccan during the third century BCE. The location of the Aśokan inscriptions in the Deccan gives a fair indication of their interests in this region.[26] In recent years numismatic research has brought to the forefront the rule of minor chiefs in many parts of the Deccan, some of whom, clearly had pre-Sātavāhana antecedents. As mentioned above the chronology of the rise of the Sātavāhanas to power is still rooted in debates. Scholars who support a shorter chronology suggest that they rose to power in the middle or the latter half of the first century BCE[27] and continued to rule till about the end of the third century CE. During the early years of their rule their contemporaries in the west were the Western Kshatrapas and in the east the famous king Kharavela of Orissa. The dynasty also had relationships with small chiefdoms, in this case as their contemporaries, known in the inscriptions as Mahārathis and Mahābhojas who were distributed in the different pockets of the Deccan. It may not be out of place here to mention that the evolution of political society in the Far South was significantly different. The Aśokan inscriptions do refer to powerful peoples outside the sphere of Mauryan control as the Satiyaputras, Cholas, Keralaputras, and

Pandyas. It is well recognized by scholars that these emerged during the early centuries of the Christian era as the three important kingdoms without any of them being able to have a centralized political authority over the region. The character of their rule could best be summarized in terms of each one of them still being controlled by the hereditary authority of a chief who in turn was supported by clans and ties of kinship. The Muvendara of the Sangam texts were therefore these chiefs gradually transiting to become kings of small incipient kingdoms under whom several other grades of chiefs existed.[28] The earliest urbanization in these parts was thus foreground with structures of power still rooted in polities emerging out of a tribal society.

Geographically the Deccan has hitherto often been depicted as merely acting as a bridge in carrying the highly evolved norms of civilized life from the north Indian plains to the Far South. This idea and its heterogeneous and complex physical locale as one of the oldest landmasses in the world has already been elaborated by us in the Introduction and Chapter 1. We have also discussed in the foregoing chapters how archaeologically the transition from the pre and proto historic to the early historic period in the context of Peninsular India shows that geographical peculiarities determined significant variations in terms of the various processes that led to the rise of the early state and urbanization. Insights provided by B. Subbarao show that historically settlements and empires have flourished in what he calls 'perennial nuclear areas of attraction', which are the major river valleys such as the Ganga, Mahanadi, Godavari, Krishna, Kaveri and so on. The availability of resources and where there is a convergence of trade routes have defined these regions. It must, however, be remembered and emphasized that historical factors also converge on what Subbarao called 'areas of relative isolation', which were important areas of communication.[29] Archaeological work in the past four decades or so has provided much data for the study of pre-urban and urban settlements of the Deccan, which are located in these so-called 'areas of relative isolation'. This data had been tabulated by us in the form of charts and appended to an earlier published paper.[30]

III

Co-existing with urban settlements of the Harappan civilization were the early farming villages of the Neolithic-Chalcolithic communities of the Deccan. The earliest pastoral communities inhabiting the Deccan are best illustrated from evidence available at Utnur. They have been called the Neolithic cattle keepers whose settlements were identified by the existence of ash mounds. Characteristically, ash mounds have been found strewn all over the hilly and dry areas of the Deccan Plateau. Other material remains of this early phase (*c.* 2500 BCE) show traces of faint dwellings, crude, hand-made reddish brown pottery and blade tools of chert and ground stone. The later mature phases of the Neolithic are best illustrated in the Krishna Valley at the site of Nagarjunakonda. These later phases (*c.* 1500 BCE) were characterized by grey ware and a stone blade industry of quartz crystals in the material remains. Most of the tool types now found indicate a greater practice of agriculture.[31] The Chalcolithic cultures in the western part of the Deccan (henceforth called the Western Deccan) that end roughly around 1000 BCE, were the first settled village communities that indicate a nascent political authority and social organization called 'chiefdoms' by some scholars. Despite the evidence of fortifications at Inamgaon, by and large, all these settlements were pre-urban as identifiable in settlements like Navdatoli, Nasik, Nevasa, Diamabad, among a host of others.[32] In contrast, in the eastern (henceforth the Eastern Deccan) and the southern (henceforth the Southern Deccan) parts of the Deccan, the Chalcolithic phase emerges as an intrusion on the already existing and well-established Neolithic cultures at sites such as Brahmagiri, Maski, Piklihal etc.[33] In the central plateau parts of the Deccan (henceforth called the Central Deccan) there is a near total absence of Chalcolithic sites.[34] The relatively more recently excavated sites of Adam and Chagtur are an exception in this sub-region.

The Chalcolithic cultures in various regions of Peninsular India, south of the Vindhyas are usually succeeded by the megalithic cultures. Significantly the latter are conspicuous by their absence in north India. The material remains associated with these cultures are identifiable by different types of burials such as urn or sarcophagi burials marked by stone circles, pit circle graves, cist burials, rock-cut chamber tombs, and so on. Menhirs or commemorative pillars and rows of stone alignments in square or diagonal form are often found associated with these burials. Among the thousands of such burials sites found, habitation areas of this culture are few. Despite the varied typology of the burials, all megalith sites were associated with black and red ware, iron tools, often emerging for the first time in the proto-historic record, and horse remains. Interestingly, after the decline of the Chalcolithic cultures the Western Deccan witnesses the apparent sudden emergence of the early historic cultures with a total absence of megalithic cultures based on iron technology. There are, however, a few sites that indicate the presence of iron without the material appendages of the megalithic culture. In contrast to this in the Eastern Deccan where urban centres also flourished during the early historical period, the megalithic and early iron-age emerges either, in an overlap situation with the Chalcolithic or, immediately succeeding it. Thus, here we have substantial evidence of iron in association with both megalithic burial and habitation areas at several important settlements that emerge during the subsequent period with urban characteristics. A similar pattern is found in the Southern Deccan generally dated to between 1000 BCE-100 CE.[35] During this cultural phase too there is an interesting variation that we find in the Central Deccan including the Vidarbha region where the megalith settlements emerge as clearly independent of the earlier cultures.[36] Their location in the midst of the easy availability of iron had a clear impact on the proliferation of settlements here during the subsequent early historical period.

The megalithic phase undoubtedly saw an expansion of settlements all over the Deccan but their heterogeneity has also to be noted. Thus in the Eastern Deccan the megalithic cultures form an essential agrarian background to the early historic phase in the fertile belts of the Krishna-Godavari basin. On the other hand, in the Central Deccan marked by the generally red soil laden infertile and rocky Telangana parts the most interesting aspect of the economy is its ability to generate a large number of iron objects because of the easy availability of iron locally. Habitation sites of the megalithic people are generally few but many have been found relatively more prolifically located here and in the Vidarbha region than in the other parts of the Deccan. These, it has been suggested, were based largely on pastoralism with the communities practicing only small-scale agriculture.[37] Both these localities and the sub-region of the Eastern Deccan can be further contrasted with the Southern Deccan where, at many sites such as T. Narsipur, Sangankallu, Hallur, Piklihal, Brahmagiri, and Maski, the megalithic cultures was superimposed on different levels of development of the preceding phase of the Neolithic-Chalcolithic settlements. This is important to emphasize because the Neolithic-Chalcolithic culture definitely interacted with the megalithic one and it is amidst this that the Mauryan intrusion took place in the Southern Deccan.[38]

Though the material culture associated with the megalithic phase in the Deccan did not begin or end in absolute terms in all the sub-regions, it did see an increase in settlements all over though some communities continued to practice pastoralism and shifting cultivation. Gradually with the expansion of these settlements from the upland regions of the Plateau to the river valleys we find the spread of an agricultural economy. Megalith cultures conglomerated in key zones all over the Deccan which, it has been suggested, indicate the existence of a stratified society based on differentiation in status. Special constructions of certain types of burials and the presence of value-oriented grave goods in them indicate clearly that they probably belonged to chiefs and important ritual specialists in the society. In other words, certain groups in society enjoyed ritual-ideological sanctions, and consequently power, though the larger kin-based networks had not totally broken down.[39] At the same time, it needs to be emphasized that there was no unilinear development from one stage of economic development to the other so that the impact of iron technology on the Deccan cultures varied tremendously in each of its sub-regions. In many areas of the Central Deccan its use did not bring about change in terms of large-scale agrarian expansion. Here, even the earlier Neolithic settlements were few and though with the introduction of iron there was a greater proliferation of settlements, these were not very large and usually connected with small scale craft production of iron related artifacts. On the other hand, in the Eastern and Southern Deccan, its use in agricultural expansion may be postulated especially since at many places it was superimposed on well-established Neolithic-Chalcolithic settlements though, here again, it varied in terms of the nature of the preceding settlement. Particularly, in the Eastern Deccan some new settlements of the iron-age also emerged for the first time clearly indicating expansion of habitable areas. Further, the situation in the Western Deccan was significantly different, as the megalithic phase here, with a concomitant use of iron on a large scale, is near totally absent. This, together with the inhospitable terrain of the Western Ghats, cut through occasionally by river courses, was not conducive for large-scale agrarian expansion. However, here the strategic location connecting the ports of the West Coast with the North Indian plains on the one hand, and the Southern Peninsular on the other, afforded it a unique environment for the development of nodal points of exchange. Large-scale trade developed with these regions only during the early centuries CE. Nonetheless, it is worth noting that from as early as the third century BCE onwards well known Buddhist monastic establishments at Bedsa, Bhaja, Junnar, Karadha, Karle, Kondane, Naneghat, Nasik among others were economically sustained. Without the support of non-religious centres and establishments this would not have been possible and evidence of these primarily non-religious centres for the same period have been found at Bharuch, Bhokardan, Bahal, Chandoli, Chaul, Kaundinyapura, and Paithan. Contact with the north during the pre-urban phase was not only commercial, in fact, cultural contact was dynamic and need not only be understood in the form of Brahmanical influence or Aryanization as conventional historiography has earlier suggested, but rather, contact through Buddhism and the Mauryan administration is evident in the archaeological record through the finds of Northern Black Polished Ware, Punched Marked Coins and Inscriptions.[40]

During this period of contact what we particularly see is on the one hand, the clear emergence of localities, each with its own identity, known to us through names like Asmaka, Assika, Mulaka in

Buddhist literature. Northern Black Polished Ware as one of the indicators of this contact is found in abundant quantity in the Western Deccan and has been dated to as early as 500 BCE at Nasik.[41] Similarly, it has also been found at important sites like Amaravati and Kesarapalli in the Eastern Deccan. Along with this it has been suggested that here the influence of Buddhism can be dated to pre-Aśokan times.[42] Similarly, the other indicators of this contact in the form of punch-marked coins and Brahmi inscriptions have been found in all the sub-regions of the Deccan except in the Central Deccan. The most spectacular in this regard is the large concentration of Aśokan edicts in the Southern Deccan[43] around areas, which were rich in mineral wealth clearly indicating the economic interests of the Mauryan state.[44]

Despite this direct contact, which can be contrasted by its absence in the Far South, there is one aspect of this period of transition to the early historic situation that needs to be emphasized in the development of the early historical sites especially in the Central Deccan. This is related to the dynamics of internal changes and transformation in, for want of a suitable and appropriate nomenclature, the so-called pre-Sātavāhana society and polity. One of these was related to the particular nature of the economy which rested on the small-scale production of iron related artifacts and the other to the substantial existence of levels of habitation not necessarily related with the megalithic material remains but in between it and those that could be clearly identified in material terms as the early historic. This can be suggested on the basis of the interesting evidence of pre-Sātavāhana coinage found from sites like Kotalingala,[45] which indicates that there was a mobilization of resources at a local level and, which, in turn meant, that the political elite had the ability to issue their own coins. Their control of the iron generating areas probably made this possible for them since at sites like Peddabankur, Dhulikatta and Kondapur considerable amounts of iron objects were present. Further, at Kotalingala, apart from iron slag and ore found here in plenty, it was the largest mound excavated in the region and where the coins of King Chhimuka (equated with King Simuka of the *Purāṇas*) as 'founder of the Sātavāhana dynasty' were also collected. Though this is most striking in Central Deccan because these coins are found along with the early coins of the Sātavāhana rulers, coins of pre-Sātavāhana chiefs have been found in other sub-regions as well though their dates vary from sub-region to sub-region.[46] Apart from this, epigraphic evidence from the coastal Andhra region or Eastern Deccan also tells us about local chiefs in the form of the names like Kuberaka *rājā* and Somaka *rājā*.[47] Their existence in the Western Deccan continues into the Sātavāhana times as is known to us from the Naneghat inscription.[48]

On the basis of this kind of information on the local power groups in the Deccan, it has been postulated by scholars that the socio-economic changes took place within these 'localities' during what can best be described as a sort of late megalithic period but it is indeed difficult to archaeologically differentiate it from the early historic. A certain degree of agricultural surplus was generated in the Deccan as a whole that provided the necessary historical forces for further economic expansion. These changes are reflected in the expansion of settlements in the Western Deccan at Bharuch and Sopara and other large settlements where *stūpas* were found such as at Navdatoli, Pauni, and Kasrawad. As mentioned above, these had already emerged as settlements as early as the third century BCE due to contact with the broader hinterland of the north Indian plains. Thus here, and in the Krishna valley, several early settlements associated with Buddhism had emerged indicating clearly the support that they received from the merchant guilds and the prosperous in society.[49] It has recently been pointed out that though subsistence data is sparse 'even before the advent of the Mauryans, the western Deccan showed precocious signs of urbanization and agricultural intensification that need not have had a north Indian genesis'.[50] However, compared to the prosperous eastern and western littoral tracts of the Deccan, evidence of early Buddhism is limited in Central and Southern Deccan. Recent researches have clearly established that trade went hand and hand with the spread of Buddhism in all sub-regions of the Deccan at chronologically different times and that its quantum varied depending on the economic strength of each sub-region to support these monastic establishments.[51] It was only under the rule of the Sātavāhanas that the

Deccan achieved a certain degree of uniformity in terms of its material cultures and in terms of active contact between the various sub-regions. Paithan in Western Deccan is generally accepted as their earliest capital and the Nasik cave inscription of Queen Balasri mentions various components of Gautamiputra Satakarni's empire. Clearly, several inscriptions and a variety of archaeological evidence indicate that the Sātavāhana dynasty began to rule beyond and over parts of the Central and Western Deccan. These had originally been their initial niches of control so that even during the early years, Sātakarni I styled himself as *Dakshināpatha pati*.[52]

This political unity of the Deccan under the Sātavāhanas is marked by an economy based on the spread of plough agriculture, increased commodity production and expansion of both internal and external trade. It must be emphasized that, what the archaeologists call the early historic period, did not represent a total change in the settlement or productive organization as is known to us from what are generally described as the megalithic societies but there were indeed significant shifts that are marked during the early centuries of the Christian era. The shifts that are represented are seen in the development of larger settlements that can now unambiguously be called urban. The spurt of urban centres all over the Deccan especially in the Western and Eastern Deccan was clearly in consonance with the spread of Buddhism as an institutionalized religion in these parts. It is also well known that from the early centuries of the Christian era the material evidence of the contact with 'Roman' trade gets clearly manifest at many of the sites in the Deccan. However, the development of internal trade with central and northern India continued as before and in Peninsular India too trade routes connecting the western and eastern parts began to develop. This is evident in the increase in the coinage that is now available belonging to the Sātavāhana dynasty. The prosperity of the port towns and inland centres in almost all the sub-regions of the Deccan can be gauged from a variety of material remains and structures that can be identified with these settlements. Buddhist cave temples, which have now come to be well known for the earliest evolution of rock-cut architecture that housed the various forms of Buddhist sculpture at sites like Karle, Kanehri,

Karadha, Junnar, Pitalkora, Ajanta, and innumerable other such caves along the western ghats, flourished during the early centuries CE. Undoubtedly, there is abundant evidence from Greek and Roman sources that Peninsular India as a whole traded with the western world between 200 BCE and 200 CE that, in turn, augmented the importance of certain settlements as nodal points of both internal and external trade that substantially sustained these centers. Thus, we have commercially important places like Baruch, Bhokardan, Kaundinyapura, Nasik, and Sopara flourish in the Western Deccan. Inland towns like Bhokardan emerged as manufacturing centres in this case for beads. Adam, Paunar, Pauni, Dhulikatta, Peddabankur, Kondapur, and Ter had their own character and flourished in the Central Deccan. Many of these were specialized settlements and the production of iron objects, terracotta, and beads is significant here though agriculture was still rooted in local conditions. Ter, for instance, was associated with textile production. Along with Kondapur, which is famous for the largest number of beads found here during this period, they both also emerged as important centres for the production of terracotta. Peddabankur and surrounding areas were well entrenched in the manufacture of iron goods such as sickles, chisels, knives, nails, spearheads, hoes, forks, etc. though it was located in areas bordering food gathering populations. It is significant to point out here that a large part of the terracotta remains found at these sites were in the form of moulds, some of them being used to make coins. Almost all these sites in the Central Deccan have abundant evidence of both punch-marked and die stuck coins in their material remains. They all also participated in the trans-peninsular trade that passed through some of these sites between the Western and the Eastern Deccan.

The Amaravati-Dharanikota complex, Jaggayapeta, Bhattiprolu, Ghantasala, Kesarapalli, Nagarajunakonda, Salihundam, Vaddamanu and Yelleshwaram in the Eastern Deccan (Map 2.2, p. 67) reveal some of the most valuable urban monumental remains. At almost all these sites early and late stages of *stūpa* building activity has been recorded and at some of them *vihāra* complexes too have been identified. Most of these sites provide some of the best evidence of the development of Buddhist art and architecture in the region. Clearly Dharanikota with its fortifications along with Amaravati were centers of political and religious importance. The best example for the development of both religious and secular architecture is seen at Nagarjunakonda that continued to flourish even after the decline of the Sātavāhana power. The development of monumental structures at most of these sites, it has been argued, was concomitant with the eastward spread of the Sātavāhanas.[53] Finally, it cannot be ignored that prosperity of the region is also evident from the inscriptional records available in both the Western and Eastern Deccan that reveal a large-scale participation of society who were generous in giving donations to the Buddhist institutions. Inscriptions have revealed particularly the participation of merchants and traders, craftsmen of a variety of kinds, farmers, and last but not least members of the royalty especially queens.[54] The urban centres in the Eastern Deccan were therefore vibrant both politically and economically participating in rich local as well as overseas trade. Lastly, Banavasi, Brahmagiri, Chandravalli, Sannati, Satanikota, and Vadgaon-Madhavpur in the Southern Deccan best exemplify the continuity of settlements at some of these towns. Some of these show significant evidence of Roman remains here but they equally reveal data associated with the Sātavāhana presence in these parts.[55] The uniformity and standardization of material remains like the size of bricks or the coins and the prolific spread especially of Buddhist monuments indicate the prosperous nature of urban settlements in the four sub-regions of the Deccan. The form that these took and their distribution pattern in relation to the Buddhist monastic settlements, however, differed from sub-region to sub-region.

For the early centuries of the Christian era, now most clearly definable as the early historic period, in the Deccan we thus find that the ecologically varied zones provided different kinds of surpluses and revenues to support urban settlements in each of its sub-regions. Even though the Western Deccan did not have a large agrarian hinterland, its prosperity rested on its trade links with north and central India on the one hand, and on the other, it was its hospitable coastline that helped it maintain contact with foreign trade. Further, here there was a close link between the proliferation of Buddhist monastic establishments and those where trade and port towns dotted the landscape. In the Eastern Deccan the immediate agrarian hinterland in terms of the fertile plains of the Krishna and Godavari delta regions, enabled a large number of early historical settlements to thrive here. As political and commercial centres many of these housed some of the best examples of Buddhist art and architecture. In contrast, to these two sub-regions, the settlements of the Central Deccan were largely dependent on their ability to produce iron objects. They were located in comparatively small agrarian niches of the Wainganga and the mid-Godavari valleys. Therefore here, with the exception of a few sites, a number of urban settlements are not marked by structures that can be considered monumental. The Southern Deccan also saw a proliferation of urban settlements but the stability of some of these was dependent on their location near mineral rich areas. It is for this reason as well that we find a continuity of settlements in this sub-region from very early times and a significant amount of Roman material remains at many of these sites.

In the Deccan, as a whole, small and big urban centres emerged within the ambit of the Sātavāhana State and the proliferation of Buddhism at about the same time. Most of the followers of Buddhism were members of the artisan and trading communities. The growth of important niches of agricultural hinterlands in the delta areas of the Krishna and Godavari rivers provided the much needed resource base for the flourishing of urban centres. There was a concomitant rise of trade and the emergence of a monetary system as well. The existence of inscribed coins go back to the pre-Sātavāhana times and during the early historic period the powerful economic and political ruling elite were able to integrate different parts of their empire through a common material culture and a coined, metallic money system issued by them. During the early historic period therefore, the political configuration of the Deccan in terms of the rule of the Sātavāhanas as well as the ideological spread of Buddhism provided a contact between the various sub-regions, on a scale that had not been known before. It also effectively cemented them in terms of economic contact and interdependence so that for this period we have a remarkable uniformity in the cultural artifacts and other material objects that have been revealed from excavations. It is generally accepted that the Sātavāhana State did not directly participate in trade.[56] Instead, both trade and production was in the hands of the different kinds of social groups and their *nigamas* or guilds. Further, a large corpus of material from long-distance trade of various centres in the Deccan tends to suggest that this too was in the hands of competing groups rather than being exclusively directed by the State. Some of the local political groups did participate in it and the functionaries of the State may have directed it and perhaps drawn some revenue out of it.[57] The symbolic role of both the Sātavāhana and Buddhist institutions in unifying the various levels of participation in the urban environment cannot be minimized. However, it is only by taking into account the antecedent cultural phases of habitation, which in the various cultural sub-regions, were often very different from each other in material and cultural development, that we can appreciate the extent to which the Sātavāhanas played an essential integrative role in a society which was otherwise still rooted in particular sub-regional economic and material moorings well up to the early centuries CE. Its so-called limited urbanization has now to be highlighted in its own peculiar context.

The attempt here has been to view urbanization in Deccan within its larger geo-spatial and economic organization and therefore, not as a mere import from the chronologically earlier and supposedly more advanced processes of urban growth augmented in the Gangetic plains. Hitherto, an overemphasis on the diffusionist theory had left little room for understanding indigenous development of cultural processes. Therefore, in characterizing the earliest urban centres here we need to understand its heterogeneous picture and emphasize the importance of the existence, or co-existence of particular sub-regions as independent, or semi-independent entities contributing to the historical development of the entire region. Particular standardized features of literature, monumental brick construction or coin hoards, known in other parts of the subcontinent did not appear evenly in all the nuclear centres of the Deccan or indeed, of Peninsular India. This however, should not lead us to make dismissive statements like 'there is no evidence of early civilization between the gold bearing zones of Karnataka and Madurai. Likewise the tract between the Godavari and the Kaveri has little to offer as regards early civilization'.[58] Most certainly, we cannot suggest a unilinear stage of development from pastoralism to agriculture and then to urbanization for the whole region taken together. In fact, as a result of these complex details of not only the economic structures but also the political and social systems that controlled and manoeuvred these, diverged conspicuously in each of the regions and sub-regions of Peninsular India. Several grades of manufacturing, market, political, and religious centres did flourish which made long-distance traders from the West flock here in large numbers.

NOTES

1. Hodder (1986: 169).
2. Sundara (1984: 13).
3. Sundara (1984: 18).
4. This obviously refers to the composite state of Andhra Pradesh before 2014 when a new current state of Andhra Pradesh was formed.
5. Krishnasastry (1990: 6).
6. Allchin (1982: 334).
7. Lynton in Kennedy and Possehl (1984: 63-4).
8. Murthy in Kamalakar (2000: 29-34).
9. Sastry (1994).
10. Collingwood (1946).
11. King in Kennedy and Possehl (1984: 109).
12. Childe (1955: 114-42).
13. Sjoberg (1957: 5-17).
14. McAdams (1966: 9-17).
15. For Europe especially see Green (1981: 8-23); Tringham in Sabloff and Lamberg-Karlovsky (1980: 472-4).
16. Thakur (1981: 20-1).
17. Subrahmanyan (1963: 351-3).
18. Banerjee (1965: 214).
19. Allchin (1982: 347).
20. Gururaja Rao (1972).
21. Nagaraja Rao (1971: 123).

22. Chakravarti (1985: 76).
23. King in Kennedy and Possehl (1984: 110-11).
24. Erdosy (1988: 2; 4).
25. Champakalakshmi (1986: 2-3).
26. Fussman (1987: 64-7).
27. Sastri, Ajaymitra (1987: 3).
28. Gurukkal (1998).
29. Subbarao (1958: 8-35)/
30. Chart—Parasher Sen in Shastri (1999).
31. Allchin (1982: 347).
32. Dhavalikar in Deo and Paddayya (1985: 68).
33. Nagaraja Rao (1971: 136).
34. Krishnasastry, (1983).
35. Chart—Parasher Sen in Shastri (1999).
36. Parasher Sen (1992: 443-70).
37. Deo in Deo and Paddayya (1985: 90).
38. Parasher Sen (1992: 443-70).
39. Seneviratne (1981: 54-70).
40. Chart—Parasher Sen in Shastri (1999).
41. Ibid.
42. Sarma, (1985: 15-16).
43. Begley (1986: 301).
44. Thapar (1987: 13 -14).
45. Krishnasastry (1983).
46. Gupta (1990: 305).
47. Sastry in Handa (1989: 71-2).
48. Burgess (1883: 59-70).
49. Amita Ray (1983: 9-10); H.P. Ray (1986).
50. Morrison (1995: 208-21).
51. Heitzman in Kennedy and Possehl (1984: 131).
52. H.P. Ray (1986).
53. Heitzman in Kennedy and Possehl (1984).
54. Burgess (1883: 84-5; 89; 109).
55. Chart—Parasher Sen in Shastri (1999).
56. Thapar (1987).
57. Thapar (1987); Begley (1986); Ray (1986).
58. Maloney in Stein (1976: 21-2).

PART II

STANDING ON THE PARTICULAR

CHAPTER 4

Kondapur: A Forgotten City on the Deccan Plateau*

And the 'Roman artist asked: 'Can I have letters of introduction to the brother Shilpins (artists) in all those places!'
The young monk from Nagarjunakonda ironically commented:
'You do not need letters of introduction to the areas of silence'

MULK RAJ ANAND[1]

In this fictive account, Mulk Raj Ananda imagined a 'Conversation' between a Roman artist who travelled with his Ethiopian slave exploring the various 'cities' of the Deccan and the indigenous people against the setting of Nagarjunakonda. This place is characterized as a major urban settlement of the eastern coastal rim of the Deccan during the early centuries CE. Mulk Raj Anand, the well-known modern Indian novelist, had, however, built this account on considerable historical and archaeological research done on the spread of Buddhism and the rule of the Sātavāhana dynasty over a major part of the Deccan that was concomitant with a period of active trade between its various ports and cities and the Mediterranean around the early centuries CE. There were some among these 'cities' ostensibly visited by the Romans and other foreigner traders that today remain 'areas of silence' as there is hardly any literary source material for this region and the period under discussion for us to use and reflect upon. At a simple level we could draw on this quote to capture the social and religious milieu of early historic

*First published as 'Unravelling the Reality of a "City" on the Deccan Plateau', in Adam Kemezis (ed.), *Urban Dreams and Realities: Remains and Representation of the Ancient City*, Brill, Leiden, 2014, pp. 89-107.

Deccan or perhaps, to highlight that many of the settlements located in the Deccan hinterland either have not been, or, have only recently been excavated and are therefore, in a sense, 'areas of silence'.

It is legitimate, argues De Certeau,[2] that since the 'real' of the historical past is a consequence of representation, the 'breadth of literary imagination' can best convincingly bring out the textures of history, its intricate patterns in symbols, actions, events and lived-in experiences of men and women in times gone by. In the present context, therefore, one is tempted to draw upon this fictive account to reconstruct the 'reality' of a city on the Deccan Plateau. But this would mean the replication of a nationalist constructed imagination of mid-twentieth century India when the above piece was written and when, flush with the newly achieved Indian Independence, archaeologists and historians were engaged in a 'discovery' or, one should say, a recovery of the classical monumentality of ancient Indian art and architecture. In the context of the Deccan, the monumentality of recovering Buddhist art galvanized the imagination of most government run departments of archaeology.[3] Apart from describing a monument in all its architectural details, its location in a particular landscape, the archaeological artefact telling its own local story, the intangibles of how the Buddhist monks interacted and lived off the local inhabitants, the opening up of local spaces to traders of all hues and colour, and the way local artists, craftsmen, technologists coped with all these changes, were hardly considered the themes that scientifically trained archaeologists were meant to focus on. In the present paper we broaden the discussion on defining a 'city' to these larger issues while simultaneously highlighting a difference in the fashioning of local built-in spaces. At the same time we address another issue, namely, the tension between objectified truth and reality. Inherent to an archaeologist's task is to place in the present, through the most stringent scientific methods of exploration and excavation, what is true about the past and what is clearly tangible, visible and describable in the best objective way possible. Few archaeologists, however, address the question of whether this can lead to a comprehension of the reality of the past. This complicated relationship between what is visible and the contingent absences that arise out of the choices we make is critical to retrieving that reality.

The Deccan was and is a terrain difficult to travel across. Even today traveling across the Deccan Plateau one is confronted with a landscape that in parts is still marked with huge granite rock-formations of what is commonly called the Deccan Trap.[4] These are considerably older than any human structural interventions on this landscape. This is combined with its primarily red sandy and patches of loamy black soils that are suitable for typical dry farming in the intermittently marked low lying areas watered by natural lakes or small river valleys. The plateau is the vast hinterland of both the eastern and western coastline of Peninsular India. It is also that mass of land through which, over historical times, peoples, products and ideas have traversed from the plains of north India to the far south marking the southernmost tip of the sub-continent. Thus, historical forces of change have converged on this unique landscape highlighting interesting economic trajectories of material change alongside socio-political interactions of confluence while maintaining a distinctness that becomes the aim of this paper to capture.

While reflecting on the urban space of early historical times, in this paper I shall focus on the archaeological site of Kondapur (Map 2.1) that has been re-excavated recently between 2009 and 2011 by the Archaeological Survey of India. It was first excavated in 1940-2 before Indian independence under the auspices of the then Archaeology Department of the Princely State of Hyderabad. What marks its location on the Plateau is its relative isolation when compared to the cluster of explored and excavated sites to its north and northeast, all dated to a similar period. Assigning an exact date for Kondapur is a major problem since scientific methods of dating the excavated material have not been applied. Based on related artefacts found at similar sites in the region, especially on the Roman finds like coins and pottery and coins of the Sātavāhana dynasty, it is broadly placed as a site that flourished during the first two centuries CE. All the sites with similar material remains have been loosely labeled as cities/urban centres, almost invariably with a Buddhist affiliation, in existing historical studies on the early historic Deccan.[5] It is often argued that it is because of Kondapur's location in the centre, connecting the Buddhist centres on the east coast with those on the west that it grew as an important junction[6] in an otherwise hostile and not very fertile terrain characteristic of the Deccan Plateau (Map 1.1, p. 40). Our central concern is to interrogate its particular character in the specific context of its location.

In terms of its specific environs and location the present archaeological mound at Kondapur (17.33' N 78.1' E) is located on a small hillock about 1 km south of the village of Kondapur in the present day Medak district of the state of Andhra Pradesh.[7] It is roughly 70 km. west-north-west of the capital city of Hyderabad[8] on a streamlet that in ancient times must of have been an important tributary of the river Mañjira which has today a circuitous course some 20 km towards the north of the archaeological site.[9] Locally, the ancient mound is known as Kotagadda (Fort Mound).[10] Kondapur would mean a 'town' if its suffix *pur* is taken literally, while *konda* is understood to mean 'hill' in the local language. The archaeological mound marked for excavation at Kondapur[11] was about 80 ha and surrounded by fields that continue to be cultivated and in close proximity of an old paleo channel (streamlet). Beyond this, abutting the mound, there is a huge modern irrigation tank; its genesis to the early historic times has yet to be established.

For a long time Kondapur was the only early historical settlement [*c.* second century BCE-third century CE] that had been excavated on the Deccan Plateau in the then state of Andhra Pradesh. But when in 1941 Ghulam Yazdani, its excavator, wrote about his work there, he noted that in his endeavor only the crust had been broken and that the lower strata still needed to be dug.[12] Jithendra Das, the superintending archaeologist, Archaeological Survey of India, Hyderabad Circle, who inspected the mound in 2008, found 'its upper strata already yielding several antiquities without digging'.[13] Since then, fresh excavations have been conducted here from the winter of 2009 till the summer of 2011 by the Archaeological Survey of India, Excavations Branch, Government of India, New Delhi, under whose authority this site continues to lie.[14] The structural remains and the diverse nature of the artefacts found during the first round of excavations done at the site between 1940-2 indicated firmly that this was a place where several crafts flourished.

There was some technological significance to the metallurgical industry here and the numismatic evidence found here was prolific and varied. Equally rich were the structural and material antiquities, amounting to about two thousand items that were unearthed here in the more recent excavations of 2009-11.[15] A unique aspect of this site is that after the early historic times, it seems to have apparently been abandoned with no evidence at all of any consequent historical strata identifiable either through excavation, or in terms of visible monumental remains in the vicinity of this mound. Against this background we take a closer look at some of these aspects based primarily on Yazdani's 1940-2 excavations.

Following the traditional lines of enquiry most archaeologists have defined early historical sites as 'urban' if they were adorned with Buddhist establishments and if there was evidence of fortification walls,[16] with the argument that political stability and an apparent ideological uniformity enabled prosperity and peace to prevail that in turn led to the rise of these townships. Thus, Kondapur qualified to be 'urban' because it apparently had Buddhist establishments even though it was felt in certain quarters that these buildings were not 'architecturally very imposing'.[17] Other interpreters of this 25 ft. high mound covering about 100 acres who officially became responsible for the site after Independence opined that 'ancient Kondapur city was larger than Amaravathi (and) skirted by a mud-fort . . . the fort's mud-wall is visible even now'[18] and reiterate the existence of Buddhist monuments here. Yazdani and many others who were first associated with the excavations here were convinced, and therefore, continually emphasized that this was one of the thirty walled towns of the Andhras that were mentioned by Pliny.[19] Even before its excavation, H. Cousens when he prepared his 'List of Antiquarian Remains in H.H. the Nizam's Dominions' published by the Archaeological Survey of India in 1900, described it as 'the *site of an ancient town* supposed to have been where the dried up lake now is, bricks, implements and coins being found in the bed of the lake'.[20] These various views on granting Kondapur a full-fledged urban status did not view its material remains as part of a larger organic whole in an inhibiting natural landscape nor, did they consider or discuss the social and economic dynamics operating behind the rise of this settlement. In fact, as has been candidly admitted by a field archaeologist of long standing, the late H. Sarkar,

> When sites like Amaravathi, Bhattiprolu or Salihundam (all along the east coast of the Deccan) were excavated our emphasis had been individual buildings or groups of sculptures and we had only vague idea about the social and economic dynamics operating behind the rise and decline of a township or settlement. . . . We focused all our attention on the Buddhist stupas as they yielded fine examples of architecture and sculptural art. . . .[21]

The same method has been applied to excavating and interpreting the remains from Kondapur as the focus has been on identifying only major structural remains that were ostensibly meant to most define the character of the site. In our current endeavour we intend to highlight on the particular difference that defined the reality of Kondapur as a settlement—was it indeed a large urban settlement, or, merely, a substantial settlement that acted as a resting point for 'transactional' and inter-dependent activity across the various sub-regions of the Deccan Plateau—be it economic, religious, social or cultural activity?

As the first excavator of the site, Yazdani noticed foundations of buildings that he labelled as 'Buddhist', although these architectural and sculptural edifices were not strikingly prominent. During the 1940-2 excavation the structures unearthed here[22] were divided into four categories on the basis of the evidence of the remnants of (a) Buddhist religious structures like *stūpas*, *chaityas* and parts of *vihāra* complexes etc., (b) plain houses built either of brick or rubble, (c) those classified as shops, areas with evidences of furnaces and large earthen basins, and finally (d) some perfunctory indications of old walls. Quantifiably, the excavator's greatest emphasis was on describing the religious buildings, ascribable to a Hinayana or Theravada sect of the Buddhists as no images of the Buddha were found then. There is a stark absence of any Buddhist images in the more recent 2009-11 excavations of the site as well. Yazdani's descriptions focused on structures located substantially in the south-western and western parts of the mound.[23] If the identification of these Buddhist monuments is accepted it would entail the most obvious conclusion that these and the body of monks they housed were financially and otherwise supported by a population around this place, some of whom were in all probability the followers of the faith.

After the more recent excavations (2009-11) conducted here Maheshwari, the excavating officer, did not find merit in labelling the foundation of several buildings excavated under her supervision as 'Buddhist'. In fact after the first season of her endeavours she reported that Kondapur could also be 'an important kshetra of the Brahmanical faith'.[24] Her work here had revealed foundations in the shape of square, apsidal and circular brick structures in primarily the western part of the main mound. Credible evidence of a non-Buddhist sect having lived at Kondapur is suggested by her on the basis of the excavation of 'a vast complex having a circular shrine facing south with one entrance and surrounded by rectangular chambers and fire altars—three metres in depth having 37 courses of burnt bricks of different shapes—triangular and *damaru*-shaped —behind the chambers.'[25] The labelling of these deep pits as fire altars by Maheshwari is based on, according to her, 'significant evidence of fire activities in them along with full pots—five in number (may be *kalasa*) with stamped impressions of a trident, *purna-kalasa*.'[26] She has further reported that 'the whole temple complex yielded plenty of animal bone pieces, perhaps for sacrificial purposes and related pottery articles such as bowls, sprinklers, spouted vessels and iron implements like spear heads and knives.'[27] Of some significance was the discovery of a Lajja Gauri (Goddess of fertility) made of kaolin and a few cult objects made of iron in the same complex in close proximity to the circular structure as reported in a newspaper interview by Maheshwari. A Lajja Gauri and other images of fertility goddesses now housed in the Kondapur Museum at the site were also found during the 1940-2 excavation indicating clearly the popularity of her worship (Figure 4.1). In fact, as is well known, her presence was common in other early historic sites of the Deccan.[28] It is pertinent to point out here that the two archaeologists who have done major excavations (1940-2 and 2009-11) at this site have characterized its religious character in diametrically opposite ways.

Source: Photos taken by ASI in custody of State Department of Archaeology and Museums, Government of Andhra Pradesh (before 2014).

Figure 4.1: Lajja Gauri Kondapur Excavation 1941-2

Though the more recent excavations have raised questions about the location of a substantial Buddhist establishment at Kondapur it is true that the larger role this ideology played in the expansion and promotion of trade and artisanal activity in the immediately contiguous coastal regions of Western Deccan and Eastern Deccan cannot be ignored.[29] The extent of this influence on the Deccan Plateau and the hinterland has hitherto been assessed in terms of the close proximity of the Buddhist institutional establishments with trade routes and market towns. Maheshwari, with data collected under her supervision during the 2009-11 field-season of excavation suggests that Kondapur must have housed some sort of cult practices that may have had nothing to do with Buddhism.[30] For this, as discussed earlier, she convincingly cites the excavation of deep pits she calls 'fire altars' and the 'circular shrine' excavated as evidence to support her views. This is an interesting hypothesis and one would have to wait for her complete report on these excavations to fully accept this interpretation. It does, however, throw light on the fact that given the varied economic activity at this site a multiplicity of social groups with different ideological orientations must have visited it or lived here. The capacity of social groups here to maintain the production of certain commodities resulted in their growing strength. They were able to also support the religious establishments located here and ultimately, the new forces of change made it possible for political elites like the Sātavāhanas to integrate this so-called isolated region into the larger-framework of their empire. Based on the current state of excavations done, Kondapur does not turn out to be a fortified town but more likely developed the character of a manufacturing and trade centre as we argue below. Tentative suggestions were made and orally discussed during the course of the more recent excavations at the site by the excavators that Kondapur could have been a place where Vedic rituals were performed. That people visited it only to participate in such rituals and/or other cultic practices prevalent here cannot be accepted as the only reason for its existence. On the contrary, driven by the material and economic resources that converged here, the local community had to generate a variety of institutions for worship for the diverse population, including the Buddhists who traveled across the Plateau to visit its innumerable monasteries scattered all over the Deccan region. Considered in the context of its similarity with the sites in the mid-Godavari valley, and also those in the Nalgonda region[31] on the Deccan Plateau, it can be said that it had linkages with this dominant ideology of the times but developed its own individual character mainly because of the ecological constraints of its location in the region. This is reflected in the simplicity of the material remains found here and the absence of large public buildings that we describe below. Should this lead us to conclude that it was not an urban centre in the Deccan during this period? Certainly it was not one that boasted of monumental buildings.

It would be worthwhile here to dwell on the social complexity of the people who inhabited Kondapur. The ground plans of the other buildings that Yazdani has referred to were not clearly discernable but these were in all probability the residences of the inhabitants of Kondapur. There are several indications to show that they housed people coming from different social strata. An indication of the economic disparity of the people that inhabited this city is that certain houses, which Yazdani calls shops, had underground chambers (Figure 4.2). Of six such chambers noted by Yazdani, three had double rooms divided by a partition wall in the centre. Their depth varied anything between 5 and 25 ft. They were built of neat courses of brick laid in mud, and their floors were either laid with bricks or small stones unevenly fixed to the ground. These interesting constructions invariably contained such valuables as coins with their moulds, seals, beads, gold ornaments, terracotta figurines and the like, thereby implying that they belonged to either rich households or were storage spaces for shopkeepers and merchants.[32]

But the overall pattern and style of architecture in these remains strikes one as being plain and simple. In fact, it is observed that it was 'not very imposing and grand, nor even beautiful, but quite efficient and skillful. . . .'[33] This is evident in the dimension, size and shape of the bricks used, which varied according to the type of

Source: Photos taken by H.E. Nizam Archaeology Department in custody of State Department of Archaeology and Museums, Government of Andhra Pradesh (before 2014).

Figure 4.2: Underground Chambers Kondapur Excavations 1941-2 building. For circular buildings like the *stūpas* and *chaityas* wedge-shaped bricks were also used.[34] All this undoubtedly implies the existence of a competent group of bricklayers, masons, carpenters and other technicians involved in construction work. An account of the first excavation of Kondapur in the Annual Report of the Archaeology Department further notes that certain structures excavated should be characterized as remnants of 'industrial buildings' defined as (i) furnaces (ii) floors and pavements for workmen and (iii) depositories for storing their valuable objects.[35] The last-mentioned we have discussed earlier as being part of either shops or houses of the rich. Yazdani clearly emphasizes the implications of this find: 'In the course of excavation remains of furnaces and of large earthen water-basins for cooling the metal have been found in large numbers and it appears that smithy work flourished on an extensive scale'[36] (Figure 4.3).

Source: Photos taken by H.E. Nizam Archaeology Department in custody of State Department of Archaeology and Museums, Government of Andhra Pradesh (before 2014).

Figure 4.3: Areas Identified as Furnaces Kondapur Excavations 1941-2

That this was indeed possible is evident by the recovery of iron objects like sickles, chisels, nails, knives, spearheads, hoes, forks and in fact a large number of 'ploughing and cultivation implements' said to have been found at Kondapur.[37] Other iron objects have been identified as weapons and those found in a carpenter's tool-kit (Figure 4.4) Furthermore, in the course of these excavations Yazdani had also noticed that the area where he had conducted trial pits was strewn all over with broken stones, pieces of brick, potsherds and iron slag; the last being found in considerable quantity.[38] Metal smiths were able to forge the metal 'only when a temperature of between 1100 degrees C–1150 degrees C. . .'[40] was reached, and thus the level of the working of iron technology was not very high. It required a large amount of fuel and also 'furnaces' which have been identified by the excavators, as well as 'working floors' for beating the metal to cast and forge it. All this, however, was possible and determined by the availability of iron.

It is pertinent to note in this context that the State Department of Archaeology and Museums, Government of Andhra Pradesh had

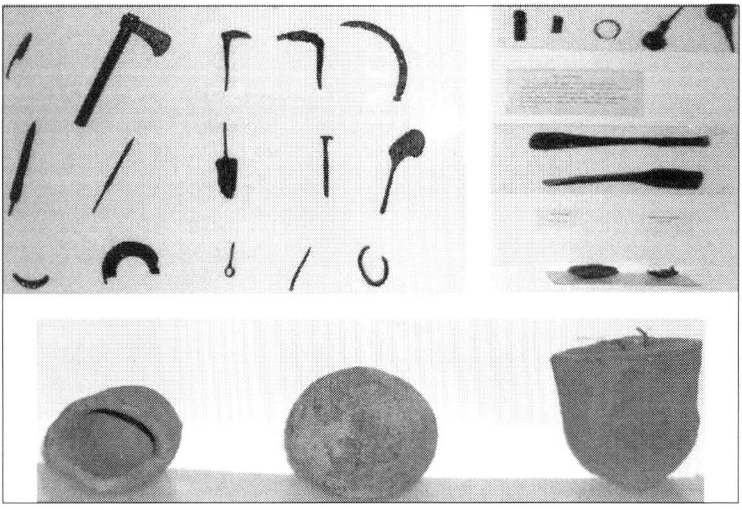

Source: Photos taken by ASI in custody of State Department of Archaeology and Museums, Government of Andhra Pradesh (before 2014).

Figure 4.4: Iron Tools and Crucibles Excavated at Kondapur 1941-2 been prolific during the 1980s and 1990s and had conducted very fruitful excavations at several early historical sites in the Karimnagar region[40] that lies roughly to the north-east of the city of Kondapur and which we have elaborately written about elsewhere.[41] hat is striking for this region as a whole, even during the proto-historic Megalith context preceding, the early historic period, is the ability of the economy in these parts to generate iron objects on a large scale. This has been particularly stressed by the excavators.[42] During the early historic period this tendency is said to have proliferated and it has been pointed out that a 'number of ancient iron working spots were located in Karimnagar region' indicated by the discovery of enormous deposits of iron slag and nodules of calcium. Indeed, here it is noted that 'the entire hill range is scattered with iron ore'. The above evidence has made Krishnasastry conclude that during the early historical times the iron industry having reached a high watermark 'may . . . have been practiced as a home industry.'[43] Against this background it is possible to see Kondapur, not as an isolated example of a centre of iron production in the Central Deccan, but as part of a large network of such centres with a common source of iron available on the Deccan Plateau. Considering that many of these settlements on the Plateau were otherwise circumscribed by a limited ecological base with an absence of large river-valley tracts of agricultural land, scholars have emphasized the importance of the role they played in providing raw material and thus stimulating and establishing networks of trade and exchange in necessary items of daily use. It has thus emerged that Kondapur during the early centuries of the Christian era was a substantial settlement with structures housing a definite population involved in metallurgy and a plethora of buildings clearly identifiable as religious establishments—their affiliation being multiple.

With the growth and expansion of internal and external trade on the subcontinent as a whole during the early centuries CE, the existing economic activity at several centres enhanced the production of not only iron objects, but also of other crafts.[44] Concretely, much has been written about the bead industry at Kondapur.[45] It is said to be a site 'unequalled by any other single site in India' where the largest amount of bead materials in hoards have been found in excavation[46] (Figure 4.5). Sarkar makes an interesting contrast between this place and others in India where beads for the early historic period have been found. He notes: 'the excavations at Nagarjunakonda brought to light 361 beads made, variously of glass, semi-precious stones, terracotta, shell, ivory, coral and faience while Bhir Mound and Sirkap, the two cities of Taxila, yielded 1,763 and 5,534 beads respectively, Kondapur in Andhra Pradesh, accounted for 23,391 beads . . . ;' and he goes on to explain that the paucity of beads at Nagarjunakonda was partly due to 'limited supply and comparatively poorer economic condition of the general people.'[47] It must be mentioned in this regard that beads in fairly large numbers have been reported from Kosam in Uttar Pradesh and in the Deccan at Paithan in Maharashtra and Maski in Karnataka.[48] The quantity and variety of beads, however, including beautifully designed earrings, amulets and bangles in terracotta from Kondapur, cannot of course be taken to mean that the industry catered only to the inhabitants of Kondapur and its surrounding

Source: Photos taken by H.E. Nizam Archaeology Department in custody of State Department of Archaeology and Museums, Government of Andhra Pradesh (before 2014).

Figure 4.5: Terracotta Beads from Industrial area Kondapur Excavations 1941-2 areas. Even the local availability of raw material does not explain its thriving there. Perhaps here again the location of Kondapur on an important arterial route, connecting the Krishna-Godavari delta to the Western Deccan via Ter, should be highlighted.[49] Buddhist monks and merchants may have found this an ideal halting spot on their long journeys. Furthermore, it was not simply bead-making that exclusively occupied the craftsmen at Kondapur, the making of terracotta figurines, both animal and human, was another flourishing art practiced here on a considerable scale (Figure 4.6). Apart from the skill with which these terracottas were modeled, many of their moulds have been discovered which means that this craft flourished as an industry here.[50] The intricate features and hair styles of the

Source: Photos taken by H.E. Nizam Archaeology Department in custody of State Depart-ment of Archaeology and Museums, Government of Andhra Pradesh (before 2014).

Figure 4.6: Terracotta Faces from Kondapur Excavations 1941-2 human figurines[51] not only attest to the artistic skill with which they were made but also give us a fair idea of the ethnic features of at least part of the population that lived here and the fashion styles of the day. Finally, evidence of a highly organized and prolific ceramic industry[52] is found consisting of ordinary plain pots and saucers for domestic use as well as ornamental pots, urns, incense burners, vases, and so forth[53] for use by different social strata and the occupants of the several religious establishments.

Some of the ceramics found at Kondapur shows influence of Roman traditions especially in terms of the glazing and shapes of pottery found, apart from pieces of Roman amphorae that have also been reported to have been found during excavation.[54] Lamps of a certain type attributed to a Roman origin have been written about[55] as these were found at many early historic sites including Kondapur.[56] According to reports of the 2009-11 excavation the site yielded a 'large number of glass vessels indicating Roman influence that indicate the existence of a separate settlement of Romans in Kondapur who had brisk contact and trade with India.'[57] Certain images too have been identified as having been either brought by foreign merchants or, having been made under influence of the Mediterranean artistic and cultural practices.[58] By far the greatest impact of this is seen in the clay imitation of coins that were found here. Like at other early historic settlements, 'though none of the representations could be identified with specific Roman emperors as depicted on Roman coins, there is striking resemblance in respect to the features and general treatment of the details, indicating that the portraits on the coins were imitated, but not actually copied. Most of them represent imitations of aurei or *denarii* of Roman emperors.'[59] These clay copies of Roman coins have been found in excavated layers called 'Sātavāhana' at Kondapur and other sites[60] (Figure 4.7). And finally, a gold coin of Emperor Augustus was also found here during the 1940-2 excavations[61] and one of Tiberius during the 2009-11 excavations.[62] This Roman-related material found at Kondapur fits in with historiographical dimensions already highlighted as having significant interpretative potential for typifying most of the early historic sites in the Deccan as 'urban' especially the coins as they help date many of these sites to

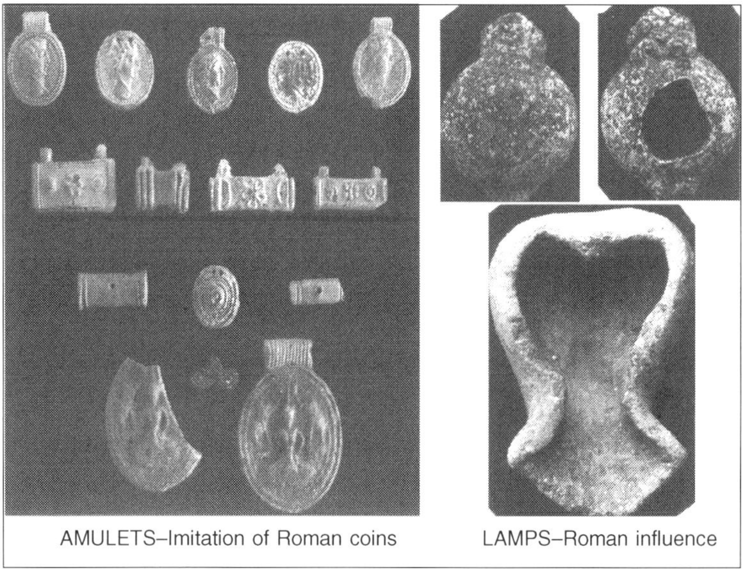

Source: Photos taken by H.E. Nizam Archaeology Department in custody of State Department of Archaeology and Museums, Government of Andhra Pradesh (before 2014).

Figure 4.7: Roman Material at Kondapur Excavations 1941-2

tentatively between second century BCE-first century CE. In a general sense Kondapur like other so-called cities of the period was impacted by the economic forces of change and prosperity emanating from the trade and commerce that flourished all over India, including the Deccan, during the early centuries CE. Some of it was generated by early India's interaction with the Mediterranean and Red Sea regions that had been actively involved in trade with the Roman empire during this period.[63] The complex nature of these so-called 'Roman' remains, however, raises serious questions about the agency and nature of this contact especially in terms of how these networks of external trade touched hinterland societies (Kondapur being located in one such) and their ability to participate in it directly.[64]

By far the most common historiographical assumption about Kondapur handed down to us is it being labelled as 'Sātavāhana', the name of a family and dynasty that ruled over many parts of the Deccan during the early centuries CE. Undoubtedly, Kondapur during the early historical period was under the influence generated by the formation of the Sātavāhana state, the first in early India to have a large part of the central, eastern and western Deccan as the nucleus of its power. It must, however, be noted that 'Sātavāhana/ Andhra' came to be adopted by archaeologists as being coterminous with the early historic urban phase in the Deccan.[65] However, the simplistic use of this label has to be questioned since it does not enable us to analyse the nature of polity at the local level that must have controlled various activities at Kondapur and other such places.[66] A critical feature that further helps us identify this character is an unusually substantial quantity of coins of different types that have been found here. First and foremost thousands of punch-marked coins and moulds to which they fitted were discovered,[67] raising significant questions about their role and circulation in the economy under the Sātavāhanas as well under the pre-Sātavāhana rulers. Under the current scope of the data found it is difficult to suggest that they were issued by members of the main ruling family alone. Of significance is the fact that a large number of early Sātavāhana coins and coin moulds were also found here.[68] Nearly 2,000 (1,835 to be exact) of the Sātavāhana coins were reported. Here again, along with their coin moulds during the 1940-2 excavations,[69] Yazdani has divided these into three varieties, namely (1) early Andhra issues with well-known symbols but without any writing; (2) some unpublished varieties of the Sātavāhana dynasty with legends in Brāhmī characters; and (3) a large number of other coins of the same dynasty which are identical to those already published.[70] In 1940 it was of considerable significance that among the Sātavāhana coins, the one of King Sātavāhana was used as evidence to indicate that Kondapur could have been their capital. Yet Yazdani concluded that 'it appears that the mound was originally the site of an important Andhra town where coins were minted.'[71] The discussion of the variety and quantity of coins found at Kondapur cannot be complete unless we also point out the similar features of the coin finds available in the contiguous region from the mid-Godavari sites like Kotalingala, some from a stratified context, and from Peddabankur that have been assessed and analysed, raising interesting dimensions for a discussion on the early polity of the region.[72] I.K. Sarma suggests that Peddabankur should also be considered a 'mint town' on the basis of a large number of terracotta moulds found here in a stratified context and the existence of hundreds of small die-struck pieces in pots.[73] Krishnasastry, who excavated at this site, locates this mint in Enclosure II, for scores of coins were found in it alongside two hoards of punch-marked coins.[74] The co-existence and succession of a variety of coin types at these centres leads to one obvious conclusion, namely, that the regional economy was dependent on trade and commercial transactions of a certain magnitude. It also suggests that the social groups involved in this trade were part of a heterogeneous polity that operated at different levels of political and economic control—the existence of punch-marked coins clearly indicates this. It is interesting that although Peddabankur and Kondapur stand out as possibly 'mint centres' there are so far no clear evidence that they were fortified towns. Dhulikatta and Kotalingala, however, which are situated not very far from each other or from Peddabankur, present substantial evidence of being fortified towns. At the former at least some kind of palace complex was located, and at the latter several coins with legends of pre-Sātavāhana local rulers were found.[75] Trade in these parts was probably stimulated not so much by an export of agricultural surplus as by the supply of iron objects and other commodities like beads and terracotta objects.[76] In contrast to this, Sarkar points out that at Nagarjunakonda, located closer to the coast in the lower Krishna valley, the excavations did not reveal any evidence of iron smelting, and that the iron objects that were found there were probably imported from outside.[77] It is difficult to determine the exact quantity of such objects exported from Kondapur and other sites, but the existence of a large number of coins here indicates definitely the prosperity of the artisan groups located here, who may have also exerted a level of political control.

The data thus far collected from Kondapur reveals complex structural remains along with significant artefacts that sometimes defy the application of a singular convenient label—'Buddhist', 'Roman', 'Sātavāhana' and, perhaps even 'Urban'—to mark the early historic period at Kondapur. We argue that discourses on the critical relationship between history and archaeology in the south

Indian context[78] have rarely been sensitive to regional contextual situations and local configurations and thus have not posited a viable explanatory model to understand the differentiated urban spaces in hinterland societies like that of the Deccan. As we have shown in detail elsewhere,[79] sub-regional and local differences begin to get reflected even in the context of the pre- and proto-historic changes in these parts, and so it is erroneous to assume that when archaeological data of the so-called 'urban centres' is presented, it proves a uniformity across the Deccan. In having detailed and described urban centres in the Deccan during the early historic period we emphasized that in each case (a) looking at issues of their continuity from the pre-urban stages of their evolution and (b) discussing their spread and nature in terms of the evolution of agrarian growth critically define the character of hinterland societies on the Deccan plateau.

In discussing the wider implications of the case study in this chapter, one would concur with Ian Hodder's[80] concerns that when one is given the task of disseminating the past, the power of theory and method necessarily control and determine the way we depict, interpret and represent the past. These control and support a wide variety of existing explanations on harking back to a past to revel in its essentialized authenticity often to project the glory of the present. Furthermore, to project a high classical and homogenous past has hitherto been done because the celebration of a singular historical identity of a contemporary political state—Andhra Pradesh[81] in the present context—has preoccupied historians and archaeologists alike. Certainly when highlighting an urban landscape there are some features that can be characterized as elite commemorative remains, which are the most visible. But within these there is a divergence and multiplicity that has survived as well. In her introduction to Archaeologies of the *Greek* Past Susan Alcock has poignantly elaborated upon how 'forgetfulness is as pivotal to this process of remembrance.'[82] In other words, her essential interrogation of what constitutes relevant data, even at a simplistic level needs attention in a broader material framework so that consequentially one can 'examine . . . the range of commemorative practices.'[83] This can only be addressed at a local level of cultural analysis and

Source: Photo taken by ASI in custody of State Department of Archaeology and Museums, Government of Andhra Pradesh (before 2014).

Figure 4.8: Neolithic Tools at Kondapur Excavated 1941-2

the pertinent question then is whose or, what cultural remains are being neglected or left out.

At Kondapur there was much excavated that was almost automatically and naturally emphasized by the excavators so as to fit the larger conception of what constituted elements of an early urban society. Today, the history, art, and culture of the early Deccan is historiographically entwined with descriptions of a close association with Buddhism. In the context of the Ganges Valley Anna King points out, 'the material remains and their chronologies have often been adapted to fit these descriptions', impeding our understanding 'of the archaeological and cultural materials' themselves.[84] The Museum near the Kondapur mound showcases a varied of stone tools identified as microliths, Neolithic tools, hand axes, copper tools and so on (Figure 4.8). Did these co-exist with the Buddhist remains? Nobody has asked this question. What were they used for and by whom and most importantly, why have they survived? Archaeologists, however, hurry to explain these as some distant hunting and incipient farming communities that ostensibly disappeared once the early historic period emerged.[85] In fact, at Peddabankur, a site lying just north of Kondapur, it was reported that Neolithic ground stone tools, were found at early historic levels suggesting the co-existence of populations with distinct economic identities.[86] A survey of the areas around the present day mound of Kondapur has revealed Megalith remains. But blinded by the shine of the 'rich' historical data found on the mound, archaeologists have not excavated or studied these. We maintain that apart from the physical configurations of a locality how the nature of the antecedent cultures over-layered or co-existed at particular sites determined their interaction with newcomers and defined the character of their later development. Furthermore, these cultures could persist as 'non-urban' forms into the early historical phase, when urbanization is supposed to have reached a high-water mark on the subcontinent as a whole between 200 BCE to 300 CE.[87] We concur with insights provided by other studies done on long-term histories that if there is anything at all that marks out South Asian history it is a 'close interaction between groups of people organized in radically different social and economic forms' as in the case of 'the sets of relationships between specialized forager-traders, many living in upland environments, and agriculturalists, merchants, and states, many based in the lowlands . . . these kinds of relationships have a long history. . . .'[88]

Kondapur's existence was short-lived and this is something we have to consider in positing tentative interpretations about how the difference and diversity of settlement patterns in hinterland societies should compel us to re-think issues about the permanence and totality of archaeological landscapes. Did it succumb to seismic changes,[89] perhaps the volcanic activity that is integral to the Deccan land mass?[90] It is significant to note that no other early historic or early medieval monuments or structures have been found remotely close to it. This absence may be connected to how we define community configurations in a given locality for a given period that could have been, to use Springborg's words, 'more transactional'[91] than the ones we use as models to discuss more concrete manifestations of city life for other regions and zones. In other words, Kondapur apparently had all the given characteristics of an urban environment as delineated by archaeologists but its location defied its solidity and duration of existence. Why have we not been able to retrieve its fortification wall, a common feature of some sites to its north? Why has 'classical' sculptural art intimately connected to the Buddhist ethos of many sites in the Deccan not been found here? These are important questions that should problematize its characterization as a typical urban centre of the Deccan even within conventional scholarship.

Thus it is challenging to deal with the 'realities' revealed by the data to discuss the profile and possible configuration of a 'city' in the larger context of the settlement patterns on the ancient volcanic landscape of the Deccan Plateau. We must begin now to accept that the so-called Buddhist structures lay side by side with other material remains that go beyond our conceptions of what we think should be 'classical' images of a city only rooted in its Buddhist links, or one that must prove to have 'legitimate' origins under dominant supervision of the Sātavāhanas. The larger materiality reflecting different, less opulent traditions needs to be brought into the canvas so that our understanding of the practice of archaeology and the theoretical burden of incorporating marginal groups can also be addressed while conflating discussions around the 'city' in the ancient world. The fundamental question remains. We began this paper with a fictive account. Contemporary debates around De Certeau differentiate between what historians seek to do, namely, to write about what they retrieve as true, which must necessarily be entangled in representation, and the more symbolic realm that concerns the retrieval of reality.[92] We drew primarily on practicing archaeologists who sincerely pursued their task of retrieving tangible objects and structures at Kondapur, but the reality of Kondapur was also that it was different, its location relatively isolated and yet inclusive. Ironically, its inclusivity can only be retrieved if one raises questions about its absences. This large archaeological mound has yet to be fully excavated, but the enigma of the past hidden underneath hinges on what is not preserved therein. Thus, the potentiality of imagination to retrieve its 'urban reality' has a place in the investigation.

NOTES

1. Anand (1965: 4-8).
2. De Certeau (1988: xv).
3. As for instance Sundara (1984: 13, 18).
4. The Deccan Plateau's famous granite formations of 'molten magma' were formed about 2500 million years ago. *Society to Save Rocks*, Hyderabad website http://www.saverocks.org/Geology.html (last accessed 31 January 2012).
5. Nagi Reddy (2008: 35, 42-3).
6. Sarkar (1986: 3).
7. In 2014 this State was bifurcated into Telangana and Andhra Pradesh and Kondapur is located in the former.
8. Dikshit (1952: i).
9. Yazdani (1941: 175).
10. ASI http://asi.nic.in/asi_museums_kondapur.asp (last accessed 8 October 2011).
11. An earlier account of this site was written by me as well Parasher Sen (1987: 82-90).
12. Yazdani (1941: 185).
13. The late D. Jithendra Das, superintending archaeologist, Archaeological Survey of India, Hyderabad Circle, reported this to journalist M. Malleswara Rao in 2008. http://www.hindu.com/2008/01/12/stories/2008011254960500.htm (last accessed 8 October 2011).
14. For two seasons of its re-excavation [2009-11] by the Archaeological Survey of India, I was able to visit the site and observe its new material configurations. I am grateful to Dr. Gautam Sengupta, the then Director-General of the Archaeological Survey of India for granting permission to do so and to Dr. G. Maheshwari, Superintending Archaeologist, Excavation Branch, Bhubaneswar excavating at Kondapur to have provided the congenial atmosphere for discussion of the work under progress.
15. As reported by G. Maheshwari to the journalist Avadhani 2011 reporting

on the excavation http://www.hindu.com/2011/02/28/stories/2011022863950600.htm (last accessed 8 October 2011).
16. Deo (1985: 94).
17. Krishnasastry (1983: 123-4).
18. Das 2008 http://www.hindu.com/2008/01/12/stories/2008011254960500.htm (last accessed 8 October 2011).
19. Yazdani (1941: 184); Dikshit (1952: i). However, no evidence of fortification walls were found during the 1940-2 season of excavations.
20. Quoted by Sreenivasachar in Dikshit (1952: i). Emphasis added.
21. Sarkar (1986: 1-2).
22. Yazdani (1941: 176) writes these structures emerged after removing 'only 20"-30" of earth from the cultivated surface'.
23. Yazdani (1941: 182-3) Those religious structures found on the northern part of the mound are reported to have been badly damaged.
24. Maheshwari 2010.http://archaeologyexcavations.blogspot.com/2010/08/excavation-work-at-kondapur-district.html (last accessed 8 October 2011).
25. Maheshwari 2011 http://www.hindu.com/2011/02/28/stories/2011022863950600.htm (last accessed 28 October 2011).
26. Maheshwari 2011.
27. Maheshwari 2011.
28. These images have been found to be fairly well distributed all over the Deccan and other parts of South India. The one found at Kondapur has been classified as one of the first type and its distinguishing marks most clearly visible. Cf. Parasher Sen (2002: 20-1).
29. Ray (1986).
30. Personal communication with author.
31. http://museums.ap.nic.in/phanigiri.htm. Official website of the State Department of Archaeology and Museums, Government of Andhra Pradesh, Hyderabad (last accessed 30 September 2011). Some of them like Phanigiri, Vardhamanukota, Gajulabanda, Tirumalagiri and Arlagaddagudem are worth mentioning as early historic settlements with clearly excavated Buddhist monastic structures and which lasted for a fairly long duration. Their architectural monumentality and sculptural remains compare well with the best classical traditions from Amaravati and Nagarjunakonda, the renowned Buddhist sites of Andhra Pradesh. See discussion in Skilling (2008: 96-118).
32. It is opined by Dikshit (1952: ii, n. 3) that in the Deccan and South India underground cells for storing of valuables and grain is a common feature even today. Yazdani (1941: 183) had suggested that these are called *chaubachchas* in Hindustani and frequently found in North India as well.

33. Dikshit (1952: i).
34. Yazdani (1941: 181-2). KEAR (1940-1) notes that the large size bricks measured 22' × 11' × 3' and the square ones measured 15' × 15'.
35. KEAR (1940-1: 17).
36. Yazdani (1941: 181). Emphasis added. There are, however, other scholars who doubt whether a separate industrial area with metallurgists' shops could have existed: cf. Dikshit (1952: iii).
37. Yazdani (1941: 184). Ray (1983: 86).
38. Yazdani (1941: 175-6) Writing in the general context of the development of iron technology in India, Bhardwaj has stated that normally 'heaps of iron slag recorded during excavations invariably contains a very high content of iron oxide and same reduced metal . . . (and thereby) . . . represent unsuccessful or partially successful reductions caused by lack of understanding the role of carbon in reductions'. Bhardwaj (1979: 152).
39. Bhardwaj (1979: 152).
40. Reported and discussed in detail Krishnasastry (1983).
41. Parasher Sen (1992: 437-77) and more recently while comparing them with those in the lower Krishna valley see Parasher Sen (2007: 231-69).
42. Krishnasastry (1983: 107; 153-4).
43. Krishnasastry (1983: 153).
44. Dikshit (1952: Introduction).
45. A total of nearly 23,391 beads were discovered here, and many of them were analysed by Dikshit (1952).
46. Yazdani (1941: 179). Dikshit (1952: i).
47. Sarkar (1986: 10).
48. Yazdani (1941: 177-8).
49. 'The system of routes connected Ter with other flourishing indigenous trading centres, viz. Kondapur , Nevasa, Paithan and Nagarjunakonda' according to Chapekar (1969: vi-vii).
50. Yazdani (1941: 176).
51. Based on the features and composure depicted on these faces, Yazdani (1941) Plates VIII, IX and X identifies some of them as Bodhisattava heads.
52. Yazdani (1941: 177)—They represent several varieties and the report on Kondapur indicates that with their help one can establish a sequence of Indian pottery.
53. KEAR (1940-1: 17).
54. Personal communication from the excavations at Kondapur 2009-11 by G. Maheshwari.
55. A point first suggested by Deshpande (1963: 603) cited by Margabandhu

(2005: 24) who writes 'they consist of small bowls with straight nozzles, circular holes for oil and circular pipe-shaped horizontal nozzles tapering to a small wick-end'.

56. The lamps of the 'Ter type' attributed to a 'foreign origin' were of a pan shape equipped with a vertical handle Chapekar (1969: vi).
57. Excavation work at Kondapur, Medak District, Andhra Pradesh, 5 August 2010.http://archaeologyexcavations.blogspot.com/2010/08/excavation-work-at-kondapur-district.html (last accessed 8 October 2011).
58. Margabandhu (2005: 166, 179-80)—There is much discussion on how Indian craftsmen were influenced by Roman techniques and traditions.
59. Margabandhu (2005: 177).
60. Dikshit (1949: 37).
61. Yazdani (1941: 180).
62. Personal communication from the excavations at Kondapur 2009-11 by G. Maheshwari.
63. Gupta (2005: 140-64).
64. There has been recent interest among scholars on this issue, especially in the fact that many of the early historic sites in the Deccan and south India were still dependent on networks established during the earlier Megalithic context. For instance, even the location of a prolifically excavated site with particularly close contacts to the so-called 'Roman' trade like Arikamedu is explained in the context of 'the local networks within the Indian subcontinent'. See Ray (1995: 103) for details.
65. Parasher Sen (2008: 316-18).
66. A question extensively addressed by me elsewhere Parasher Sen (2007: 261-5).
67. KEAR (1940-1: 19-20), Yazdani (1941: 180), Dikshit (1952: iii).
68. A total of 1,535 coins were reported at the time of excavation KEAR (1940-1: 16) Along with these, moulds probably used for punch-marked coins were also discovered.
69. Yazdani (1941: 180). Similar coin finds have also been reported from the 2009-11 excavations. Personal communication given by G. Maheshwari
70. KEAR (1940-41: 19). These coins were considered the most important data for dating the site.
71. Yazdani (1941: 180).
72. Details of the various views on these discoveries have been analysed in Sastry (1981: 1-16) and Sastry (1979: 134-5) and assessed in Parasher Sen (2007: 246-50).
73. Sarma (1980: 35).

74. Krishnasastry (1983: 139, 200, 100).
75. Krishnasastry (1983: 125, 132, 136-8).
76. Krishnasastry (1983: 179-85) describes a variety of terracotta objects found at Dhulikatta and Peddabankur.
77. Sarkar (1986: 10-11).
78. Discussed earlier in Parasher Sen (2008: 313-17).
79. Parasher Sen (1992: 438-46).
80. Hodder (1986: 169).
81. Today Kondapur is located in the State of Telangana.
82. Alcock (2002: 16).
83. Alcock (2002: 2).
84. King (1984: 109; 110-11).
85. Krishnasastry (1983: 22, 24) points to the existence of microlith tools in abundance from Mesolithic times, through the Neolithic phase and up to early historic times.
86. Parasher Sen (1992: 473).
87. Champakalakshmi (1986: 2-3).
88. Morrison (2002: 21).
89. Barness (2012: 50) informs us that 'the landscape of plateaus and cliffs known as the Deccan is the result of a cataclysmic volcanic flooding 65 million years ago (11: 39 pm)'.
90. A point made by D. Jithendra Das, superintending archaeologist, Archaeological Survey of India, Hyderabad Circle, to journalist M. Malleswara Rao, 2008. http://www.hindu.com/2008/01/12/stories/20080112549 60500.htm (last accessed 8 October 2011).
91. Springborg (1992: 6).
92. White (2005: 147-57).

CHAPTER 5

Vihāras and Water Storage: Thotlakonda and Phanigiri

It is inconceivable to look back at the early history of the Deccan without dwelling on the social and cultural landscape that was provided by the arrival of Buddhist communities here. The spread of Buddhism in the modern states of Andhra Pradesh and Maharashtra was prolific during the early historic times. In Telangana and Karnataka too Buddhism has left a considerable impact. A substantial amount of historical detail is available to us in the form of monographs on Buddhist art and architecture, its literature and philosophy and also its patronage by political elites and laypersons alike. One would imagine that with all this information we have exhausted all that there is to be known about the early Buddhist contact with the Deccan where Buddhism flourished in early historic times. Fortunately that is not so. In this chapter we take a detailed look at efforts of the Buddhist monks to organize their habitational spaces in monasteries and, in particular how they managed an important resource for their existence at their *vihāras*, namely water.

Historiographically, studies on sites with only Buddhist monasteries (Map 5.1) have been erroneously labelled as urban centres. In fact, often these monasteries were built on hilltops or excavated in caves and were actually dependant on the rural countryside for their subsistence and possibly connected to agricultural production in their immediate hinterland.[1] There are divergent opinions among scholars whether monasteries were totally isolated settlements[2] or important centres linking critical trade networks.[3] A relatively recent study on the monastery of Thotlakonda suggests that: 'taken

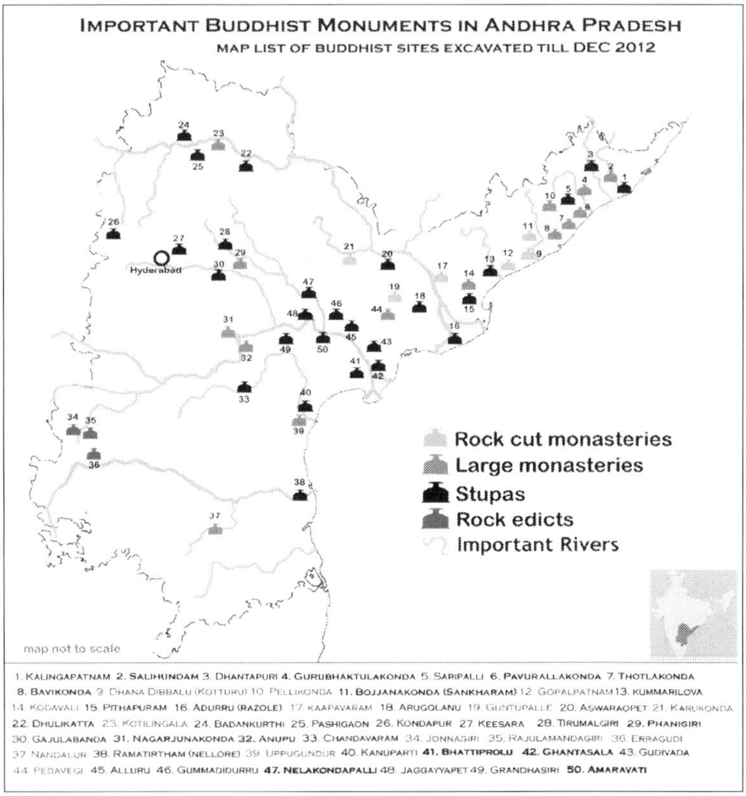

Source: Accessed and reproduced from Wikimedia Commons N. Aditya Madhav, 2013.

Map 5.1: Monasteries Thotlakonda (No. 7) and Phanigiri (No. 29)

together, it is clear that the monastery was not isolated from its local context, but enmeshed within a landscape of relations, both economic and religious, tying monks to the laity in the local area'.[4] It is therefore important to look at the particularity of the largely monastery based sites from those that existed on the plains and other locations that were more amenable for their transformation into urban centres. As discussed in Chapter 3 urban centres necessarily required certain economic pre-requisites for their transformation from small rural settlements into urban ones.

Source material for the late centuries BCE and the early centuries CE all over the Deccan are of course embedded in structures, art-historical material, inscriptions and texts of Buddhist affiliation in their monasteries but, how and where exactly these are found is of immense importance for us to highlight. This inseparability gets most clearly reflected in the intensive excavation and conservation work that has been done in relation to the discovery of Buddhist *vihāra* and *stūpa* complexes ever since the latter half of the nineteenth century. The unearthing of such remains has continued well into recent times. It is creditable that the State Department of Archaeology and Museums, Government of Andhra Pradesh[5] was very active in this regard as is evident from the relatively recent publication of the report on the site of Thotlakonda. An interim report[6] was published by them on the site of Phanigiri. Both these give valuable descriptions of the various structures at these two important Buddhist sites. The former is located in the state of Andhra Pradesh and the latter in the new state of Telangana. The report on Thotlakonda is substantially a presentation of the details about the various types of Buddhist structures excavated here ranging from *stūpas*, votive *stūpas, vihāras, chaityagrihas*, congregation pillared halls, a kitchen or refractory complex, water cisterns and so on (Figure 5.1). Of all the material and structural remains excavated here the last of these, namely, water cisterns located on the hilltop shall be the focus of our descriptions on this site. Similarly, at Phanigiri a *mahāstūpa,* votive *stūpas,* both in brick and stone, apsidal *chaityagrihas*, several *vihāras*, a sixteen pillared congregation hall, a stone pillared congregation hall, a brick square shrine, other platforms and a refectory were excavated (Figure 5.2). The focus of our descriptions at this site shall be the residential layout of the *vihāras* in relation to the overall settlement on this hilltop site.

Dominant architectural forms associated with Buddhism have received considerable attention primarily because they have survived for posterity and thus, have defined the way we look at the Buddhist heritage. Many of the earlier studies were fascinated by the architectural magnificence of its buildings or, on its brilliant sculptural portrayal of the events related to the life of the Buddha and of the *Jātaka* stories that were found prolifically depicted at many sites.[7] It is the lesser known features about these large

Source: State Department of Archaeology and Museums, Government of Andhra Pradesh (before 2014).

Figure 5.1: Overview of Buddhist Monastery at Thotlakonda

Source: State Department of Archaeology and Museums, Government of Andhra Pradesh (before 2014).

Figure 5.2: Full view of the Mahāstūpa, first-second century CE, Phanigiri

Buddhist establishments that have only partially been addressed that we want to bring to the fore as part of our interpretations. For instance, in the case of the monumental remains at Thotlakonda, as also other Buddhist monastery sites, the rock water cisterns or water troughs at the site have hardly drawn the attention of scholars. In fact, they can be seen as extremely important for the very existence of the religious habitation area. At Thotlakonda are found intricate patterns of water storage and management without which the life of the monks would have been impossible on the hillock where their habitation was located. In using the methodology of landscape archaeology, Lars Fogelin for the first time has done a systematic archaeological survey of the areas around the Thotlakonda monastery in coastal Andhra Pradesh to examine the nature of early Buddhist monastic life. His analytical approach has pertinently enabled us to learn about the tension between the ostensible isolation of the monastery and the engagement of the monks housed there with the lay community in their vicinity that was of mutual benefit to both during the early historic period. This study thus throws light on how ritual workings of early Buddhism known from the material remains studied by Fogelin impacted the practice of the faith in this region.[8] His analysis clearly indicates that the monastery did not live in complete isolation but did its own management of resources on the hilltop habitation. However, construction of the complex and the maintenance of the structures must have required labour from the lay community.

At Phanigiri too, the importance of water storage was recognized and its very location ensured this. It is perhaps due to this availability that a large *vihāra* settlement emerged on this massive rock hillock, which must have housed a large number of monks. Like with reference to other important Buddhist sites, here too what has drawn the attention of scholars are the remarkable sculptural remains found, comparable, in style and form, with sculptures from the famous early Buddhist sites of Amaravati and Nagarjunakonda that have hitherto been considered the custodians of the classical arts that flourished under Buddhism in the Deccan.[9] Skilling's approach to lay bare the new archaeological material found on this hillock site is to focus exclusively on the rich sculptural remains at Phanigiri and how they reflect on the nature of Buddhist ideas and thought. Apart from Fogelin and Skilling, few scholars have dwelt on discussing these two sites. Unlike at Thotlakonda, the excavators of Phanigiri do not give details of the water cisterns found on the hilltop though they are mentioned briefly in the interim report.

Experts today readily tell us that by the turn of this century, unless we make consistent efforts to conserve water, it will become a rare resource. In the context of the arid and semi-arid regions of the world this is particularly highlighted. The situation in countries like India, which are dependent on the monsoons, is particularly fragile as we get too much water in a season when we do not need it and too little in the seasons when we desperately require it. Thus, it is often articulated that India does not lack water resources per se but that it does not have an effective and appropriate system to manage its containment. Overburdened with the achievements of modernization and industrialization, the era of big dams to conserve this resource came to India in a big way. Today, it is losing its charm because of the rightly projected concerns of the environmentalists and activists that the costs of these constructions are not only high in financial terms, but also because of the irreparable damage they do to the natural and human elements of survival.[10] It sometimes seems that the bright lights of modernization in this regard have succeeded in blacking out information on how an ancient society like India, which has always been dependant on the vagaries of the monsoon rains, had experimented with various methods to conserve and manage water sources.[11]

We illustrate one such method with data from the above-mentioned site of Thotlakonda in coastal Andhra where a small community of Buddhist monks effectively stored water, primarily got from the monsoons, to live a monastic life on a hillock. This takes us back to the early centuries of the Christian era and is an effort not exclusive to the site of Thotlakonda only but was a method well-known to other early Buddhist establishments. Indeed, Krishnasastry informs us that even during the life time of the Buddha, monks were advised on the various ways in which they could store water for use during their seclusion period of rest in the rainy season.[12] It may be pointed out at this stage that the prescriptions for the making of water troughs was also laid out in the early Buddhist texts and these have been followed while making the water cisterns in the Buddhist Cave temples of western India[13] datable to around the same period or a little earlier when compared to Thotlakonda and Phanigiri. This, we are informed by the excavator was made necessary because the monks were required to live in secluded and isolated areas and often no regular or perennial supply of water may have been available in their near vicinity. This explanation may only be partially correct. In fact, at Phanigiri water sources were available in the vicinity but water cisterns were made on the hilltop for easy accessibility and use. Though initially the idea of the monks living in these *vihāras* was for the temporary season of the rains, it soon became their permanent abode and the institutional base for the propagation of their particular school of Buddhism. Along with this development went the increase in the population of monks at particular *vihāras* and, therefore, the requirements of storing water for this reason also became a crucial concern for the monks. The technology to make the water cisterns had not only to be sound, but it also had to go hand in hand with the management of the water resources thus stored. Though many Buddhist monasteries had lands attached to them for their maintenance, the water cisterns at Thotlakonda were primarily meant for the domestic use of the monks and the daily needs of bathing, cooking, cleaning and probably also for the conduct of burials of the monks at the *vihāra*. Fogelin's research points to the fact that outside the monastery complex per se, his survey found that a maximum of material evidence was of 'small memorial cairns, most likely erected for dead monks and devout laity'. The local population seem to have been actively engaged with regard to mortuary rituals. Other archaeological evidence found similarly was of reservoirs and water cisterns among other things. He interestingly also points to finding a 'small monastic village' outside the main monastery.[14] At Phanigiri as well a water tank is found located near cairn burials at the base of the hill there.

The site of Thotlakonda (17' .82° N, 83' .41° E) is situated on an important route running north to south along the eastern coast of Peninsular India. It is about 15 km from Visakhapatnam on the way to Bhimunipatnam and near the village of Mangamaripet. The site was excavated for several seasons during 1988-92. This monastery was surrounded by others, which have also been excavated by the State Department of Archaeology, Government of Andhra Pradesh. Most prominent among these was the site of Bavikonda (Map 5.1) excavated during 1982-7.[15] This site was famed for the gold and silver relics found in a casket here and, like other Buddhist sites, a *mahāstūpa*, several smaller *stūpas*, about fifty living cells and several *chaityas* around a central congregation hall were identified. Another important monastery excavated, located about 7 km from Thotlakonda, was Pavuralakonda. The overall plan of structures found here is similar to Bavikonda.[16]

Excavations[17] at Thotlakonda revealed a large monastery with as many as sixty living cells, a *mahāstūpa* (Figure 5.3), about a dozen smaller *stūpas* and a few *chaityas*. On the western side a refectory was identified. As in other monasteries in the centre of the complex a large, rectangular hall was located. Surrounding the site

Source: State Department of Archaeology and Museums, Government of Andhra Pradesh (before 2014).

Figure 5.3: Main Buddhist *Stūpa* at Thotlakonda

numerous cisterns and a large reservoir were also identified. It is extremely significant to note 'the name Thotlakonda appears to be of recent origin, derived from the presence of rock-cut troughs of various shapes and sizes hewn in the bed rock of the hillock'.[18] The site is on a hillock and in the proximity of a stream locally called Peddagadda. Near the south-eastern part of the hillock there was also a large tank that has now dried up. Further, the location of the water troughs on the north-east and south-western parts of the hillock is significant as these sloppy parts would be most suitable for the maximum collection of rain water. With regard to the major excavated monuments on this hillock, it was noticed that the main *stūpa* or *mahāstūpa* was found on the highest elevated part of the mound, which is in the north-east corner. The other votive *stūpas* were also found in this area whereas the location of the *vihāra* or the residential complex was noticed on the other three sides of the hillock. One set of the water cisterns (nos. 1-3) are interestingly on the north-eastern side near the main *stūpa* and the other set (nos. 6-10)[19] are on the diagonally opposite side, i.e. the south-western part of the site, outside the *vihāra* complex.

A total of eleven cisterns were found at Thotlakonda revealing a well-organized water supply system. They varied in size and depth and many of them had steps leading into the trough (Figure 5.4). It has been suggested by the excavators that these cisterns or *kupas* were excavated from solid rock and covered with lids so as to avoid seepage of water and its evaporation. This care had to be taken because the water supply into the cisterns was primarily in the monsoon months only. After long use some of the lids were found broken lying at the bottom of the cisterns. Seepage, however, did take place as is indicated in the case of cistern no. 10 at this site where lime mortar was used to plug fissures in the walls.

Further, serious efforts were often made to barricade the cisterns so that the excess rainwater did not flow over. Traces of boulders to suggest the existence of one such barricade were found to the southern and western sides of cistern no. 6. More clearly, a stone wall alignment was seen on all four sides at cistern no. 7. The most significant example of this kind is the 'L' shaped cistern no. 10, which had a masonry barricade wall and here, it is clearly sug-

Source: State Department of Archaeology and Museums, Government of Andhra Pradesh (before 2014).

Figure 5.4: Water Cistern with Steps on Thotlakonda Hill

gested that it was to arrest the flow of rainwater.[20] On the other hand, the traces of a stone enclosure wall on three sides of cistern no. 1 may have been made 'to prevent the accumulation of dust in the water due to the high velocity of winds'.[21] Besides lids, around some of the cisterns (nos. 6, 7, 8), post holes have been found which indicate that a cover made of palm leaf or some other such perishable material was used since no piles of tiles have been found around the cisterns to indicate their use for roofing of these sheds. These protective measures were important since the monks used some of these cisterns for bathing. For instance, cistern no. 11 has been given a local name of *Mangalitotti* or barber's cistern, which suggests that the monks bathed here after they had tonsured their heads. This was an essential religious practice for monks in order to be initiated into the Budhhist Sangha.

By far the most significant aspect of the technology of water management with regard to these water cisterns is the aspect related to the regulating of excess water from the cisterns located at a higher level to those at a lower level. Sometimes, as in the case of cistern no. 1, room was made to adjust for excess water during certain seasons at the same level itself. Thus, here we find wide sunken spaces towards the east probably meant to accommodate the overflow of water from this well cut and rectangular shaped cistern. Here were also found water channels leading to the trough or *kupa* for collection of overflowing water from the *kupas* of the upper levels. At cistern no. 3 a rectangular deep pit was scooped in the centre for collection of additional water making its total depth to be 2.80 m so that it had to have eight steps to lead down to the water. In the case of cistern no. 7 the excavators tell us that 'a sloppy surface was made at the bottom to collect (last vestiges of) water at one corner to maintain depth'.[22] Around cistern no. 9 channels are found cut into the rock and this seems to have been a common method of connecting cisterns. These were provided in such a way keeping in view the gradients for facilitating a free flow of water from the high contours.

It is worth noting that at other sites in the near vicinity of Thotlakonda, rock-cut water cisterns have also been found. At Pavuralakonda, lying west of Bhimunipatnam, for instance, sixteen rock-cut cisterns were found to be larger and deeper than those found at Thotlakonda;[23] a clear indication perhaps that a larger number of monks or residents must have inhabited this place. At another site called Gopalapatnam, near Visakhapatnam a rock-cut cistern, about 20 ft deep, was noticed indicating that this probably served the water needs of the entire settlement. What is interesting here is that this cistern is cut into the first terrace of the hill on which the settlement was located and the settlement itself existed on varying upper levels.[24]

Thus, today the active concern amongst scientists and social scientists alike to explain to society the importance of the conservation of water and the methods of doing so can draw on the ancient experiences. Since these water troughs were scooped out of locally available hard rock, the costs of making them were probably not very high. The technology to do so also required tools that were already well known since around the late centuries BCE and early centuries CE. The inhabitants had mastered the techniques of excavating rocks to build *vihāras* and *chaityas* for residential purposes all along the Western Ghat region. Each community probably had contact with stone cutters and others skilled in the task so that major purchases of tools and skilled labour did not have to be brought from outside. Fresh efforts on these lines were always necessarily small in scale and most pertinently, kept the local environmental needs in mind. The above case study has illustrated limited water available at the site of Thotlakonda, which could only be replenished during the heavy downpours of rainfall in the monsoon season. This was contained and managed in such a way so that monks could live a comfortable life without water shortages to cope with the dry season.

We now turn to take a closer look at the way the newly excavated monastery at Phanigiri was organized. It was located on a big granite rocky hill top and therefore, brick structures on it had to be carefully located. The village of Phanigiri is located at Lat. 17' 25° N and Long. 79' 29° E on the banks of a rivulet called Aleru, locally also called Bikkeru.The hillock with the Buddhist remains of the early historic period is 150 ft high and located on the northern side of the village (Figure 5.5). It is suggested that it seems to have derived its name from the shape of the southern

Source: State Department of Archaeology and Museums, Government of Andhra Pradesh (before 2014).

Figure 5.5: View of Phanigiri Hill

portion of the hillock, which looks like a snake hood. Scholars further point out that in Sanskrit, *phani* means 'snake', *giri* means 'hillock' and hence the name Phanigiri. From Hyderabad it is at a distance of 110 km via Bhongir and Tirumalagiri, which is the mandal headquarters in Nalgonda district. Its strategic location on this route must have connected it to settlements on the east as well as the west of the Deccan plateau and the coast in early historic times. It is of considerable importance to note that as primarily a Buddhist monastery, it was surrounded in the north-south direction by other Buddhist establishments, particularly Vardhamanukota, Gajulabanda, Tirumalagiri and Arlagaddagudem, that are also on the banks of the Aleru. These Buddhist establishments must have been in touch with each other for religious as well as economic reasons of sustenance and communication since they were all located within a radius of 6 km from Phanigiri.

An idol of a standing Buddha with an inscribed slab of first century CE Brahmi characters, coins and broken sculptural panels were reported from Vardhamanukota. Later trial excavations of the ancient mound encompassed by a brick fortification wall, which is locally known as *kotadibba*,[25] brought to light alignments of limestone columns in a row, broken panels, beads, terracotta figures, Sātavāhana and Mahātalavara coins, early historic pottery, etc., assignable to first century CE. Brick structures such as a *chaitya, vihāra*, a brick platform, etc., were also revealed. Trial excavations[26] at Gajulabanda, 3 km away from Phanigiri to its north-west, unearthed a monastery with a *mahāstūpa*, a *vihāra*, votive *stūpas*, platforms and other early historic materials. Associated with these brick structures and fragments of sculptural material, were found Sātavāhana coins datable to first-second centuries CE. Tirumalagiri, the other Buddhist site near Phanigiri has its present habitation over an ancient mound. Here similar Buddhist related material remains have been found and even today brick alignments can be seen at certain places in the village. Arlagaddagudem is at the most distance away from Phanigiri and here trial digs conducted brought to light brick structures and potsherds of early historic period. Importantly, from this site Roman gold coins of Augustus, Tiberius and Nero were reported.

Explorations in and around Phanigiri village had brought to light a cluster of Megalithic burials away from the hillock towards north and north-east direction overlooking a big tank. At the foot of the hillock on the eastern side near a Kakatiyan temple complex, was noticed a disturbed habitation with brick alignments. However, the exact relationship of this earlier historical evidence with the monastic complex has not been clearly established. The Buddhist habitation on the hill has seen several seasons of exploration and excavation. The Nizam's government did the first preliminary excavations at this site during 1941-4. They were then taken up again six decades later, by the Department of Archaeology and Museums, Government of Andhra Pradesh in four field seasons during 2001-7. Inscriptions found here were datable to the Sātavāhana and Ikshavāku period. The other cultural material found here has been dated to the first century BCE and the third century CE by the excavators.[27] These excavations were taken up while making an integrated plan of the monastic complex. The ancient habitation on hill top thus described covered an area of 10 acres in extent. The excavators have briefly summed up the discoveries at Phanigiri in the following words:

> It is observed that the Mahastupa, votive stupas, apsidal chaityagrihas, sixteen pillared congregation hall, stone pillared congregation hall, brick shrine and refectory are *located at an higher contour, on the south and western side of the site,* whereas the viharas, pillared congregation hall and platforms with staircases are *located at the lower level on the eastern and northern side of the monastery.* To connect the structures, located at different levels, several staircases were provided wherever necessary. It appears that the architects (*Navakammikas*) might have surveyed and studied the contours on the hilltop and rightly exploited the contours and developed several terraces by leveling the undulating surfaces with rubble mixed with soil as packing material and finally planned the structural edifices of the religious and secular nature at appropriate places as per their requirement. Further, *rock-cut tanks and cisterns on sloppy summits of the hillock were built to collect and store rainwater to cater the needs of the monastic complex.*[28] [emphasis added]

As detailed above it had been important to highlight the particularity of the location of Phanigiri. Being surrounded by other Buddhist monasteries of near contemporary period[29] and surrounded by the agricultural plains of the Deccan plateau (Figure 5.5a), it is

Source: State Department of Archaeology and Museums, Government of Andhra Pradesh (before 2014).

Figure 5.5a: Hilltop view of the Plains below, Phanigiri

clear that the Buddhist inhabitants at Phanigiri did not live in absolute isolation. Since not much has been written on Phanigiri, Skilling postulates that 'Phanigiri's interactions with the surrounding landscape, with settlements and centres of power, with long-distance trade routes, and with downstream and deltaic sites remain to be determined. One may assume that the river valley would have been a natural route since pre-historic times.'[30] Despite its location near a rivulet, excavations here have revealed water tanks and rock cut cisterns on the hilltop and also tanks at the foot of the hillock that must have served as the main water source for the inhabitants. Near the cluster of megalithic cairn circle burials at the foot of the hillock, on the north-eastern side, there was a tank locally known as Nadimi Cheruvu. On the hilltop too, in the north-western side of the Buddhist habitation cairn heaps were located by the excavators and these too were adjacent to a tank (Figure 5.6). One can postulate that these were in all probability the burials of the resi-

Source: State Department of Archaeology and Museums, Government of Andhra Pradesh (before 2014).

Figure 5.6: Water Tank on the rock surface, Phanigiri

dential monks. Similar ones had been noticed at other Buddhist sites, namely, Thotlakonda and Pavurallakonda in Visakhapatnam district and Chandavaram in Prakasam district. Ensuring a steady supply of water for the monastery was of prime importance at Phanigiri too. However, what we intend to highlight further is the massive organization that was done by the monks to build their living cells on the hilltop. Next we turn to describe these as they give a magnificent idea of the layout of an active and communicative monastery.

At the Phanigiri complex the *mahāstūpa* (Figure 5.7) was the biggest structure located elegantly on an elevated area on the southernmost part of the monastic complex. It had a diameter of about 18 m, with four projecting *āyaka* platforms at the cardinal points, each measuring 4×1.25 m.[31] Seven votive *stūpas* were unearthed on the east and south-east corners of the *mahāstūpa* at two different levels. Three votive *stūpas* were on the upper level and four votive *stūpas* in a row in north-south orientation on the south-east

Source: State Department of Archaeology and Museums, Government of Andhra Pradesh (before 2014).

Figure 5.7: Mahāstūpa first-second century CE, Phanigiri

corner of the *mahāstūpa* were found to be at a lower level. Those at the upper level were made of brick while those at the lower level were 'exclusively built of random rubble masonry with mud mortar and externally plastered with lime,'[32] suggesting two phases of construction here.

Two apsidal *Chaityagrihas*, facing east were located on north western side of the *mahāstūpa* and connected to it by a flight of steps. We are informed that they belong to two phases of construction. Apsidal *Chaityagriha* I had foundations of brick and Apsidal *Chaityagriha* II was encased by limestone slabs. In between the two *Chaityagrihas* was exposed a small rectangular room (3.00 × 7.00 m) that was probably meant for a person of high rank or head priest of the monastic complex. While removing the debris in between the two apsidal *Chaityagrihas*, several fragments of sculptured panels and images were recovered. Skilling suggests that this area 'might be called a sacred complex', since 'one component . . . is a brick platform with two gigantic pairs of footprints of the Buddha, carved with auspicious signs'.[33]

A large area of the hill was kept for setting up the living quarters of the monks residing there as six *vihāras* have been excavated here. The *vihāra* complex was on the northern and eastern side of the *Mahāstūpa* and connected to it by platforms and staircases. The excavators found a certain amount of uniformity in the layout of the living cells (Figure 5.8) They write: 'Each *vihara* is in rectangular plan with common verandah in front with the entrances decorated with *Purnaghata* motifs moulded in brick. Each cell has a sill followed by semi-circular stone step (*chandrasila*). Pathways were laid to reach the *mahastupa* from each *Vihara* of the monastic complex'[34] (Figure 5.9).

The layout of the monastery (Figure 5.10) indicates that the *vihāras* at the site were all located on its periphery with the congregation hall in the centre. This was a multi-pillared Congregation Hall opposite apsidal *Chaityagriha* II with a forty-eight stone pillared square demarcated with well-dressed limestone blocks.[35] Near the entrance of this hall, broken sculptured panels with label inscriptions and pottery pieces were recovered. Another sixteen pillared congregation hall was found located a few yards away from

Source: State Department of Archaeology and Museums, Government of Andhra Pradesh (before 2014).

Figure 5.8: Close view of a *Vihāra* Plan, Phanigiri

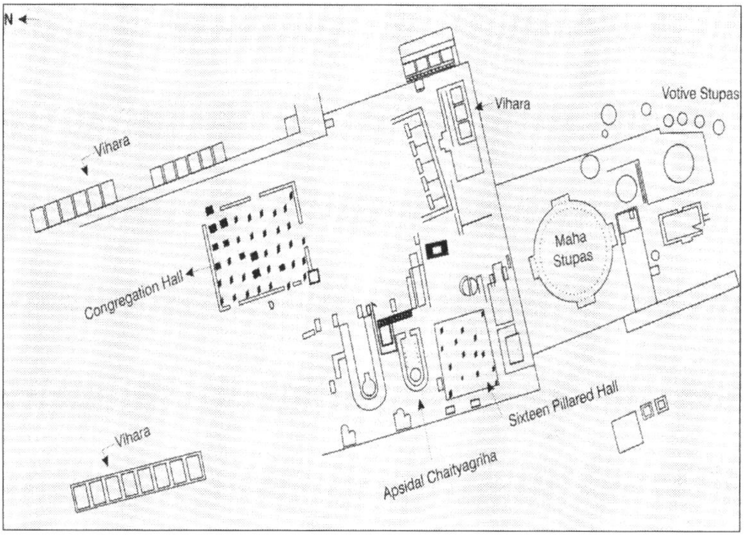

Source: Reproduced from Subramanyam et al. (2008: 14).

Figure 5.9: Ground Plan of the Excavated Monastic Complex: Phanigiri, 2001-7

Source: State Department of Archaeology and Museums, Government of Andhra Pradesh (before 2014).

Figure 5.10: *Vihāra* Complex at Phanigiri

apsidal *Chaityagriha* I on the eastern side, with an entrance facing south.[36]

Vihāra I was located on the north-eastern side of the *mahāstūpa* and consisted of three cells. Each cell measured 2.40 × 2.30 mts. They were built in an east-west orientation with a verandah connected by a flight of steps facing north. The extension of the *vihāra* was further done and another three cells were added making it a total of six cells in the first phase of construction at this *vihāra*. The occurrence of broken lime stone pillar stumps and clay tile pieces in and around the structure suggests that the cells and verandah of the *vihāra* had a tiled roof supported by limestone pillars and wooden rafters.The use of tiles was a common feature found at other Buddhist sites as well. *Vihāra* II, located to the north of *Vihāra* I had six cells, each measuring 2.50 × 2.50 m. The floor of the cells and the verandah had floors of Cuddapah stone slabs that were then treated with fine lime plaster to attain a smooth finish. In between these two *vihāras* a narrow passage was found that was connected by a flight of steps on its western side to reach the *Mahāstūpa*[37] (Figure 5.11).

Source: State Department of Archaeology and Museums, Government of Andhra Pradesh (before 2014).

Figure 5.11: Layout of *Vihāra* Cells, Phanigiri

Vihāra III lay to the east of *vihāra* II and outside the retaining wall of the monastic complex, on the eastern slope of the hillock. It had twelve cells and a common verandah oriented in north-south, facing west. From this *vihāra* as well one could reach the *Mahāstūpa* area through a narrow passage in between *Vihāras* I and II. *Vihara* IV was located at a distance from the apsidal *Chaityagriha* II. It had nine cells in north-south orientation. Each cell here measured 2.70 × 2.70 m and it is observed that they would have easily accommodated two monks. *Vihāra* V measured 28.00 × 4.50 m and was located away from the *Vihāra* IV oriented in a north-south direction. It had eight living cells. Finally, *Vihāra* VI was located in the extreme north-western portion of the complex in an east-west orientation. It measured 18.40 × 4.00 m and had six cells for the monks to live in.[38]

While all the *vihāras* were to the northern side of the *mahāstūpa*, the refectory was found and excavated to the south-east of the *mahāstūpa* and on the western side of the third votive *stūpa*. This was a rectangular brick structure with a partition brick wall, encompassed by a brick wall on east, west, north and a stone masonry wall on the south. 'The occurrence of huge quantities of ash mixed with potsherds of dishes and conical bowls on the eastern and northern side of the structure obviously indicate that it might have served as a kitchen complex'.[39] Overall the construction of this monastic complex was done in two phases as is evident from 'renovations and modifications' that were found to be done by way of blockage of earlier entrance ways to cells, etc.[40]

The brick walls of *vihāras, chaityagrihas* and other structures were all plastered externally and internally with lime plaster and decorated with stucco figurines of lotus medallions, floral motifs and human figures, mythical animal figures, etc. Several broken lime stone sculptured panels were unearthed particularly near the *mahāstūpa*, apsidal *Chaityagrihas*, staircases leading to the *Chariyagrihas*, at the entrance of stone pillared congregation hall and in front of *vihāras*, etc.[41] During the course of excavations, a total number of forty-two Brāhmī inscriptions belonging to the Sātavāhana (first-second centuries CE) and the Ikshavāku (third century CE) were recovered. Of these about forty were label inscriptions.[42] Some of them have been found in fragments and, therefore, difficult to decipher. As in the case of other Buddhist monasteries donations to the monastery have been recorded on the inscriptions found at this site. A few examples here would illustrate the trend found at Phanigiri. One inscription records the installation of a *Dharmachakra* at *Sadivihāra.* A number of gifts in the form of land and cows were given by one Vinayadhara Dhammasena along with members of the family, friends and relatives. An interesting gift of four *kahapanas* (gold coins) is recorded that was given by the monks (*bhikshu-samgha*).[43] While exposing these *vihāra* cells, a good number of Sātavahāna and Ikshavāku coins were found,[44] which clearly indicates that the monks had access to coined money. By far the most important inscription from the perspective of our reading is the one that mentions a *Mahānavakammika* or Chief Superintendent of Works. Obviously such professional groups must have been an integral part of those that worked to plan, set-up, build, execute and organize the monastic structures on the hill top at Phanigiri.

For both Thotlakonda and Phanigiri we have used reports that were brought out by the then Andhra Pradesh State Department of Archaeology and Museums. The two sites were located in different ecological zones though both of them were made on hilltops. In terms of the essential aspects of the Buddhist features of setting up a monastery, both the sites had the requisite *stūpas*, *chaityagrihas*, *vihāras* and other such structures. However, the particularity of the immediate environment around them defined the way these were built. The challenges of living on these relatively high altitudes meant that knowledge of the soils, types of rock formation, wind direction, seasons and other such climatic and geographical features had to be kept in mind. Both provide us examples of such attempts. In the case of Thotlakonda we were able to describe in detail the way the water troughs or water cisterns had been made to conserve water in the monastic complex. At Phanigiri the nature of the hill being of hard granite meant that water tanks were made at the base of the hill. Here, the creation of suitable soil conditions on the hilltop was essential to be able to lay out a full-fledged monastic complex. These descriptions have thrown light on the fact that though its situation was at a high altitude there was no compromise made in the perfection with which both the architectural and sculptural art was worked on and found embedded into the monastic complex.

We began with raising questions about the specific nature of monastery sites and other settlements that have been called urban centres. In the case of both the sites discussed by us we have to conclude that they were located near hinterlands of agricultural land. Further, they were both connected to other Buddhist sites and monasteries in their near vicinity. Though these habitations cannot be termed as 'urban' per se, we must emphasize that the Buddhist monks lived at places that were connected to the large urban economy of the times. Within the confines of the monastic establishment, the evidence of coined money, precious stones and material, inscriptions, names of merchant and other professional groups on them, etc., all indicate that the monks had certain relations with larger economic order of the times. Furthermore, the very construction of the monasteries and the sculptural art that they were adorned with the much needed donations that could not have been generated in the monastery itself. Apart from this, concurring with the views of Fogelin discussed earlier with reference to the monastery at Thotlakonda, we could generalize that during the course of daily activities as well the monks had to have interactions with the laity and society at large. For their religious practices in following the rules of the Sangha, the *vihāra* and *chaitya* complexes had to be particular spaces for the monks to dwell in away from the rest of the society and this is what gives us the particularity of the habitation areas occupied by monks of the different schools of Buddhism across the Deccan. It must be emphasized in ultimate analysis that how these enclaves were prepared and executed depended very much on the local resources and local conditions, which the monastic orders had to define relationship with from time to time.

NOTES

1. Heitzman (1997).
2. Basham (1954).
3. Thapar (1966).

4. Fogelin (2011; 2005: 483).
5. Krishnasastry et al. (1992). These excavations were conducted by the government under the former state of Andhra Pradesh.
6. Subrahmanyam et al. (2008). These excavations were conducted by the government under the former state of Andhra Pradesh. Phanigiri is now located in the state of Telangana.
7. Some of the early works in this regard were classic studies like Mitra (1980); Ray (1983).
8. Fogelin (2011).
9. Skilling (2008: 97); Subramanyam et al. (2008: 30).
10. Baruah (1989: 4-13) gives a telling account of the socio-cultural and ecological impact of the chain of big and small dams that the Narmada Valley Project of the Government would bring about.
11. Explained and illustrated in Pande in Agarwal and Narain (1997: 11-23)
12. Krishnasastry (1992: 55).
13. Nagaraju (1980) describes several cisterns or small troughs where water could be collected. Most of them were attached to the cave shrines and *vihāras* at several sites where these caves have been excavated in the Western Ghats.
14. Fogelin (2005: 483).
15. Prasad (1993).
16. Prasad (1994).
17. Sastry et al. (1992).
18. Krishnasastry et al. (1992: 15).
19. Krishnasastry et al. (1992). This is how the excavators have numbered the cisterns in their report.
20. Krishnasastry et al. (1992: 58).
21. Krishnasastry et al. (1992: 56).
22. Krishnasastry et al. (1992: 57).
23. Krishnasastry et al. (1992: 11).
24. Krishnasastry et al. (1992: 11).
25. Annual Report, APDAM (1984-5).
26. Annual Report, APDAM (1978-9).
27. Subramanyam et al. (2008: 6).
28. APDAM https://web.archive.org/web/20120310124143/http://muse-ums. ap.nic.in/ phanigiri.htm
29. Subramanyam and Reddy in Parasher Sen (2004: 365-8).
30. Skilling (2008: 97).
31. APDAM https://web.archive.org/web/20120310124143/http://muse-ums. ap.nic.in/ phanigiri.htm

32. Subramanyam et al. (2008: 7).
33. Skilling (2008: 97-8).
34. Subramanyam et al. (2008: 8).
35. Subramanyam et al. (2008: 27).
36. Subramanyam et al. (2008: 28).
37. Summarized from Subramanyam et al. (2008: 9).
38. Summarized from Subramanyam et al. (2008: 27).
39. Subramanyam et al. (2008: 28).
40. Subramanyam et al. (2008: 29).
41. Subramanyam et al. (2008: 31).
42. Subramanyam et al. (2008: 30).
43. Subramanyam et al. (2008: 32).
44. Reported during the course of the 2001-2 excavations at the site APDAM https://web.archive.org/web/20120310124143/http://museums. ap.nic. in/phanigiri.htm

CHAPTER 6

Patancheru: Cultural Heritage of an Ancient Market Town*

Conventionally history is written of large entities like dynasties, nations and countries, which are based on sources—literary, archival, and archaeological—that provide hard core evidence. Regions and small localities often lack systematic source material, which leads us to depend on fragments of information. When one begins to write about individual centres, sites and places, a major challenge one faces is the lack of official records that one can draw upon. This silence impacts the methodology one has to adopt in order to reconstruct narratives of the past of these kinds of settlements. The history of the small and the fragmentary is almost always absent in the metanarrative of even regional histories. The aim in this chapter is to address these absences at Patancheru[1] and retrieve historical vestiges wherever possible.

In the existing historiographical and archaeological literature on the city of Hyderabad and its environs, there was an absence of a systematic history of its village and semi-urban settlements. District Gazetteers provied limited information on some broad parameters of the site or place location and its prominent features. In many ways a project we undertook to document heritage of places between 'Dargah and Patancheru'[2] (Map 6.1) becomes the first to begin to write a History of what could earlier be safely called 'rural' settlements. Each was couched in its own sense of the past,

*An earlier version of this paper co-authored with R. Himabindu entitled: 'Understanding Local History: Archaeological Remains at Patancheru' was published in the *Journal of Deccan Studies*, vol. IV, no. 2, July-December 2006, pp. 5-27. It has been updated with new data collected between 2012 and 2016.

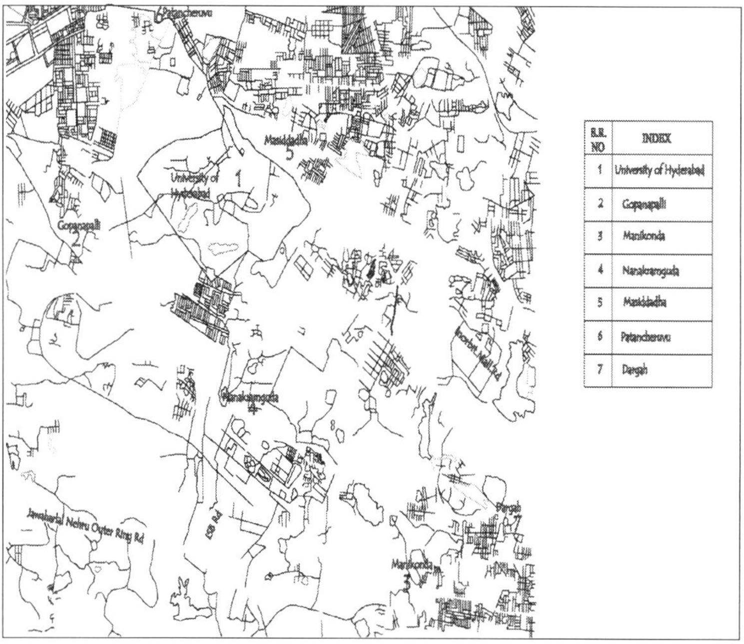

Source: Map prepared by the author.

Map 6.1: Location of Villages studied in vicinity of the University of Hyderabad

central to their survival and identity, which was primarily articulated through their seasonal festivals and rites of passage. It needs to be emphatically stated that these communities had safely guarded their rocky environments by making most of their shrines deep inside the rocks or at their base. For generations then these natural formations have remained protected. Apart from this visible connection between human urge for the sacred and the necessity to protect the natural environment, our journey with the inhabitants between 2014 and 2016 with the help of their oral narratives, festival celebrations and discussing with residents their earlier means of livelihood, revealed how dependent the people were on their environment. Thus, this turned out to be a different kind of history as the inhabitants became providers of sources of information.

Hitherto, under the rubric of 'Local History' studies, we have noted that place histories get encapsulated in what is commonly and conventionally called 'Place Names Studies'.[3] This is holistically possible if a plethora of epigraphic and literary data is pronounced in its availability at the given location being studied. If this kind of source is not available in abundance scholars usually turn to the archaeological and monumental remains *in situ* to restore visibility to its past in terms of the extant heritage of a given place.[4] Thus, the details of Local History get overwhelmed with the magnitude and glare of national and even pan-regional histories. Our submission is that in the case of Patancheru none of these sources of information has been found intact or, in a systematic manner. In fact, one can state that most of it was in a state of disarray, partially visible, disturbed at various sites around the place or, housed in museums and in private locations. There is therefore, something lost about the history of Patancheru and something found. However, piecing together what has been found and museumified or, worshipped in today's temples, poses a challenge. A small aspect of this challenge is taken up in this chapter, namely, by providing a peep into the rich sculptural heritage of this place now housed on the premises of the International Crop Research Institute of Semi-Arid Tropic (ICRISAT). This was one of the major institutional campuses that came up in this village whose existence has protected the original landscape and water bodies of the area. But before this is done a brief account of the disturbed nature of what must originally have been the core of the place called Patancheru today.

Patancheru at 17'.52° lat. and 78'.26° long, marked the outer limits on the west of the project we had taken up for study. Today, it is in the Patancheru mandal of Medak district and is the gateway for travelling to the towns of Sanga Reddy, Medak, etc. It has today become one of the largest industrial zones which is located about 32 km from the centre of Hyderabad in a north-westerly direction on the now busy Hyderabad-Sholapur national highway. With the global inching its way into the local, Patancheru of today is bustling with institutions, industrial units and new housing colonies that may erase away the past beyond recognition. The area is also home to a large number of pharmaceutical manufacturers, which has resulted in the local river water being the most drug polluted water in the world according to scientists. This has affected the quality of life in and around the village. Towns and markets of the past usually lay on either important routes of communication or, in the vicinity of abundant water resources. This is a common phenomenon through historical time. In fact, the significance of Patancheru is its location on a major highway connecting the southern and western parts of the Deccan and for this reason it has always been an active place for habitation. Though Patancheru of the past had both these advantages but, ironically, the forces of 'development' have resulted in damage both to its historical heritage and its water sources. In fact, we are informed that with 'the wave of industrialization that began in the 1970s the complexion of its once placed landscape' has now changed to become 'one of India's worst hotspots' where lakes, streams, as well as the groundwater of Patancheru and surrounding areas are laced with 'toxic heavy metals and chemicals'.[5]

The known history of Patancheru goes back to at least the fifth century CE with remnants of Buddhist and Jaina sculptures as well as a larger number of those belonging to various Hindu sects alongside the thriving of local cults found here. It has been considered an important centre that thrived in Chalukyan times. Along with highlighting its antiquity, we have built on the fragments of historical evidence still available in the form of innumerable sculptural remains from the Chalukyan to the Kakatiyan period and beyond to weave a long term history of the region. Some of this historical sculpture has been carefully preserved on the ICRISAT Campus where much of the material was found. As a market town it also saw various travellers pass through it as is evident in the building structures of the Qutb Shahi times. The most interesting feature noted during the course of documentation, however, was the large number of Naga/Nagini sculptures in stone found on the ICRISAT campus, many of which were still under worship. The Sarai area of the Patancheru village has of course become overcrowded with its old monuments, shrines and temples becoming dilapidated or being renovated for continuing worship. The nomenclature *sarai* for a part of the village suggests that it was located on an old trade route and thus its history as an ancient *pattana* (town) can be traced. It is said to have originally been on the banks of a natural *cheruvu* (lake) and, according to some scholars, that is how it got its name *pattanacheruvu*, now shortened to Patancheru.

Several etymologies and historical names for this place have been suggested. As mentioned above the most simple one being that it could be a combined form of two commonly known words inherent in it, namely, *pattana* meaning 'market-town' and *cheruvu* meaning 'lake'. Both these words thus got shortened to form Patancheru signifying that it was an important market town in the vicinity of a lake. There is an interesting local story that informs us that it got its name because a Pathan got a *cheruvu* or 'lake' dug here and that is how the place name Patancheru emerged. These renderings of the name are not supported by historical evidence and it must have been given to the place in relatively recent times. In fact, a rather early inscription found at Patancheru itself gives us its historical name as Pottalikanagaraa. King Vijayaditya of the Western Chalukyan dynasty issued this inscription during his fourth regnal year (696-733 CE) and we are informed that he stayed at this place.[6] A variant form of this as Pottalakere[7] occurs in remnants of Kannada inscriptions found here. Many of these belong to the Rashtrakuta and Kalyani Chalukyan periods. An inscription of the latter dynasty, during the reign of King Bhulokamalla Someshsvara III dated to 1127 CE, in fact refers to a locality called Cintamanipura of Pottalagere.[8]

The antiquity of Patancheru goes back to the Paleolithic phase and numerous sites with material remains of the old stone age times dating back a couple millennia or more have been located in its environs. More concretely, a megalithic stone circle had been found near the Patancheru village. It consisted of a double concentric circle of stones; the outer being of about 30 metres in diameter and the inner being of about 60 metres. 10 metres away were located the remains of an enclosure formed from large stone slabs.[9] Scholars frequently refer to the Hindu and Jaina architectural and sculptural remains, belonging mainly to between the twelfth and fifteenth century CE that have been found scattered in and around the Patancheru village.[10] However, on a field visit to the village it was noticed that an image of Lord Buddha of some antiquity is today found located at the village Panchayat office. It is well known that during the early historic period, not far from Patancheru, about 40 km, in a further north-westerly direction the site of Kondapur is located, which has been considered an important Buddhist and commercial centre of the early historic times.[11] Similarly, early remains and relics belonging to Jaina religion have also been found in Patancheru village. About forty years ago in the playground near the village bus-stand at the entrance to the village, two elephant-heads flanking a Jaina sculpture were noticed.[12] Today, only the elephant-heads remain in what has now become a crowded market area. Further, not far from Patancheru, near Shankarapalli, it was recently brought to the notice of the Superintending Archaeologist, Hyderabad Circle that on a hilltop there were Jaina Caves located.[13] Thus, apart from Hindu images, primarily of Shaivite affiliation, the Shramanic sects too were popular in this sub-region of the Deccan at different points in time.

The material evidence at Patancheru is undoubtedly prolific for the Rashtrakuta and Kalyani Chalukyan periods, but on a close study of the sculptural remains it is noticed that during Kakatiyan times too this place was well endowed with patronage, which continued into Vijayanagar times. Some of the scattered and now dismembered Jaina and Hindu temples had additions of *mandapas*, pillars, doorways and sculptures that on stylistic grounds can be clearly dated to the Kakatiyan period. Roughly, these temples belong to between the twelfth-fifteenth centuries CE. Lastly, the presence of an Ashruf Khana, a mosque and a masjid constructed in the style of other Qutub Shahi monuments in and around Hyderabad indicates that Patancheru continued to be sought after as a place to settle well into the sixteenth century. The above outline of its long prehistory and history only indicates the critical and strategic location of Patancheru along a route that connected the western with the eastern and southern Deccan. Its continued habitation with successive political elites coming, conquering and occupying it from time to time had its toll on the monumental heritage and, as we shall discuss below, many of the material remnants are today found in a broken and dilapidated condition.

There is little historical research that has been done on Patancheru beyond the noting of what was discovered and reported from time to time in the annual reports of the Epigraphy and Archaeology Departments of the Archaeological Survey of India and the State Department of Archaeology and Museums, Government of the composite state of Andhra Pradesh. On the basis of these reports some critical information about the place has been put together that gives us a rough political background against which we can describe the core of the material evidence we propose to discuss as the main part of this research. Patancheru seems to have been a major political centre during Western Chalukyan, Rashtrakuta and Kalyani Chalukyan periods. The following inscriptions found at Patancheru give us a glimpse of their association with this place: (1) A Kannada fragmented inscription located on a stone built into the southern gate of the extant Jama Masjid records a tax-free gift probably of land to a certain god at this place called Pottalakere in characters of about eleventh century CE. (2) An inscription issued by King Vikramaditya VI of the Kalyani Chalukyan dynasty written in Kannada and located at two sides of a slab built into the wall of the southern gate behind the extant but unused Ashruf Khana records the genealogy of the Chalukyan kings of whom Trailokyamalla (Someshvara I), Someshvara II and latter's younger brother are mentioned in characters of about the twelfth century CE. (3) A fragmentary stone inscription located on a fragment slab built into the extant Shasuddin's well behind the Ashruf Khana refers to a deity called Ramanathadeva. It also refers to Pottalacherla, Paragimattu and Narrakallu, probably localities in and around Patancheru in thirteenth century CE characters.[14] We next go on to describe the extant archaeological, architectural and sculptural remains at Patancheru in the sections below defined by us as those being 'In Context' and those 'Out of Context'.

'IN CONTEXT': DISARRAYED, DISMEMBERED AND ABANDONED

Patancheru village is situated on the main Patancheru road and is 5 km north of ICRISAT. The historical material remains here was scattered all over the village and especially concentrated around that part of the village called *sarai*, which is about 1 km interior from the Patancheru main road. At the end of the Patancheru main road, two tombs with a height of 5 ft from the ground level, datable to the Qutb Shahi period, were found located. On our field trip,[15] beside the present day Patancheru Mandal Revenue Office, which is on the *left side* of the Patancheru main road at a modern Hanuman temple, a broken Vinayaka and a Naga stone idol were seen. However, our field trip to the village mainly concentrated on the old structures and sculptures *in situ* found on the *right side* of the Patancheru main road. Heralding this entry we are welcomed by two elephant heads—their style indicating that they probably belong to the Chālukyan times[17] (Figures 6.1 and 6.1a).[18] On entering the main village, at a distance of about half a kilometre, on the right was located a structure with pillars deep into the earth (Figure 6.2). This seems to have earlier been part of a Hindu temple but in later times its pillars were reused to construct what is today called an Ashruf Khana, a popular religious centre of the Shia

Source: Photo taken by the author.

Figure 6.1: First Elephant head Chalukyan period, Patancheru Village

Source: Photo taken by the author.

Figure 6.1a: Second Elephant head Chalukyan period, Patancheru Village

Source: Photo taken by the author.

Figure 6.2: Medieval Ashruf Khana: Reused Pillars of a Temple, Patancheru Village

Muslims that is no longer in use. On the same road, which is today called the Ram Mandir road, is the Panchayat office. Just before this office, on the road itself was found a seated Buddha image (Figure 6.3) in *dhyāna mudra* posture that the people worship even today.

Moving further into the *sarai* part of the village many loose sculptures were found lying all over place on the roadside and some at various temples located here. We were informed that during the course of the construction of modern houses an interesting household object in the form of a square grinding stone came to light. Today it is lying on the roadside beside a newly constructed house. At the area called *sarai*, on the left side, there is a Shiva temple of some antiquity. This is a temple under worship and has been whitewashed by the local people. It has a *linga* in the *garbhagriha* with a big Nandi inside the temple facing the *linga*. In the open space courtyard of this temple remains of another Nandi image was found, some mutilated pillars and stone sculptures of women in various postures that seemingly must have been part of door frames of an original temple.

Source: Photo taken by the author.

Figure 6.3: Lord Buddha in *Dhyāna Mudra,* Patancheru Village

From this site moving downwards, on the right side a Shivalayam was noticed. Here, two Shiva *lingas* and a Nandi image were found half immersed into the earth. Alongside these Shaivite images was also found a Hanuman idol, some loose sculptures of *nāgas* and *nāgins*, Buddha figures (Figure 6.4) carved on a narrow monolith black stone—all of them must have been lying around at different locations and have been now assembled in the premises of this temple. Near the Shivalayam, on the same road, and moving further downwards on the right side were noticed some more loose sculptures. These were also unearthed while the construction of modern houses was being done. Today they lie on the road. Some of the broken and mutilated images and also a broken doorway have been placed in premises of another nearby temple. Further, two recognizable stone idols were found located on the right side of the road at a short distance from the Shivalayam. One of them is clearly an image of Veerabhadra, locally known as 'Bayyannna (Figure 6.5) and today it is placed under a tree for worship. At a short distance from the above place and beyond the *sarai* part of the village, on

Source: Photo taken by the author.

Figure 6.4: Buddha Figures on a narrow Monolith Black Stone, Patancheru Village

Source: Photo taken by the author.

Figure 6.5: Bayyanna—Veerabhadra, Patancheru Village

its outskirts another old Shiva temple is located. On one side of the doorway to this temple shrine was found a broken Nandi image without a head and on the other side, a sitting elephant sculpture. Some loose sculptures of *nāgas* were seen in between the pillar remains (Figure 6.6) lying outside this temple.

Amongst all these mutilated remains the pillars are important signifiers of the style and probable date of these old temples. Radhakrishna Sarma observes that most of the pillars found at Patancheru reveal the following features—'The *aśvapādam* is molded and carved with a sculptured medallion on each face of it. The shaft combines square, circular and octagonal shapes . . . on the whole, the pillars are not highly ornamented'.[18] This latter observation was made by us also and it clearly indicates that they can be dated to early Chalukyan times. The other features of the architectural fragmentary remains that suggest this are the parts of door-frames, ceiling slabs and carved slabs with flowers, creepers

Source: Photo taken by the author.

Figure 6.6: Early Chalukyan period—Pillars lying around the Temple, Patancheru Village

and geometrical designs. Even the limited extent to which our fieldwork was done in and around the Patancheru village, strikingly brings out the prolific nature of the artistic remains still lying around un-attended to except for those pieces, which were located in temple premises. Exposed equally to the natural forces of the sun and rain as well as the rapid pace of development these may soon be lost to posterity. It was our observation that the local people wherever they found the unbroken idols they placed them in nearby temples and began to worship them and thus, to some extent, the images were restored and protected as symbols of the extant culture and heritage of the place. In other cases there was lack of concern and a general air of neglect. Though this was in ancient times the context in which the settlement flourished and in the midst of which the original structures were built, the surviving remnants of an eclectic and diverse nature reveal only a tip of the iceberg of what must have been a flourishing settlement that was visited again and again by conquering armies, traders and the ordinary traveller alike.

'OUT OF CONTEXT': FOUND, ORGANIZED AND PROTECTED

The story of the extant cultural heritage of Patancheru does not end with what has been described above. Some of it found its way to another context, alien to its original context but here, it survives for posterity to examine and study. In 1972 an International Organization—the International Crop Research Institute of Semi-Arid Tropic (ICRISAT) was established in the environs of what is today generally called the Patancheru area. It was established by the shifting of two existing villages, namely Kachireddypalli and Manmool.[19] This site was apparently chosen because of a unique combination of black and red soil found here, which was critical for the crop research that they had to undertake. The census and gazetteers of the composite Andhra Pradesh state note that in the Sanga Reddy *taluk* of Medak district regar or black cotton are found.[20] What was unique about the above location chosen was that the black soil was on the surface till a depth of about 5 ft and below it was found the red soil—a combination of both making this an unusual location. We submit that this must have also been the reason why earlier historical settlements had flourished here. Officers at ICRISAT explained that this unique sedimentation was due to volcanic eruptions that must have happened several thousand years back. Today 75 per cent of the soil under their control is of this type and in the other 25 per cent area there is only red soil.[21] Both types help them carry out research on different types of crops grown in the semi-arid tropics and the potentialities of improving on their quality.

The inhabitants of the above dislocated villages were settled in Ramachandrapuram, an existing village in the proximity. We were informed that, at the same time, some old historical sculptures were also shifted to this village. Clearly, the historical context of these objects was now changed. At this, what is now called the old Ramachandrapuram village, we noticed some loose sculptures at a new temple constructed here, which was about 1 km from the main road. This new temple, however, has housed an old stone idol locally known as Kshetrapala but that is all we get to know about it. Similarly, one knows little about a Hanuman idol of some antiquity carved on a pillar located here. Once the process of work on the ICRISAT campus started with the development of their farmlands, laying of roads on their campus and digging land for the storage of water in the form of a lake, they increasingly discovered the remains of buried temples and sculptures. The then Director of ICRISAT, E.W. Nun showed interest in retrieving these historical remains and contacted the archaeological experts to help him to do so. We give below a brief description of some of the sculptures and structures found on their premises. Most of them have been removed from their original context and location. We describe them thematically based on their sectarian affiliation rather than chronologically since it is very difficult to date most of them or suggest how they must have originally been placed.

Located at the entrance of main office door of the ICRISAT office is seen an image of Vishnu with a lady *chauri* bearer as attendant (Figure 6.7). The plaque below this image notes that the

Source: Public Relations Officer, ICRISAT.

Figure 6.7: Vishnu with *Chauri* Bearer, Western Chalukyan period, ICRISAT, Patancheru above sculpture is of a late medieval period. However, the characteristics of Vishnu, carrying the conch shell and discus are clearly visible and the style suggests that this image belongs to the late Western Chalukyan and early Kakatiyan period of around the twelfth century CE. The Huntington Archive of Buddhist and Related Sculptures hosts a stone sculpture of about 2 feet of a *chauri* bearer from Patancheru. They have dated it to the Western Chalukyan period (900-100 CE) now located in the National Museum, New Delhi. Its style is strikingly similar to the image under discussion.[22] Another stone idol of Vishnu in a damaged condition with a broken nose with only half its body is found on the lawns in front of the office and can be dated to Kakatiyan times. A popular deity of worship generally but, more so among the Vaishnavites, is Hanuman. An image of his engraved on a slab, that was probably part of a pillar earlier, is today placed on the lawns of the main office building at ICRISAT. On this slab are clearly seen the emblems of Vishnu, namely, the conch shell/*śankha* and discus/*chakra* on both sides of the image (Figure 6.8). Its carving style clearly

Source: Public Relations Officer, ICRISAT.

Figure 6.8: Hanuman Image, Western Chalukyan period, ICRISAT, Patancheru tells us that it is of the Western or Badami Chalukyan times. Amongst the loose sculptures in the workshop area of ICRISAT is found another Hanuman idol but it is now fully coloured in vermilion and therefore difficult to date.

At another location on the premises there is a Hanuman temple with a stone pillar or *dvajastambha*, probably of a very recent date, in front of it. Yet another idol of Hanuman, which is coloured profusely and is worshipped even today, is found in this temple. In this temple we also have coloured stone idol images of a *nāgin* and a Vinayaka, which are also under worship. It may be noted that the Vinayaka image on stylistic grounds can be placed to the Chalukyan times. In origin this temple seems to be of medieval times, probably of the Vijayanagara period that has now been renovated and white washed and therefore looks like a new temple. A Vishnu temple undoubtedly of the Chalukyan times is located near the groundnut godowns of ICRISAT. Some of its architectural features, the floral design and the character of its pillars enable us to date its origins to the Chalukyan times but it has features of the Kakatiyan times too. The capital pillars that are standing are definitely of the later times but some of the ones that are lying on the ground can be dated to the late Chalukyan times. The floral design on the outer wall, the only remaining part of it, has to be dated to the Kakatiyan times. Recently, its floor and door have been painted. On the both sides of the door we can see the *dvārapālas* and on the lintel we prominently see symbols of Vishnu *śankha* and *chakra*. This inclusion was probably made in the nineteenth century as it had then become important to signify the Vishnu-nāma in this way. Local folklore informs us that this temple has survived the vicissitudes of time because a huge peepal tree that is today seen growing out of this temple, protected it. The tree has its roots beneath the *garbhgriha* inside the temple. The emergence of the tree from the temple has created several cracks on the walls of this temple.

The sculptures affiliated to the Shaivite form of worship also abound on the premises of ICRISAT. At its main foyer entrance we are welcomed by a broken seated granite Nandi in front view. Its side view (Figure 6.9) shows some simple decorations on it and

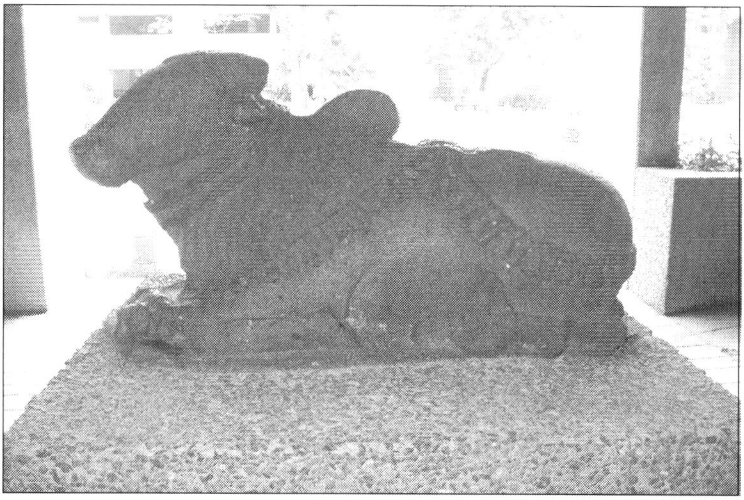

Source: Public Relations Officer, ICRISAT.

Figure 6.9: Seated Granite Nandi of Late Kalyani Chalukyan Period, eleventh century CE, ICRISAT, Patancheru

this enables us to date it to the late Kalyani Chalukyan period of probably the eleventh century CE. Another broken Nandi in granite is placed at the foyer entrance lawn, which can also be dated to the Chalukyan period. A huge monolith Lord Ganesha image, magnificent in proportions, is located outside the office building under a peepal tree. We were informed that this was found while the workers were digging land to make the lake on the ICRISAT campus. It was deeply embedded in the earth and, we are also informed that before it was removed workers thought that it was only a huge stone slab—in fact, it was the large surface of the head of this image. Today it is under worship. All of the features of the image point to the fact that it belongs to the early Western Chalukyan period. For instance, its head is without any decoration or headgear and its hands are carved into the image and are not visible separately (Figure 6.10). Another loose image of Vinayaka, now coloured in vermilion, is located near the workshop of ICRISAT and can be dated to the Kakatiyan period. Beside it, also of the same period, is an image of Goddess Kali. Among these loose im-

Source: Public Relations Officer, ICRISAT.

Figure 6.10: Monolith Ganesha, Early Western Chalukyan period, ICRISAT, Patancheru

ages in the workshop area is also found an early image of Bhairava in a *jatabhara* form dated to the Western Chalukyan period. In this group of sculptures located at the workshop there is an interesting slab with a stone inscription carved out on four sides. In the middle of this slab is a Shiva *linga* with Surya and Chandra on either side. Below them a Nandi image is carved. The images on this slab have been coloured and the inscription below them, though uncoloured, is unclear but the language used is clearly Kannada. This enables one to suggest that it was probably made in the Chalukyan times with additions to it during the Kakatiyan times.

At a short distance from a 'castle like building' on the Campus, which is 5 km from the main office building at ICRISAT, there is a Shiva temple, probably of recent times. The temple is today white washed. It has a *linga* in the *garbhagriha* and a seated Nandi of granite in front of the *garbhagriha,* which are both white washed. A broken idol of Surya is seen outside at the entrance of this temple and this can be dated to the late Chalukyan times. Also of Shaivite affiliation, a small shrine is found near a bushy area close to a medieval masjid. Inside this shrine is seen a beautiful and unusual image of Goddess Pārvati (Figure 6.11). She holds a lotus known as *nilotapala* in her right hand and her left hand is free in a downward position as *dolahasta*. Her eyes are prominent and her hairstyle is clearly visible. Based on all these features it can be dated to late medieval (Vijayanagara) times. In front of the 'castle like building', locally called 'Manmool Castle' by the people working at ICRISAT, is found a small dilapidated temple, which can be dated to very early times. It is most certainly of the early Western Chalukyan style because of the way the plain monolith stone slabs were used to construct it (Figures 6.12 and 6.12a). At its entrance, on the right side a single vertical slab has a hooded Naga carved on it and this can be dated to late Chalukyan times.

Among the sculptures that defy classification based on sectarian affiliation are the innumerable images of *nāgins* found on the grounds of the ICRISAT campus. One set of these was found while digging a lake and they have been placed under a peepal tree. There are five *nāgins* (Figures 6.13 and 6.13a) each made in a different

Source: Photo taken by the author.

Figure 6.11: Image of Goddess Pārvati, ICRISAT, Patancheru

Source: Photo taken by the author.

Figure 6.12: A small Temple Shrine (front view) in Early Chalukyan style, ICRISAT, Patancheru

Source: Photo taken by the author.

Figure 6.12a: A small Temple Shrine (back view) in Early Chalukyan style, ICRISAT, Patancheru

Source: Photo taken by the author.

Figure 6.13: Nagini, Early Chalukyan period, seventh century CE, ICRISAT, Patancheru

Source: Photo taken by the author.

Figure 6.13a: Nagini, Early Chalukyan period, seventh century CE, ICRISAT, Patancheru way. Popular belief is that they are the protectors of the fields and are generally worshipped as fertility goddesses. Out of five of these images three of them are clearly of the early Chalukyan period of the seventh century CE because characteristically in this period *nāgins* were made top half in the form of a woman and the lower half in the form of a snake. All of them hold a sword in the right hand and a shield in the left hand. The other two images (Figures 6.13b and 6.13c) are today profusely worshipped especially on Nāgapañchmi day and therefore, are full of colour and have been robed with a saree like cloth. These images are in the form of two entwined snakes with only hoods and no human face visible. This is a special feature of the *nāgins* in the later Chalukyan period.

Another set of *nāginis* was found in the workshop area of ICRISAT. Along with several (about twenty or so in number) loose sculptures lying here about 10-12 images of *nāgini* are placed around the wall encircling a tree. None of these are worshipped today. Most of them are in half woman and half snake form and

Source: Photo taken by the author.

Figure 6.13b: Nagini, Early Chalukyan period, seventh century CE, ICRISAT, Patancheru

Source: Photo taken by the author.

Figure 6.13c: Nagini, Early Chalukyan Period, seventh century CE, ICRISAT, Patancheru

they hold a sword in the right hand and a shield in the left one. Some of them have a lotus in the right hand and it has been suggested that they are of a later period. A few of them, which are not too clear are only in the form of intertwined *nāgas* with hoods. Similar sculptures, six in number are clearly seen with hoods in half woman and half snake body in the quarantine isolation area of ICRISAT in the premises of a renovated Shiva Temple. In front of the *garbhagriha* was found seated a granite Nandi. We are informed that this temple was renovated by the then Director of ICRISAT, Mr. E.W. Nun with his own expenditure. The ceiling above the *garbhgriha* shows the recent construction and renovation work. Keeping in mind the popularity and immense number of *nāga* and *nāgini* sculptures, people of the area have recently constructed a small shrine over a big naturally formed anthill for daily *nāga* worship in the middle of the fields owned by Shri Sankarayya. This is located near a deep and very broad well, which is not in use at present and is surrounded by a fence. The steps into the well are seen to be in an old style of construction.

A few stray sculptures that seem to have been part of the doorways or outer walls of the now destroyed and dilapidated temples are seen in the collection of images displayed at ICRISAT. A woman's sculpture (Figures 6.14), probably as a part of a doorway (*torana*) holding a lotus in the right hand is seen on the lawn in front of the office building. This can be dated to the Kakatiyan period based on the beautiful and heavy ornamentation characteristic of images made during this period. Another image of a woman holding a lotus (may be of Goddess Lakshmi?) is placed in the office building but little can be said about it as it is not very clear.

Two very interesting sculptures of typical warriors generally called *viragals*, of the Kakatiyan period of the thirteenth century CE are found displayed—one on the lawn and other in the office building. Both these images (Figure 6.15) are made on square stone slabs. Both hold a spear in their hands and are seen in a moving

Source: Public Relations Officer, ICRISAT.

Figure 6.14: An Ornamented Doorway sculpture of a Woman Kakatiyan period, ICRISAT, Patancheru

Source: Public Relations Officer, ICRISAT.

Figure 6.15: A Warrior (Viragal) Kakatiayan times, ICRISAT, Patancheru

posture. The spear is aiming at an animal, probably a horse, being killed and over their respective heads is seen an *apsara* like figure seemingly beckoning the warrior to the heaven. Their headgear is particularly visible and characteristic of innumerable such warrior sculptures of the Kakatiyan period found all over Telangana.

The so-called 'Manmool Castle' (Figure 6.16) seems to have been built during the Qutub Shahi times and was used for different purposes—probably as a fort, a hunting lodge, a taxation centre or, simply as a shelter. A local legend told to us by the workers most probably perpetrates a myth that beneath this castle *golden coins and treasures lie buried that are guarded by a Jinn.* Not far from this place is also found a Masjid built in the style of the Qutub Shahi period. The architecture of this mosque is very simple and plain with some floral designs on the *minārs* (Figure 6.17). There is a tomb in front of this Masjid, which has a single *minār*, which is about 2-3 ft in height. It is suggested that this tomb may have belonged to some local ruler during the late medieval times. It

Source: Photo taken by the author.

Figure 6.16: 'Manmool Castle' Qutub Shahi period, ICRISAT, Patancheru

Source: Photo taken by the author.

Figure 6.17: Masjid built in the Qutub Shahi period, ICRISAT, Patancheru may be noted that just behind this Masjid several fully demolished small shrine like structures were noted and we are informed that they are most probably burials of the Lingayata Vishwakarmas dated to late medieval times.

By default the imperatives of writing a political history of the nation or its states meant writing the history of dynasties or their monuments. By extension local history has hitherto been confined to archaeology-based studies especially of the prehistoric times or, had became individual temples studies, numismatic and epigraphical studies and the like. In 1987 was published a history of Hyderabad district.[23] Several scholars contributed to this endeavour but each contributed to themes of historical interest between 1879 and 1950 only, and did not discuss any aspect of the ancient or medieval history of this district. Interest in regional and local history of the region under discussion has therefore been limited.[24] It would be correct to argue that just as the spurt in writing regional history in the post-independent era was methodologically an offshoot of the national school[25] of historical scholarship, the subsequent in writing of local histories was seen as an avenue of increasing the data base for bolstering the interests of how regional identities had to be projected. Ultimately, this method advocated that local details would enhance and glorify a region's cultural heritage. In fact, writing in another context Devahuti suggested that scholars need to form and use regional frames of reference on which the classification of facts, problems of periodization and so on could be done but, at the same time, also wrote: 'we need to know the past in order to know our identity. The resultant rootedness has the potential of universality necessary for an objective view of history.'[26]

However, scholars emphasizing the importance of writing local history[27] do not want it to merely provide the 'grains' that make up the 'sand dune' of national history. Rather, they suggest that a holistic and total local history be written for the interests of the local.[28] In this perspective then everything—the small, the fragmentary, the broken, the dislodged, the resurrected—all need to be documented. This research is one such endeavour. At the same time, the challenge of putting together such documentation runs the risk of misrepresentation if interpretations based on this kind of data are pushed very far to make the local unique and unconnected to its surrounding areas. The political data from the site under discussion is minimal, that on the economic totally absent and generally, the written record is scarce. For this reason mapping the historicity of Patancheru in existing historical literature was difficult. One of the interesting aspects of this exercise has been to show that locations like that surrounding the present day Patancheru area have multiple histories. The remains are primarily those that were originally part of religious monuments but nonetheless, the above descriptions clearly point to the fact that the site had successive waves of occupants each with their own ethos and historical identity. The fact that despite destructions and displacements at the site we were able to put together a mosaic of intertwining histories of different religious communities that made Patancheru their home should make the writing of local history a necessary part of the historian's craft.

NOTES

1. The research article on which this chapter is based was originally written based on data collected for our collaborative project: 'A Digital Historical Atlas of South India' funded by the Ford Foundation and coordinated by the French Institute of Pondicherry (2004-8). Subsequently, the data was updated while working on another project (2012-16): 'From Dargah to Patancheru-Documentation of Tangible and Intangible Heritage in the Environs of the University of Hyderabad' funded by the UGC under the University of Hyderabad's UPE-II programme.
2. Parasher Sen (2018).
3. A classic example for Andhra Pradesh is Ramachandra Murthy (1985).
4. In the case of Patancheru a good example is a three page account in Radhakrishna Sarma (1972: 61-3).
5. Sharma (2006).
6. Venkataramanayya (1975-6).
7. *Annual Report of Indian Epigraphy* 1960-1; 64, p. 48, Inscription no. 2, which is in Kannada refers to this name. There is another name found in Inscription no. 1, namely, Poþþalacherla in characters of about the thirteenth century CE.
8. Radhakrishna Sarma (1972: 61).

9. Venkataramanayya (1975-6: 1).
10. *Census of India,* Medak District, Government of Andhra Pradesh (1997: 13).
11. Parasher Sen (1987: 82-90).
12. Sarma (1972: 63); Hiebert (1975-6: 4-5) refers to literary sources to reflect on the Jaina and Shaivite religious competition in the history of Patancheru.
13. Sashi Sekhar and Jitendra Babu—orally communicated. The then Superintending Archaeologist, Dr. Jitendra Das of the Hyderabad Circle of the ASI was proposing to undertake a serious study of these Caves and the sculptures housed in them.
14. All these inscriptions have been reported in *Annual Report of Indian Epigraphy* 1960-1; 1961-2; 1964.
15. The small account put together on the sculptural remains at Patancheru by Radhrkrishna Sarma (1972) was also based on the field observations that were done at this site. However, it needs to be mentioned that some of the sculptural remains that he made note of are now not available at the site.
16. Sarma (1972: 63) has also referred to these elephant heads, which he notes were flanking a Jaina sculpture. He further notes that these elephants must have earlier been placed beside the entrance to a temple. Today no Jaina image is found and instead of a playground as noted by Radhakrishna Sarma where these images were found, we have several shops that have come up in the area.
17. We sincerely acknowledge the permission given by the authorities of ICRISAT to take photographs of the historical material on their premises. We would especially like to thank Shri M.M. Sharma, the then Public Relations Officer at ICRISAT and Shri Ishwarayya who had worked there for all the help rendered in this regard. Photographs of the sculpture and buildings taken in Patancheru Village and the Sarai area have been taken by the author.
18. Sarma (1972: 61).
19. Workers at ICRISAT inform us that this village name is formed out of two words, namely, '*mandu*' and '*mool*', which means in Telugu 'medicinal roots' that were grown here and are also found in the nearby villages.
20. *Census of India*, Medak District, 1981, p. 14.
21. Based on oral information given to us on our field visit to ICRISAT. Also reported by them in *Historic Relics at ICRISAT Centre* published by them (Cummings 1973-4).
22. Hosted on their website no. 0021397 in the John C. and Susan L. Huntington Archive of Buddhist and Related Sculpture.
23. Sarma (1987).

24. Hiebert (1975-6: 1-12) is an exception as it has the political history of Patancheru with immense detail based on inscriptions.
25. Thapar (1984: 16).
26. Devahuti (1979: xi).
27. Stephen (1977: 4-9).
28. Local scholars when writing about the regions and localities often express the view that 'mircro-history' or 'local history' has received little attention or totally ignored by scholarship at large. See for instance Hussain (1985: 165).

PART III

ACCESSING THE OTHER

CHAPTER 7

Conversations at Nagarjunakonda*

My conversations with Professor R.S. Sharma always revolved around the particularity of the Deccan and how literary sources primarily focusing on regions north of the Vindhyas often portrayed peoples of the Deccan as the cultural 'other'. With the arrival of Buddhism into this region even during the lifetime of the Buddha as some scholars suggest, people of the Deccan did not necessarily remain the 'other'. R.S. Sharma had also taught us that whatever information we got from the literary perspective of texts should, as far as possible be corroborated with material evidence from archaeology and inscriptions. In a small measure this paper is an attempt to do so. His interest in looking at the horse and ship symbols on Sātavāhana coins and interpreting them in relation to the meaning of the term 'Sātavāhana' too resonates with the attempt below that looks at the deep connection between travellers to the region both by sea and inland routes and their conversations with the local people. However, since the Deccan of

*This chapter is based on a paper published as 'History and Literature: Unravelling Conversations in the Local Context of Buddhist Deccan, in D.N. Jha (ed.), *The Complex Heritage of Early India: Essays in Memory of R.S. Sharma*, Manohar, New Delhi, 2014, pp. 327-46.

An earlier version of this paper was orally presented at the International Seminar on: 'Buddhism beyond Buddhism: Buddhist Themes in 20th Telugu Literature', organized by the International Telugu Centre, Potti Sriramalu Telugu University, Hyderabad, 6-7 January 2007 and published as 'Fiction and History—Painting the Social Fabric in Early Deccan', in P. Chenna Reddy and E. Siva Nagi Reddy (eds.), *Bodhisiri: A Festschrift to Annapareddy Venkateswara Reddy (Buddhaghoshudu)*, Research India Press, Hyderabad, 2014, pp. 287-99.

early historical times has very few literary sources, I draw on a more contemporary account of the past to bring out the textures of social history in a region that has generally been understood as the home of the origin of Mahayana Buddhism. How does one recover the sensibilities of emotions, conversations, feelings, through historical data that are nonetheless part of our collective heritage now frozen on stone or an ancient script? The domain of literature has an intimate relationship with our memories of the past. I am drawing on ideas in some recent issues of the journal *Rethinking History* that suggest that the 'historical and fictional can be mixed for certain literary purposes but ought never be confused'.[1] In one such article Hayden Whyte concurring with Richard Slotkin's work quotes him to the effect that on the one hand, 'history-writing requires a fictive or imaginary representation of the past' and, on the other, that 'the writing of historical fiction can be a valuable adjunct to the work of historians in their discipline'.[2] In the present context we shall focus on a reading of a fictional account that throws light on the lesser known intangibles of who lived at Nagarjunakonda, how the Buddhist monks who stayed in the monasteries here interacted with the local inhabitants, how the artists and other specialists viewed the essence of their art and interacted with foreign travelers to the place and so forth. Towards the latter half of the chapter we dwell on fragments of inscriptions and other historical data that compliment this reading to argue how a literary representation and hard core evidence both infuse life into a historical discourse.

And the "*Roman artist asked: 'Can I have letters of introduction to the brother Shilpins in all those places!'*
The young monk from Nagarjunakonda ironically commented:
'*You do not need letters of introduction to the areas of silence*'" [emphasis added]

MULK RAJ ANANDA[3]

The above quote is from a literary account written at a time, namely, the mid-twentieth century when both in literature and the arts there were serious attempts made at the resurrection of the so-called 'Indian' elements of our cultural heritage. In the particular context of the Deccan, the mid-twentieth century led to a 'discovery' or, should one say, a recovery of the monumentality of Buddhist art. In particular, in the making of the vision of Pandit Jawaharlal Nehru—the temples of modern India—a concomitant aftermath was the destruction, displacement, replacement of the older temples. One telling example of this was the building of the magnificent Nagarjunasagar Dam which simultaneously meant a massive archaeological salvage operation as the dam was meant to unleash water over what was once the home and core of civilization in early Deccan. Nagarjunakonda, the site (Map 2.2, p. 67) Nāgarjuna, the great Buddhist philosopher, the Sātavāhanas, the first 'imperial' patrons of Buddhism in the Deccan and a whole gamut of the history of the lower Krishna Valley was about to be eroded. Today its vivid monuments and sculptures remain intact for us only as memory of their original extant locations and contexts (Figures 7.1 and 7.1a).

Source: Photo taken by ASI in the custody of the State Department of Archaeology and Museums, Government of Andhra Pradesh (before 2014).

Figure 7.1: Buddha's Statue Relocated at the New Site on the Nagarjunakonda Hill

Source: Photo taken by ASI in the custody of the State Department of Archaeology and Museums, Government of Andhra Pradesh (before 2014).

Figure 7.1a: Reconstructed Apsidal Shrine, Nagarjunakonda Hill

What came to be resurrected that is now visible on the island Museum is in fact, a mere commemoration and the putting up of a kind of memorial of what we need to remember both in symbol and actuality. The submergence of areas around Nagarjunakonda for the building of the dam therefore led the archaeologists and art historians into a race against time to document as much as possible about that era of the glory of Buddhism in the Deccan. In 1965 a special issue of the Indian Art Journal *Marg* was brought out on the art of Nagarjunakonda. In moving away from mere descriptions of the historical remains and the plastic arts, in this issue Mulk Raj Anand penned down for us a fine fictional account that has often gone unnoticed entitled: 'Conversation in Nagarjunakonda'.

Travelling across the subcontinent, we submit, was an integral part of the way different regions of the subcontinent interacted, which subsequently shaped linguistic communication and social understandings. It created temporary social milieus in contrast to the apparently permanent social spaces of the village, town and province.

It is the totality of understanding both these that would ultimately give us a historical account of a moving and dynamic society rather than one based on only a normative view of it (Figure 7.2). We emphasize that to create the imagination of such a thinking, feeling and dynamic social order we must first turn to literature that enables us to draw on both memory and history. It is the end of Mulk Raj Anand's fictive conversation that emboldens us to graft it on to the past as it most strikingly reflects on historical places and processes and artistic and philosophic urges that are inherent

Source: State Department of Archaeology and Museums, Government of Andhra Pradesh (before 2014).

Figure 7.2: Sculptural Art at Nagarjunakonda depicting ordinary people in any ethos of travel. The last part of the conversation is of the Andhra Shilpin suggesting to his Roman counterpart via his interpreter the following:

'Your master must go to Amaravati soon. The chisel is finer there'

The Gandhara monk added: 'The way in which it moves with a caressing touch expressing the love of life with a more subtle and warm sensuousness. In fact, it would be wonderful if the Roman made a pilgrimage to all these sites—Ajanta, Karle, Bedsa, Sanchi, Barhut and Mathura. . .'

The Ethiopian told his master warmly of this suggestion because he himself was enthused at the thought of going to all these places'.[4]

In this fictive account Mulk Raj Anand's essential aim was to bring out the relationship between phenomena and consciousness, the real and the unreal in the artistic wealth and philosophical maturity of the people who made that era at Nagarjunakonda come alive. There is an interesting social context that also comes through providing the setting to this conversation amidst the local and devout Madhyamika monk, the Theravadin monk from the island of Tambapanni (Ceylon), the liberal Mahayana monk from Gandhara residing there temporarily, the Roman artist who came along with a merchant and his shipload of wine and other goods to the region, the Ethiopian slave, speaking Prakrit and the Roman's interpreter, the Andhra Shilpin, the perceptive young monk from Nagarjunakonda and last, but not the least, the Chenchus who were central to the habitation around Nagarjunakonda. The credentials of each would suggest that it would hardly be possible for each of them to converse with each other. But they did as Mulk Raj Anand imagines they must have. A few extracts of these conversations would best illustrate the point being made:

'. . . The monk recited the formula 'Buddham Sharanam Gachhami' every now and then.

The Indian Shilpin talked at great length, like a preacher preaching the gospel of his art.

The Roman artist looked ubiquitously at the eloquent mouth of the monk and wondered how such a Ganges of words could issue out of such a small gorge.

As the foreigner could not, out of politeness to the host, ask him to speak slowly, so that he may understand, in the little vocabulary he knew, the content of the sermon, he brought forth a beautiful bottle containing red wine and two glass tumblers (Figure 7.3).

The sight of the liquor perturbed the monk, so that he recited again 'Buddham Sharanam Gachhami' to evade the consequences of disaster and turned his face away.

The Roman tried to tempt him by pouring the wine into his mouth, and with the bottle held in his right hand, so that the rich liquid gurgled down his throat without the mouth of the container touching is lips.

The miracle fascinated the devotee.

Also it brought a few other Shilpins and Chenchus to witness the scene.

One of the young aboriginals came forward with cupped hand adjusted to his mouth and signifies his wish for a taste of the red "poison"...'

Source: State Department of Archaeology and Museums, Government of Andhra Pradesh (before 2014).

Figure 7.3: A foreigner with wine cup depicted at Nagarjunakonda

'. . . At this the Roman called for his slave, shouting in a prolonged accent his orders for more wine. The slave, a handsome young Ethiopian, came out in his Roman toga bearing a large glazed jar. The Roman master ordered the slave to serve everyone around with one tumbler each and to drink himself.

The monk was now purple with suppressed fury and got up to go in protest, muttering that it was not proper to drink wine in a Buddhist vihara.

At this another monk who was from Gandhara came forward and said:

'The Buddha had never forbidden the drinking of wine, the eating of meat, or the living of the worldly life. All that the Enlightened One had said was that one should cut out desire which is the cause of pain.'

Whereupon, the protesting monk called a passing brother who hailed from the island of Tambapanni (Ceylon), to bear witness to the falsehood uttered by the brother from Gandhara. The Tambapanni monk smiled evasively, shrank into the shell of his own being, sat down and looked at the red-faced Roman devil, who was offering temptations to all and sundry. And he waved his head in pity for the drunkards. . . .'

'. . . The protesting monks could not displease the stranger. Anyhow, the monk from Gandhara had already been sipping from a tumbler with some taste and he held forth:

'According to the Enlightened One, *ragha* or attachment brings misery. One perceives objects through contact with sense organs. And if the object is pleasing, attachment develops to it'. . . . [Full explanation omitted here][5]

'. . . The protesting monk spoke:

'The sage Nagarjuna has repudiated this proposition, by saying that attachment grows with the respect to an object. And the mind (*chitta*) in which attachment dwells, called *rakata* is not logical. . . ,' [Full explanation omitted here]

'. . . The Roman threw up his hands in the air at his ignorance of a language spoken so fast and with such subtlety of utterance. And he beckoned to the Ethiopian to explain. But the slave had not understood the argument either.

The monk from Gandhara made bold not only to enable the Roman to understand, but to refute his brother from Nagarjunakonda by quoting the exact words of Nagarjuna.

'If the opponent argues that *rakata* (attached) does not exist before *ragha* (attachment), so *rakata* (attached) is the resort of (*asaraya*) of *ragha* (attachment)' . . . [Full explanation omitted here] And I can drink without *ragha* (attachment)'

At this the Chenchus laughed out aloud, because they had not understood the argument at all, and only wanted to hear the last phrase.

The protesting monk accepted defeat for a while and sat down.

The monk from Tambapanni sighed and then smiled gently.

The Roman ordered another round of drinks.

Between serving the drinks the Ethiopian tried to explain to his master that Nagarjuna was the sage after whom the Madhyamika philosophy in the local school of Buddhist doctrine was called. Further, he said that Nagarjuna had studied at the University of Nalanda in Eastern India, a place not far from Bodh Gaya, where the Buddha achieved Enlightenment. Then Nagarjuna had come to the valleys of the Krishna river. . . ,' [Full explanation omitted here]

'. . . There were monks here from as afar as China, Kashmir, Gandhara, Tosalli, Apranta, Banga and Vanavasa. *But the place had seen so many centuries that nothing was certain. People spoke in legends and myths and proverbs.* [Emphasis added]

The Andhra Shilpin nodded assent to all that the slave had said. But, after taking another tumbler of red wine from him, he wiped his mouth and smiled and licked his tongue in pleasure.

'Tell your master in Roman speech, the essence of Nagarjuna's point of view'. And pulling at the man's toga, he made him sit down and listen.

'Nagarjuna says that the simultaneous origin of *ragha* (attachment) and *rakata* (attached) has been proved to be illogical. It can also not be stated that they are not of simultaneous origination. . .' [Full explanation omitted here]

'. . . The Ethiopian turned to his master and explained slowly, the meaning of the difficult jargon, but became confused as he could not interpret the whole thing properly.

The Roman artist blushed at his ignorance of philosophy, swallowed the spittle of embarrassment, and turned to the Andhra Shilpin with the words.

'If, as the monk says, no *moha* (illusion) and no *muha* (illusioned), then what purpose in the figures carved by you?'

The Chenchu lads suppressed their laughter at the broken Prakrit speech of the Roman. At the same time they were pleased at the sober common sense of the foreigner. They were no philosophers, but happy-go-lucky people attached to the earth in all the pleasure-pain of the humdrum world, almost like dark marigolds growing wildly amidst the scanty habitation of the valley.'

In the piece written by Mulk Raj Anand at this point there is a long conversation between the two artists—the Roman and the Andhra one on form and what lies behind it, the role of senses, touch and silence in the making of art work. [Full explanation omitted here]

In this part of the conversation as narrated by Mulk Raj Anand there is now a shift from philosophy to the meaning of art and life. The move from a world of abstract ideas to actual lived in experience. I would read this as a shift from an impregnable space of the void to one that was located in the humdrum of the region and its people that welcomed Buddhism and its various schools of thought but, now without understanding themselves in the midst of all the other worldly message that was being brought to them. Thus both the Andhra Shilpin and the Chenchus play a significant role in defining the nature of art, its form, its sensibilities and its content that we see today. History rarely recognizes this since art historians and archaeologists are busy documenting facts and dating these extant remains rather looking around for the society that lived through the experiences that made the historical environment that was throbbing around the third century CE. The rest of the conversation by Mulk Raj Anand brings out this flavor with éclat, something that historians would shudder to trend on.

'. . . The Andhra Shilpin withdrew into his shell for a while and then cocled his head like a tortoise advancing from the long patient wait and spoke:

'All is in flux—everything changes, everything moves and life is lived.

We all, workmen, apprentices, masters, building caves, grave mounds, carving vibrant images, whose radiance thrills Our hands sometimes tremble, push and pour forth, the exuberance of our inborn skill. We climb up on to the scaffoldings, hammers and chisels in our hands, drunk with the hangover of the dances in which the Chenchus swing heavily, from side to side, to one, two, three beat of a music which makes the darkness bright.

The protesting monk frowned and turned away his eyes from the company in disgust against such an expression of the love of life. Like a policeman of the faith, he was vigilant about any shifting of emphasis from thinking to feeling. He raised the finger of admiration and said:

'The carvings with which you are obsessed are only necessary as mediums of meditation. The adept is supposed to fix his attention on them, while trying to convert the apprehensions, of the senses into a concept as clear and distinct as the object he sees with the open eyes—to achieve the *upacara* stage of mediation. ....' [Full explanation omitted on stages of mediation]

'...The Roman artist sensed that the man of religion was against the temptations of colour. So he said:

'In my country, colour is much valued. Colour delights the eyes. Colour soothes the temper. Colour sets the spirit on fire. Colour nourishes the body. . . .'

'. . . The Andhra Shilpin found his familiar feelings confirmed and dared to opine even against the monk. . . . Some people learn to talk in big words. Others learn to think without words. Most people can only look.

The artisan learns to express what he cannot say with words. He is inspired to seek the flow in space, which is not visible. He is like a dog barking at the shadows. He lives in the area whose whereabouts he cannot explain.

'May not end of meditation be the rapture which cannot be explained.'

The protesting monk was relentless. He spoke harshly:

'Says the *Dhamapada*':

'Even the Gods aspire towards those who are enlightened and mindful, who are wise and devoted in meditation, who take delight in desirelessness and in tranquility.'

The stranger was cowed down by the firmness of this utterance.

Even the Ethiopian dared not translate.

The monk from Tambapanni looked elated.

The monk from Gandhara was puzzled.

The Andhra shrugged his shoulders and said in a meek voice:

'Perhaps priest, princes and merchantman tend to loose the human capacities. . . .' [Full explanation omitted here]

'. . . The protesting monk murmured:

'If it was not for the respect we owe to the foreigner, I would go and tell the abbot of the goings on here.'

The Andhra Shilpin turned to him with an appeal in his gentle eyes:

'Your anger is totally unjustified. Perhaps, you remember having seen the frieze, the Temptation of the Buddha, carved by one of my ancestors. The Enlightened One is here represented symbolically, as was enjoined by the early masters. . . . The Temptresses, with big breasts and heavy hips, are redolent with the charm of the senses. The hosts of the demon, Mara, are the embodiments of sheer physicality. The elephants of the hosts of Mara also exhude power. *The ancestors of our ancestors at Barhut and Sanchi, Bhaja and Amaravati have infused into us the affinity with all forms of life which the Enlightened One preached.* [Emphasis added][6] But it is in the clash of energies, recreated in the carvings, in which the artist lives, as though possessing the tensions in the zone of silence. The Buddha himself *was* [Emphasis in original] awakened by his actual experience of the pain of the sick man who he saw, of the peasant he beheld toiling behind the plough, of the dead body being carried away. '*Outsiders* cannot impart what goes on within. *Insiders* live too much within. We must try to be *outsiders-insiders* at the same time. . . .' [Emphasis in original]

A young monk, who had sat listening patiently to the elders lifted his chin from where it was cupped on his right hand and spoke now:

'The sage Nagarjuna, the prophet of the Madhyamika, believed in the dialectic of opposites. To him everything was relative. Motion exists because its opposite rest exists. Darkness exists because light exists. Therefore, a denial of *this* involves the rejection of *that*. ....' [*Full explanation omitted which highlights the issue of there being no rigid elements of existence as understood by Mulk Raj Anand*]

"... The monk from Tambapanni said: 'Then the Nagarjuna dialectic means the rejection of all views because they are absurd.'

The young monk nodded his head.

The Andhra Shilpin opined:

'Perhaps all oppositions can be got over by accepting everything in humanness...'

The protesting monk intervened:

'He speaks like the Brahmins. Dung is God—God is dung!...'

The young monk spoke in a conciliatory mood.

'The sage Nagarjuna did not deny philosophy, not because there is no Real for him, but because it is inaccessible to reason. The sage speaks of a higher faculty, called intuition (*Prajana*), with which real is identical... So art works are admissible...'

The protesting monk insisted:

'The sage Nagarjuna pointed out that the root cause of pain and imperfection is *avidya* or the tendency to conceptualize the real. By mistaking this or that for the real, we get attached to things or evince aversion towards them....' *[Full explanation omitted here on what Nagarjuna says on the issue of Freedom and Sunyata in Mulk Raj Anand's understanding of it]*

'... The speakers were silent for a while, almost as though they were convinced of the Buddha's suggestion that, from the heart of silence we break off and find our way.

The Roman artist looked to his mentor.

The Ethiopian said:

'They have decided that words are of no use.'

The Roman artist enthusiastically hailed this verdict and said:

'Then painting and sculpture and music are the real key to understanding.'

The Andhra Shilpin intervened:

'Poetry also, by its contrasts, resemblances and transparent phrases, reaches depths. In fact, all arts are one. Only the critics want to understand meanings and have no room for suggestion. Therefore, they bark and howl and protest against the inner thing....'

The Ethiopian translated these words to his master.

The Roman artist nodded his head with approval, but pointed out:

'You seem to reject Nature. We measure the model by units of geometry *before* we sculpt. . . .' [Emphasis in original]

The Andhra Shilpin looked to the Ethiopian, and having got the meaning of his contemporary's assertion asked:

'How do you measure things in movement? The changing moods, the harmony and the disharmony? In fact, the alternation of various rhythms. . . .' [*Full explanation omitted—conversation between two artists on their respective methods of executing art works as imagined by Mulk Raj Anand*]

'. . . The Andhra Shilpin said: 'The vital, powerful and *emotional flow of the carvings in Nagarjunakonda owe themselves to our pagan faith—we like the naked body*. . .' [Emphasis added]

The Andhra Shilpin interrupted:

'Your master must go to Amaravati soon. The chisel is finer there. . . .'

It is with the fuller version of this above quote that I had begun this chapter with. While the narrative of the Andhra Shilpin emphasizes on the special characteristics of the art at Nagarjunakonda and Amaravati, there is nonetheless an awareness of the Buddhist art as it had flourished in other important Buddhist centres of learning and art on the Indian subcontinent. But it is not simply this. There was also a continuous interaction with the outside world that this fictional account brings out forcefully—something that was integral to the way the host community defined itself in relationship to the 'other' and it is for this reason that the initial quote at the beginning of this chapter is so important to emphasize upon. I repeat:

The Roman artist asked: 'Can I have letters of introduction to the brother Shilpins in all those places!'

The young monk from Nagarjunakonda ironically commented:

'You do not need letters of introduction to the areas of silence'.

'At this juncture the Chenchu brought the jars of Arek to the guest. . . .' [Emphasis added]

The Roman artist gingerly partook of a small thimbleful. He liked it.

The Chenchus served the liquor to all those who wished to drink.

Soon there was audible the beat of the drum.

Some Chenchu boys were coming dancing now, beating the drum with mighty strokes. Even as they ran to and fro with the vibration. . . .'

'. . . The drum beats spread from the earth to heaven and on beyond the frontiers of vision, obliterating the silences.

The Chenchu boys began to dance fast, faster still faster.

The Roman artist caught the contagion of their spirit and joined in.

The Ethiopian followed suit.

The Andhra Shilpin clapped his hands in accompaniment to correct their steps.

The young monk plunged into the vibrant group.

The other monks stared, inspite of themselves at the miracle of diathrymbic movement before them.'

[The End of the 'Conversation' as imagined by Mulk Raj Anand]

This fictive 'Conversation' began with the Roman artist's gesture of friendship by sharing the wine that he had brought with the local community and it was the Chenchus who had relished it the most. It ends interestingly with the Chenchus reciprocating by sharing their Arek with all those who wished to share it and it is the Roman artist who is the first to welcome their gesture. Beyond the message of Buddhist teaching that is the core of this conversation, there is the fundamental vibrancy of life that is being brought into focus in this piece of creative writing. Though apparently they seem marginal, the Chenchus, as the original inhabitants of the Valley become most central to the discourse as, both in terms of the ethos that is represented in the sculptural art as well as in defining the essence and joy of living they define the contours of this 'Conversation' in very critical ways. The Andhra Shilpin and the young monk from Nagarjunakonda become the inoculators of conveying this essence to all the three other Buddhist monks—from Gandhara, Tambapanni and the one who upholds the Madhymika doctrine. This has a special meaning because they bring into focus the special flavour of the regional and local while, at the same time, being the new entrants to espousing the Buddhist faith. In other words, their understanding of the way Buddhism evolved in the particular context of the Deccan is highlighted in their questioning and reinterpreting the doctrine to suit their particular context and relevance.

The question now arises as to why Mulk Raj Anand wanted to weave into his narrative this intricate social relationship between the foreigner, the monks from the surrounding regions of the Indian subcontinent, the new converts from the region as followers of

Nagarjuna's teachings and the local Chenchu inhabitants. As a creative writer of the mid-twentieth century this was the vision of a symbiotic interactive society that was being projected on the horizon of newly independent India. Pakistan had been formed but Gandhara was seen as part of our civilizational heritage in more ways than one. Tambapanni or what is Sri Lanka today had played a critical role in upholding the early Theravada Buddhist message and conserved that which had been lost on the Indian mainland but with which, over historical time, the island country had had extremely intimate and critical relations. Regional states of the Indian union were beginning to assert their particular identities and the role that Andhra had played in being the intellectual centre of Mahayana Buddhist preaching had to be highlighted. After all, it was this particular Buddhism that went beyond the boundaries of the subcontinent and became the religion par excellence of many countries in Asia. Finally, the heyday of independent India was also about integration of a different kind. All castes and communities had to be brought under one umbrella and the sensitive writer in Mulk Raj Anand could not forget the Chenchus in this regard. In *summam bonum* it was the realities of the contemporary that compulsively took him to memories of the past. Maybe the local communities of the Krishna Valley would not remember the happenings of their past in this way. The role of memory in traditional cultures is very important and distinctively different from how official and collective memories from outside the region are constructed.[7] The latter are mainly seen as regenerations of celebrating national entities and visions and are rooted in modern attempts to retrieve the past and which may not be the way the local communities wish to remember it.

What is reflected above in the fictive narration, not only raises questions of memory and imagination but also that the ethos of early Deccan civilization was marked by an ideological variance of views, a social diversity and an artistic freedom, all of which were essential features of defining a dynamic cultural landscape. In the latter half of this chapter, I now supplement the above perceptions from modern literature reflecting on the past with historical sources of information located in the past. Unlike the connected and holist narrative presented above, by their very nature the latter emerge in fragments and thus have to be woven around key but short pieces of data that reflect on a larger hidden phenomena that we are forced to imagine. I particularly draw on the fragmentary inscriptional data that we have from many Buddhist sites that throw up several personal names that suggest a social and economic diversity in and around Nagarjunakonda and the region as a whole. In fact, as one peruses through the early inscriptions from the Buddhist sites all over the Deccan dated to roughly between the second century BCE and the fourth century CE, the variety of the data strikes one immediately. The special location and close proximity of the Buddhist caves to the important passes along the Western Ghats has been discussed at great length by earlier scholars showing how critical these trade routes, across these inaccessible ranges, was for different types of travelers across the region.[8] In an analysis[9] of the way these names occur at the various sites/locations in this region it is found that there are only a handful of examples of names that refer to members of the artisan communities and those that we may define as *nīca* (low) *kulas.* However, cutting across caste lines many were lay followers of the new faith who as donors, as builders, as scribes, as a variety of craftsmen, as traders and merchants travelled to these *chaitya*, *stūpa* and *vihāra* sites and recorded their proper names. In many cases these names themselves do not enable us to fix their original caste affiliation. In the western Deccan amidst several references to names of *gahapatis, vaṇijas, seṭṭhis*, etc.[10] who necessarily emphasize on their kinship relations, there are a few names of gardeners, garland makers, goldsmiths, ironmongers, ploughmen, etc. who also do the same but more frequently assert their identity in terms of the places they hailed from. Though coming from the less privileged sections of society, they also give donations to the Buddhist Sangha and in the process asserted their individual identity. Thus, we have at Kuda three examples of the names—Sivapirita, Vadhuka and Muguda—of *mālakāras* (gardeners),[11] an ironmonger named Mahika,[12] from the famous cave site of Bhaja, the reference to the wife called Bahda of a *halika* or (ploughman)[13] and from Sailarwadi another name of the wife of a ploughman called Siagutanika who makes a gift along with her husband named Usabhanka and the *gahapati* by name Namda. Usually craftsmen made minor gifts like in the case of a *vadhaki* (carpenter) who made a door of a cave at Karle.[14] Similarly, even a *suvanakāra* (goldsmith), named Saghaka from Junnar could only make the gift of a cistern even though he was better well placed than a ploughman.[15] Another striking feature is the existence of a great variety of names that clearly reflect a Buddhist ethos and which enables us to categorize them as Buddhist names—Buddharakshita, Dharmarakshita, Samgharakhita, Nāga, Nāgapalita, Saghaka and so on can typically be considered Buddhist in nature and so also others like Buddhi, Nāgatisa, Sidhātha, Makhabudhi, Rāhula.[16] For some of them there is little indication of their caste identity but in the mention of their professions we learn that they belonged to the wealthy *gahapati* or *seṭṭhi* communities. Though the overwhelming data here is on individual names, it is pertinent to point out that in rare cases we have the explicit mention of a *varṇa* in this type of data.[17] However, we must conclude that all these highlight a Buddhist social milieu asserting an individual identity beyond *varṇa* or *jāti*.

In the eastern Deccan, however, emphasis on kinship identity was more apparent. Even in the context of an example from Amaravati wherein the craftsman belongs to the lowly caste of a leather-worker the kinship identity is asserted in the midst of a large majority of the names of *gahapatis* found on these fragmentary label inscriptions at Amaravati. This example refers to a gift by Vidhika, son of the *upajhāya* (teacher) Nāga belonging to the generally understood ritually impure *carmakāra jāti*. It draws our present attention because he gave the gift of a slab with an overflowing *purṇaghaṭa* or auspicious vase (Figure 7.4) along with his mother, his wife, his brothers, his son, his daughters and other relatives and friends as follows:

camakārasa nāgaupajhayāputasa vidhikasa samatukasa sabhayakasa sabhatukasa putasa ca nagasa samadhutukasa sanatinitabaindhavasa deyadhamma. Punaghatakapato.[18]

Apart from having a proper name for a member of the outcast leather workers community for such an early period, this inscrip-

Source: State Department of Archaeology and Museums, Government of Andhra Pradesh (before 2014).

Figure 7.4: Purnaghata from Amaravati with Inscription

tion points to the important question of these communities now taking to teaching within the confines of the new intellectual order provided by Buddhism—it was a *cammakāra* (leather worker) called Vidhika, the son of a teacher called Nāga who gifted this slab with an auspicious pot (*purṇaghaṭa*).[19] There is another interesting example of a gift by one Attha, the *kāmika* (labourer) from Sanchi but with no other details given.[20] Besides labourers, engravers or scribes, excavators, architects and sculptors of the cave sites were essential for the construction and maintenance of cave settlements. These people were in fact the creators of the data we use for historical research. We have an interesting early inscription from Guntupalli datable to the first century BCE that gives us the name of a scribe called Culla Gomaka.[21] Another such early example comes from Amaravati dated to the second century BCE that refers to a *rājalekhaka* named Balaka; probably an official scribe of a local chieftain.[22] In some examples we get the names of those individuals who worked in stone to build monuments as in the case of Siddhārtha and Nāga Chandra who donated some slabs and pillars for the *toraṇadvāra* of a local *stūpa* at Jaggayyapeta. They are referred to as *avesanins*, meaning 'stone cutters' or 'foremen of artisans' in this inscription.[23] As is well known from the literary sources in general there was considerable specialization of crafts in each of the categories so that the particular skill in each case probably defined the status of craftsmen and artisans vis-à-vis each other. This is what probably made them refer to their skill alongside their names. From Kanheri[24] we have the mention of one *maṇikāra* called Nāgapalita who hailed from Soparaka and got a cave excavated there. Being a skilled artisan of crystal and diamond working he had substantial wealth to shower his munificence in getting this cave excavated for the Buddhist monks to reside in.

Probably the highest social status was that conferred to sculptors and architects (Figure 7.5). It is perhaps for that reason that the qualities of a perceptive Shilpin were creatively brought out in the 'Conversation' discussed above. We have epigraphic evidence from Amaravati and Nagarjunakonda datable to the first–second century CE that mentions them by name and designation. At Amaravati, *navakammikā* Buddharakshitā, *mahānavakammikās* Aditya and Dharmarakshita and *pradhānanavakammikā* Chanda were said to be in charge of the renovation of works of the *stūpa* and *vihāra* at Dhanyakataka.[25] Similarly, the Buddhist structures at Nagajunakonda were built and maintained by *navakammikās* Ananada and Chandramukhi.[26] Such detailed examples of names and professions of individuals that were so essential for the excavation and construction of cave settlements for the monks are not found with reference to the Tamil Brāhmī inscriptions of the Far South dated to around the same period. Nonetheless, we must accept that these names reflect a critical mass of human population around these sites with whom the pilgrims, monk inhabitants of the Buddhist cave sites and the merchants/traders must have interacted for the purpose of using their skill and knowledge. It also throws light on the fact that livelihoods of artists were closely linked with the way the Buddhist ideology proliferated during these centuries.

Source: Photograph by Professor K.P. Rao, University of Hyderabad.

Figure 7.5: Buddha Pada (Feet) finely sculpted with Inscription at Base—Nagarjunakonda

Similarly, we need to highlight the names of Yavana or foreign merchants (Figure 7.6) and travelers that formed a critical, though initially small, community of outsiders who interacted with the local society for both economic and cultural reasons. In the 'Conversation' narrated above the Roman artist is supposed to have come along with a group of merchants. Both the Deccan and the Far South, during the early centuries of the Common Era had witnessed a dynamic contact with the Greaco-Roman world that has been well documented primarily with textual data available from outside the subcontinent.[27] The textual data from within the different regions of the country is sketchy to say the least and the

Source: State Department of Archaeology and Museums Government of Andhra Pradesh (before 2014).

Figure 7.6: Foreigners as Gaurds depicted at Nagarjunakonda

archaeological data only gives us detailed site-wise information[28] that cannot generally be applied to other sites in the region. It is well known that the Deccan inscriptions give some of the names of these Yavana travellers who were most certainly merchants but who had perhaps become recent coverts to Buddhism—their names indicating this transformation read like Dhammadeva, Dhamma-rakhita, Yasavadhana, Culayakha and so on.[29] These are noted in the context of them making donations in the same manner that the other visitors to these cave sites had done. In the Tamil Brāhmī inscriptions, as noted above, we do not come across any direct reference to the names of Yavana merchants though, as is well known, they are referred to collectively in the Cankam texts. Here, they are regarded as aliens although some of their cargoes are much welcomed.[30] The archaeological artifacts from areas around Arikamedu suggests their living as a segregated group and therefore, unlike their votive inscriptions in the western Deccan, they seem less integrated during this early period in the towns and cities of the Far South. Making reference to the data on the Yavanas from the Deccan and the Far South together, Dhavalikar in a significant article elaborates for us the deep impact their presence had on the artists and writers of the times.[31]

Women *do not* figure in above fictional narrative account and this is one absence in the fictional account that does not reflect the social ethos of the Deccan based on historical sources. In fact, there is enough historical data on them for this period and region suggesting that women were ardently drawn to Buddhism. The inscriptions of the Deccan and central India that refer to the names of women donors substantiate this. This is of course invariably in their capacity as mothers, daughters, daughter-in-laws and wives. In the present sample survey there are three examples of names of women in the Tamil Brāhmī inscriptions, two are of nuns who were not donors[32] and, in another example[33] it was the mother of the nun who made a substantial donation. A tabulation[34] of all the examples indicating women donors discussed by us indicates that out of a total of eighteen gifts made at Amaravati, six of them were by women, related in some way or the other to *gahapatis*[35] and, sometimes, they gave gifts along with male members of their families. In the western Deccan sites we have noted that six out of twenty-six women in these examples gave gifts.[36] Two of these were by wives of ploughmen[37] and one was a Brāhmaṇa woman who gave a gift.[38] The remainder four women were part of the *gahapati* families. The Sanchi examples in the sample taken up for scrutiny in this paper give only a few names of women and all of them were part of *gahapati* families.[39] However, detailed research related to early Buddhist sites especially in central India and the eastern Deccan indicates that a very large number of women made donations to the *sangha* and were fervent followers of the faith. For instance, from the two important sites of the eastern Deccan, Amaravati and Nagarjunakonda, we are informed that inscriptions prolifically give names of women coming from the *gahapati* or merchant classes at both the sites. At the latter site we also get innumerable names of women from the royal families. Their kinship ties are prominently noted in these descriptions indicating a long line of supporters for the Buddhist faith in their respective families. This also indicates that they were not making donations in their independent capacity as women. The names of *bhikkuṇis* (nuns) are also found in the context of them making donations but in comparison to the above they are few.[40] Some scholars like H.P. Ray, however, suggest that they were actually making the donations in the name of ordinary donors.[41] Nonetheless, this points to an interesting trend in the context of the Deccan, namely, that the monasteries here played a major role in the accumulation and distribution of funds received by them for purposes of the piety from their followers.

The above data from fragmentary inscriptions has hitherto found mention in historical accounts of the region but only in a perfunctory manner to highlight the larger spread of Buddhism and its success in the Deccan during the early centuries CE. We, on the other hand, have chosen to highlight this particularity to make them central in the formulation of a larger picture that defined the social fabric of the times. Alongside the fictive account that prefaced the historical data in this paper we have tried to build an argument that for a concretization of the Buddhist built-in landscape and its economic sustenance, social groups like the ones discussed above and their interaction with each other was indispensible. The literary imagination of Mulk Raj Anand made it possible for us to visualize a social landscape that would otherwise have been impossible to do since the nature of the historical sources are limited for this purpose. Read in this way and against the background of the fictive account above on the possible social interactive space across the ancient Deccan, we suggest that this was one region of the subcontinent where peoples, cultures, and ideologies met to fructify the solid basis for a life affirming ethos of celebrating conversations.

NOTES

1. White (2005: 153).
2. White (2005: 154).
3. Anand (1965: 4-8).
4. Anand (1965: 8).
5. Extracts have been shortened when details of the philosophic issues were discussed in depth by the writer.
6. This part clearly reflects on notions of the past and history as perceived by the artist and generally understood by his audience.
7. Lewis (1987) makes critical distinction between remembered, recovered and invented histories and suggests that the latter two are the ones that resurrect a contemporary view of the past often ignoring what the particular society being written about thinks of its own past.
8. Ray (1986: 20-29).
9. Parasher Sen (2007a: 47-90).
10. Parasher Sen (2007a: 84-5) See Appendix IIA, Sl. Nos. 2, 4, 16, 17, 18, 27, 28 and 29.
11. *Epigraphica Indica*, (henceforth *EI*,), vol. X, H. Lüder's List (1973), Ins. Nos. (i.e. Inscription Numbers) 1051 & 1061, p. 112.
12. Lüder's List (1973), Ins. No. 1052, p. 112.
13. Lüder's List (1973), No. 1084, p. 115.
14. Lüder's List (1973), Ins. No. 1092, p. 117.
15. Lüder's List (1973), Ins. No. 1177, p. 135.
16. Parasher Sen (2007a: 84-8), see details Appendix IIA and IIB.
17. Parasher Sen (2007a: 84-5), see Appendix IIA, Sl. Nos. 7, 24.
18. Lüder's List (1973), Ins. No. 1273, pp. 151-2.
19. Few people know that this was the official emblem of the former Government of Andhra Pradesh. Efforts were made to make a replica of this *purṇaghaṭa* with its inscription so that it could be widely known to the people at large.
20. Lüder's List (1973), Ins. No. 181, p. 28.
21. Subrahmanyam (1968: 2).
22. Sivaramamurthy (1942: 277).
23. Lüder's List (1973), Ins. Nos. 1202, 1206.
24. Lüder's List (1973), Ins. No. 1005.
25. Sivaramamurthy (1942), Ins. No. 33.
26. *EI*, vol. XX, p. 17.
27. An overview of these trends see, Boussac Jean-Francois Salles (1995), and Romanis and Tchernia (1997).

28. For instance, Begley (1996).
29. Mitra in De et al. (1969: 621).
30. Thapar in Romanis and Tchernia (1997: 17, 21, 37).
31. Dhavalikar in Parasher Sen (2005: 114-27); Jean-Francois Salles (1995) and Romanis and Tchernia (1997).
32. Parasher Sen (2007a: 79, Sl. No. 8).
33. Parasher Sen (2007a: 81, Sl. No. 35).
34. Parasher Sen (2007a: 90).
35. Parasher Sen (2007a: 86-7), Appendix IIB, Sl. Nos. 1, 3, 11, 12, 13 and 16.
36. Parasher Sen (2007a: 84-5), Appendix IIA, Sl. Nos. 3, 8, 10, 17, 19 and 22.
37. Parasher Sen (2007a: 85), Appendix IIA, Sl. Nos. 19 and 22.
38. Parasher Sen (2007a: 85), Appendix IIA, Sl. No. 8.
39. Parasher Sen (2007a: 88), Appendix IIC, Sl. Nos. 2, 4 and 6.
40. E. Siva Nagi Reddy, 'Benefactresses of Buddhism in Early Āndhradeśa', *Suhurlekha*, pp. 1-6.
41. Ray (1986: 193-4).

CHAPTER 8

Renunciation and Jaina Tīrthas*

Tirthayatra brings an end to a number of beginnings, success in money, devotion of *sangha*, fortune for good people, renovation of old *chaityas*, development of *tirthas*. It helps in following the sayings of *tirthankaras* in correct way, bringing *moksha* closer and gaining higher status of human and god.

JNANAVIJAYAJI, *Upadeshtarangini*, 1938: 25[1]

This quotation succinctly expresses the purpose of pilgrimage for devout Jainas but it also simultaneously suggests that this would bring them closer to *mokṣa* or spiritual liberation. It befittingly encapsulates for us the purpose of this chapter, namely, to reconcile the two main pillars on which Jainism as a religion grew in India and entrenched itself in particular localities. Contrary to contemporary perceptions that Jainism seems confined largely to Western India during the early years of its spread and prosperity, Jainism also had a considerable following in the Deccan and south

*This is a slightly revised version of a paper entitled: 'Renunciation and Pilgrimage in the Jain Tradition', published in S. Rajagopal (ed.), *Kaveri Studies in Epigraphy, Archaeology and History* (*Professor Y. Subbarayalu Felicitation Volume*), Panpattu Veliyiittakam, Chennai, 2001, pp. 465-83. I am grateful to the 'Professor Y. Subbarayalu Felicitation Committee' and to Dr. Rajagopal, the editor of this book for giving permission to reprint this article as 'Renunciation and Pilgrimage in the Jaina Tradition: Continuity and Change in the Deccan', *Journal of Deccan Studies*, Special Issue on Jainism (Guest Editor: Aloka Parasher Sen), vol. V, no. 1, January-June 2007, pp. 157-76.

India. There are several views put forth on how Jainism spread into these parts. The origin of Jainism in the Deccan according to one opinion goes back to the days of the lifetime of Vardhamāna Mahāvīra himself.[2] Generally it is accepted that Jainism began to flourish during early historic times. Textual evidence in the form of legends and the recording of oral memory inform us that this began around the third century BCE when Bhadrabāhu and Chandragupta (the Mauryan emperor who had abdicated his throne to become a Jaina) traveled to Sravana Belgola along with several thousand Jaina followers.[3] Though details of this early period are still shrouded in uncertainties what is generally agreed upon is that despite the tough competition from Buddhism, it stayed on with intensity for a longer period of time. Sastry has put forth archaeological evidence from early historic sites in the Deccan especially Vaddamanu to shed light on the fact that it co-existed with Buddhism and that both the religions had royal patronage.[4]

Its development during the early medieval period is significant to emphasize upon in the present context for understanding the spread of the concept of *tīrtha* (pilgrimage).[5] It is during this period that certain transformations in the faith took place providing it a new form that enabled it to meet several challenges from both the spiritual leadership as well as the laity. New methods were adopted to make the followers understand the value of renunciation that involved a rigor that was awesome for most of the lay followers. The duration of its survival is important because only then we can appreciate how important centres of Jaina learning and congregation led to the furtherance of their faith. It may be noted that it is during the same period that the collective Jaina tradition, assignable to between the sixth and fifteenth century CE, in the form of its great literature was systematized and put down to writing. Most of this literature was in an oral form from the days that Lord Mahāvīra preached and even after his attainment of ultimate bliss. Through it the important message of renunciation was conveyed to people in a variety of ways. Prominent among these was a recounting of stories and tales explaining the life achievements of great renouncers through pilgrimage, texts, epics, spiritual autobiographies, and folktales in general.

It is our submission that the study of *tīrthas* enhances our study of both *local* and *religious* history.[6] We would like to emphasize at the outset that our attempt is not a mere description of the temples, buildings, and images located in centres of Jaina pilgrimage. In this chapter we intend to elaborate, with the help of one or two examples of Jaina pilgrimage centres in the Deccan, the broad socio-economic and changing historical framework in which these centres flourished without damaging the essential principle of the Jaina faith in renunciation as a desirable goal. Our chronological focus will be limited to the early historic and early medieval times. For understanding the continuity of such practices we have to first take a close look at the ideological impetus that motivated people to set up institutions of worship and learning. All these factors can be put down in terms of generalities but our attempt shall be to put them in the context of a local or micro-level situation. This has to be closely analysed since it poignantly reveals how such local *tīrthas* received financial and material support from the larger group of the Jaina laity. Without periods and regions of prosperity, the sanctity of such centres would be short lived. Thus, in our ultimate analysis we wish to highlight that faith and economic support went together.

The core of Jaina doctrine was centred on the idea that the blissful, bright and all-knowing soul was present in every *jīva* and *ajīva* entity. These entities enveloped not only human, animal, and plant life but stones, rocks and running water as well. However, the existence of this soul was understood to get clouded and dull by *karmic* action and matter which was born as a result of an unending cycle of transmigration. The main focus of attention in Jaina belief is therefore, the annihilation of this *karma.* It was believed that this could be done through penance. This, in turn, required a long course of fasting, self-mortification, study and meditation that was ideally to be done by the most rigorous means so that fresh *karma* could not enter the soul. In simple words, by a carefully disciplined conduct the dangerous qualities of *karma* could be prevented from entering the soul so that it could be set free. This simple and clear Jaina teaching remained unaltered even though Jaina philosophers developed with great subtlety many other aspects of their doctrines and epistemology in general at a later period.

The early Jainas recognized, however, that full salvation for the layman was not possible. To attain *kevala* and *mukti* one had to necessarily abandon all aspects of luxurious life including the clothes one was wearing. The rigorous penance could therefore, not be followed by the lay folk. Further, it was also recognized that monastic life was essential for salvation but since the Universe was fast declining very few souls could indeed achieve spiritual liberation in the foreseeable future. Nonetheless, some popular Jaina stories[7] on how members of families, wives and children in particular, were effected by the resolutions of renunciation undertaken by those who wished to go in search of truth, were popularized as an ideal for all to respect. Though the stories revealed from time to time that social ties, friendships, emotional bonds between man and wife, mother and child, father and son and so on, were painful and often generated anger and helplessness, these narratives were so written that they went beyond the single life of an individual to show the ultimate efficacy of the decision of renunciation being the only goal. In other respects of the Jaina teaching too a lay follower of Jainism found it difficult to even take up the profession of agriculture since it involved the destruction of plant life and many other living beings in the earth. The Jainas most ardently followed this insistence on *ahimsā* when compared with any other Indian religion.[8]

The close association of the Jaina Order of monks and nuns with the laity has to be emphasized. Herein, lay the difference between them and the Buddhists. The layman in Jainism was encouraged to live the life of a monk for specific periods. In his ordinary life he was encouraged to inculcate commercial virtues of honesty and frugality. The Jaina Sangha therefore consisted of *bhikshus* (monks), *ajjikās/sādhvis* (women ascetics) and *shravikās* (lay worshipers) so that the promotion and interests of the Sangha was made a pious duty of everyone.[9] The admission of the laity into the Sangha was acclaimed as the genius of Mahāvīra for organization because this enabled the Jainas to have a root in India, which the Buddhists never obtained.[10] In other aspects there were similarities with the other faiths that were prevalent on the subcontinent. For instance, very early on Mahāvīra and the other Tīrthānkaras began to be worshiped in the same way as the Buddhist and Hindu gods. Further, it has been pointed out that the notion of austerity that was so central to the Jaina faith got reflected in the images of the Jaina Tīrthānkaras that were marked by a lifeless and rigid monotony absent in other contemporary sculptures.[11] Soon the donation of the laity to the Jaina Order, along with support by kings and nobles, led to the building of splendid Jaina temples—two extant outstanding examples are Mt. Abu and Sravana Belgola. Though the core of Jaina belief did not falter, the tradition of explaining the importance of pilgrimage or *tīrtha* gradually began to evolve with the emergence of these institutional bases of the religion.

In a country like India the concept of *tīrtha* was already popular and it is likely therefore, that to compete with others, the Jainas had to adopt it as well. In Puranic Hinduism the idea of *tīrtha* was well entrenched by the early centuries of the Christian era and had effected the psyche of the Indian mind as a valuable social and religious mode of worship.[12] The concept of *tīrtha* emerges out of the notion of a sacred place and *tīrthayātrā* or pilgrimage is a popular form of piety and devotion to these places of significance in a particular religion's ecology of sacred places. Over time, around these *tīrthas* or sacred places there emerges a mythology that further sanctifies the place, while at the same time, publicizing its importance. Usually, at these places *dāna* or gift and charity rituals are performed and the proclamation of such rituals at important *tīrthas* gives that place a special importance for the devotee who is supposed to get unparalleled religious merit by such acts. Thus myth, belief and ritual get intertwined in a complex way to how the concept of *tīrtha* develops in different religions particularly on the Indian subcontinent. In the case of Jainism, we argue, that it also got entwined with the concept of renunciation since many of the places of Jaina pilgrimage were immortalized in the name of the brave and sincere *ācārayas* and *munis* who had given up ordinary life to achieve *sallenkana* or ritual death.

It would not be an exaggeration to suggest that in other aspects there was a considerable influence of Hindu rites and rituals that affected the overall texture of the Jaina concept of worship. For instance, between the tenth and the fifteenth century CE, detailed rules regarding the ritual of almsgiving (*dāna*) appear in almost all the texts that deal with the duty of the Jaina laity. This, it is argued, was essential to formulate as it would assure the monastic fraternity of adequate and permanent support.[13] Along with this the details of formal worship of the Jaina images or *pūjā*, taking these images in procession or *yātrā*, etc., also become central to Jaina belief. However, it is important to emphasize that the idea of pilgrimage in Jainism originally began to be associated with the activities of the great Jaina *ācārayas.* Visit to such places came to be considered a sacred duty and a purifying and meritorious act. The idea is put forth that the Tīrthānakaras themselves made some *tīrthas* but the choice that they could be made by others was also given in the later Jaina texts. Primarily, they were understood to have come up in places that were identified as the *kalyāna-kshetras* or those areas associated with the birth and other noteworthy events in the life of the Tīrthānakaras. Next in importance were the *siddha-kshetras* that were those areas where the Tîrthānakaras and other saints had attained spiritual liberation. This was followed by the *atisāya-kshetras* that were associated with the miracles or myths important for the Jaina believers and finally, the most common were the *kalā-kshetras* reputed for their artistic monuments, temples and images.[14] By early medieval times the idea of *tīrtha* had become rampant in Jainism and an integral part of its religious practice. It was the *siddha-kshetras* that acquired a special significance for propagating the ideal of renunciation and were highlighted in a big way in the literature of the times.

Scholars of Jainism suggest that it was in the Jaina literature of the early medieval and medieval times that fundamental changes began to take place in its doctrines, rituals, and monastic organization. By this time there had also emerged different Jaina sects. The proliferation of these sects particularly in the southern region of the subcontinent is important to emphasize upon. Scholars like R.N. Nandi suggest that that the changes and deviation in this regard can be explained in terms of their relationship to the changing social and economic milieu of what he calls 'the early middle ages'. This was marked by the decline of the market economy of towns and the rise of small-scale subsistence economy of agriculture.[15] We discuss below some of these changes as reflected in medieval Jaina literature that has relevance for the development of the idea and practice of *tīrtha.*

The *Bṛhat Kalpa Bhāshya* that can be dated to 'the early middle ages' illustrates the growing popularity of the practice of *mathavāsa*, i.e. permanent residence of monks. This necessitated a change of the old canonical rules restraining monks from taking a permanent residence. The above text refutes the earlier view that monks must stay away from the society and live in the forest in order to avoid contact with people in general and women in particular.[16] Another writer Hemachandra, a Śvetāmbara author of the twelfth century CE also commends the settled life of monks in monasteries and refers to the provision for lodging (*upāśrya*) like food, drink, clothing, beds, etc., which is said to be most beneficial to the ascetics.[17] Devendra, another Śvetāmbara author of the thirteenth century CE states that the best form of *dāna* or charity is the gift of a dwelling place (*vasti*) since this gives the monks and ascetics an opportunity for study, meditation and development of religious life. Many inscriptions published in the *Epigraphica Carnatica, Bombay Karnataka Inscriptions* cited by Nandi give evidence to the above fact and we find kings, nobles and other wealthy clients undertaking to build residential houses for the monks and to furnish them as best as possible.[18]

From the above, as gleaned from both literary and inscriptional sources, we can deduce that the changing lifestyle of the monks began to necessitate a change in monastic laws. Permanent residence greatly affected the monastic ideal of non-possession or non-attachment (*aparigraha*). Thus changing conditions from the early medieval period led to possession and attachment to worldly things. In fact, literature of the period, especially on *dāna*, tried to justify *parigraha* (possession) by the monks. Hemachandra goes to the extent of questioning those who suggest that there was no canonical authority for *dāna* in any form other than food and drink and goes on to quote texts permitting the offering of clothes, blankets, etc. These items were almost like the amenities of life that the householders enjoyed with the only difference that the monks had a code of conduct to abide by.

Puritans, however, continued to emphasize that living in forests or taking to the life of a wandering monk was an ideal. They resented upon the increasing popularity of the *mathavasti* monks. Thus, texts continued to mention transgressions that monks should not commit as listed by Haribhadra in the eighth century CE. These included the making use of water, flowers or other substances containing live matter, bathing in cold water, applying oil to the body, decorating the body, making use of perfumes and the erection of postmortem memorials at burial places. The puritans also objected to and criticized the settled monks who derived income from agriculture and admitted women as disciples.[19] The literary perceptions and restrictions were based on what was happening in reality. Information from inscriptions show that the monks had started encouraging the construction of temples and did indeed derive subsistence from land donated to them as free holdings. From epigraphs it also becomes clear that in the temples they used water, flowers, milk, curd, clarified butter, grass, etc. for different services. That, women were allowed to become nuns, and as senior nuns, had monks as disciples as well as the fact that there were lady disciples under male monks is also clearly visible in the data from the epigraphs, which give frequent references to these aspects. Similarly, it was for all to see that numerous *nisidhis* (memorial stones) came up as postmortem memorials and all these substantiate Haribhadra's allegations that all those who indulged in the above were to be treated as 'false ascetics.'[20]

The above ideas on the change in the concept of the monastic ideal and particularly the gradual but certain process of the building of *mathas*, temples and other permanent structures have a considerable bearing on our present concern on the simultaneous growth of the *tīrthas*. The tension between these changes and the ideal of renunciation also gets reflected in the literature of the times and great efforts were made to emphasize on the latter in the form of stories so that the message did not get diluted in any way. We shall dwell on some of these stories below. The above changes also led to the rise of a large number of monastic units in different parts of the country who vied with each other in attracting the layman to their particular ideas, beliefs and practices. Going on pilgrimage was one of the most visible and material means of expressing support to these various monastic orders. Indeed, their success very much depended on where they could receive a regular hospitality of their clients in order to further build temples and institute cults of more Jaina deities.

We now turn to take a close look at one of the most well known Jaina *tīrthas* that not only has a long recorded history but is also one site from where a great abundance of inscriptional data had been collected especially on the number of nuns and monks who offered *sallenkana* (self-mortification) at this place and thereby, upheld the important Jaina doctrine of renunciation. This is the site of Shravana Belgola near Mysore, in the present-day state of Karnataka. This example enables us to see how the idea of pilgrimage developed in Jainism given the changing socio-economic context in which the religion was also transforming. However, most importantly, at the same time, its main tenets of belief and the ultimate aim of how salvation should be attained were constantly interrogated and re-formulated by preachers, teachers, and seekers of salvation who flocked to this site from very early times. This also gives us a valuable insight into how, over a period of time, the followers of Jainism sanctified the earlier memory of the ascetics and monks who had visited this site but had preferred to remain anonymous. Thus, gradually at this site we are able to study the initiation of certain practices into Jainism that involved both collective and individual ritual and this, in turn, fostered the growth of pilgrimage as a mode of being a devout follower. That this *tīrtha* was a Digambara centre also makes this a unique case study because usually the settling down of monks and *ācārayas* is emphasized upon in the Śvetembara sects.

Shravana Belgola is located in the Hassan District of Karnataka State and covers a topographical area of about 5 sq km. It has a continuous history of about 1,500 years and is the foremost Digambara Jaina centre in India, revealing for the historian and the scholar the largest number of Jaina records at one place. Besides having the tallest colossus in the country of Gomateśvara it is also a place that has the largest number of Jaina Digambara temples concentrated at one place. Last but not least, it has the highest number of *nishidhis* or commemorative monuments located here, which is how the recorded history of the place first began. Settar whose study *Inviting Death*[21] provides us with the above details has further analysed that the Hill at Shravana Belogola at first, simply 'invited the devout to death'. Only later, he informs us, did it begin to attract pious pilgrims to this place who were initially awe struck by the severe austerities being done by the monks. It was still later that the place began to attract prosperous patrons who began to shower resources for the construction of temples and pavilions. The natural barren rock formations thus gradually began to be surrounded by man-made structures that then became the focal point of pilgrims over the ages.

Based on the data provided by Settar some examples of the above can be given. Shravana Belgola is in fact a place that was known for its two hills called Candragiri (Small Hill) and Vidhyagiri (Big Hill). The historical name that occurs in the inscriptions frequently to describe this place is Katavapra or Kalvappu. This occurs with several suffixes in the inscriptions of the period between the seventh to the twelfth century CE like *giri* (hillock), *śaila* (rock-bed), *tīrtha* (holy centre), *durgā* (fort), *parvata* (mountain), *rishigiri* (hillock of monks), and *tīrthagiri* (hillock of pilgrimage). After the excavation of the colossus in the tenth century CE the entire complex came to be called Gommatatīrtha or Gommatapura. In fact, it has been pointed out that it was only after the twelfth century CE that Belgola is mentioned as a *tīrtha* in several inscriptions from there.[22] Settar further informs us that '. . . the *tīrtha* seems to have attracted visitors to settle down around the pond' and therefore, the connotation of it being a *nagara* or town only occurs in the records of the fourteenth century CE and after[23] when the composite term Belgola-nagara occurs. Thus, Belgola, literally meaning the white pond, was first hailed as a *tīrtha* in the early twelfth century CE when it gradually began to grow as a township between the twelfth and the fourteenth century CE to finally, become the headquarters of the *nādu* in the fifteenth century CE. In some records of the nineteenth century Shravana Belgola is hailed as the Kashi of the South because of the substantial increase of its spiritual importance.[24] The general impression is that it is only because of the presence of the Gomateśvara colossus, carved in the tenth century CE that pilgrims thronged to this place through the ages. However, contrary to this, Settar writes: 'Though the colossus is the most important object which attracts millions of visitors today, its importance is subordinated to the sepulchral hill and the holy pond throughout the history of Shravana Belgola.'[25]

The sanctity of this place to the Jaina laity must now be explained. During the third century BCE and even as late as the seventh century CE the environs of Shravana Belgola were anything but hospitable to the householders. It was surrounded by high peaked mountains and situated amidst lowlands and a valley that was still inaccessible. Legend informs us that the first migrations here were due to the fact that there was a famine in north India. The monks who wanted to perform austerities were of course drawn to the place because of the secluded environment that was most suitable for them if they desired to mortify their body and invite death. This can be contrasted with the urges of a pilgrim who comes to a place to show reverence and then wants to record his or her gift or *dāna* to the place. In this way the laity left an inedible mark of their visit that becomes the reference point for later generations of pilgrims to follow.

The pattern of how Shravana Belgola grew in sanctity is clearly explained by Settar. These explanations and the statistical data that accompanies them help us to argue that pilgrimage as a concept has to be located in the broad historical context of the times, which enable its underlying growth and prosperity. The role of the individual aspirations and spiritual urges of the followers are not the sole factors that determine the form and the structure of the pilgrimage centre. At Shravana Belgola by the seventh century CE about seven hundred pious men had invited death voluntarily on the rocks at Katavapra. The anonymity of these early saints is important to note and none of them had their memorials made. About 100 commemorative records have survived to this day.[26] The history of these hills at Shravana Belgola during the early years was therefore, not made by outstanding events or, the achievements of great monarchs and rulers in the furtherance of the faith. On the other hand, the obscure monks and nuns waged a war against worldly desire through the weapon of self-mortification. *This of course was fundamental to their original teaching and belief.* It is further interesting to note that in the few details known about these individuals none of them were attached to any *sangha*, society, or association. They also did not inform posterity about their high spiritual pedigree or their list of disciples.

Gradually over these hills there emerge records when young monks begin to tend to the dying monks during their last stages towards death. From the records we gather that they seem to have taken pride in honouring the dead by engraving brief inscriptions at Katavapra. Among these monks commemorated, about 30 did not name their *sangha* at all nor, did they name their teachers. Statistics analysed by Settar show that only 6 monks took pride in referring to their *sangha,* which are mentioned by name like those located at Kittur, Kalattur, Sandviga, etc. This perhaps indicates that these *sanghas* must have approved of the ritual termination of life of their members. A few records are also available that mention the names of the teachers only and not of the Orders or *guruvādis* that these monks belonged to. In contrast to the monks, the nuns who mortified themselves between the seventh and eleventh century CE, it is noted, always mentioned the names of, either their *sangha* or, their teachers. It is further noted that almost all the nuns came from the Navilur Sangha. During this early period, except for an isolated record that mentions that the false doctrine was destroyed by a king, there are hardly any references to royal patronage of any kind.

It is between 900-1100 CE that records begin to mark a significant change that clearly is an erosion of the simplicity that was the hallmark of the earlier period. The tenth century CE is marked by the rise of institutions and by the twelfth century CE we definitely see at Shravana Belgola the fall of the individual and the rampant rise of the institutional life with all its frills of ritual. Ironically, this is marked by the considerable entry of the laity into the religious life of the Digambara Jaina establishment both as seekers of spirituality as well as rich donors for the construction of temples and *mathas.* Initially of course, the laity had been drawn to the hills to witness the awesome mortification rituals of the early monks. As a next step they started erecting *nishidhi* memorials for them. Among the significant commemorators were engravers, sculptors, scribes, and members of the order and sometimes lay disciples. During the sixth to the tenth century CE the patronage of the ruling kings and people of affluence is largely unsolicited.

The evidence from both the hills at Shravana Belgola indicates that the number of pilgrims increased between the tenth and the eleventh century CE. Several of them left behind their names on the rock bed. The names of pilgrims had been known from the eighth century CE onwards but they were just a trickle then. From the tenth century CE onwards they mention clearly that some of them had come to pay obeisance to the *tīrtha* and some others to 'bow before the god'. For instance, an interesting example of the tenth century CE tells us that one Andamarayya came with Sankayya desiring to see the monk Aggaladeva but being enchanted by the holy place both of them stayed on at Belgola till the end.[27] Though the total number of pilgrims who came to the place must have been many, only a few of them inscribed their names. From the names engraved on the rocks like Ranadhira, Sri Ratta, Sri Bamma, Isarayya, Sridhara we presume that most of them were ordinary laypersons. In fact, for the period before the eleventh century CE, Settar has analysed to write: 'it is interesting to note that this sizable number of pious visitors never made an attempt at enriching the holy centre either by cash or land grants.'[28] It is also deduced that during this early period the majority of the pilgrims were local people including some who were non-Jainas.

From the above discussion it can be clearly seen how Shravana Belgola emerged an important centre of pilgrimage for the Jaina community. The increase in the number of pilgrims brought the laity closer to the monks. Whereas, during the first four hundred years, i.e. between 600 and 1000 CE we do not find any examples of lay disciples terminating their lives, the evidence for the period after the tenth century CE increases in this regard. It is noticed that in the early days the pilgrims came to meet the monks by whom they were inspired. However, later after the nineth century CE, on the engravings left by them they mention that they had come to pay respects to god. This further leads us to argue that after this period temple building had become an important activity and so now the pilgrim's aim was to pay respect to the gods housed in the temples.

The emergence of temple building activity and the land grants as well as cash grants that began to be given to them totally changed the character of this pilgrimage centre after the twelfth century CE. The increase in the number of monuments at the place went hand in hand with the activities of the Sangha and in this case it was the Mūlasangha that began to enrich the religious life of this region as a whole. From the open hill where the early monks had mortified themselves, there gradually emerged caverns, rock-shelters, etc., which gained sanctity. The earliest such cave was the one associated with Bhadrabāhu that emerged into prominence only between the nineth to tenth centuries CE. However, proper temple worship became popular between the tenth to thirtenth centuries CE. The Sangha's new role emerged in the context of controlling the resources that were being generated by the laity for this worship and organizing this worship in a proper manner. Thus, we find that by the end of this period the individual monks who had earlier committed self-mortification and to whom the laity had come to see, more or less, disappear from the hill. The clergy now became engaged in temple building and temple management. The spiritual and religious activity now engulfs the entire valley around Shravana Belgola and not merely the hills because lands began to be given in the surrounding villages for the management of these temples. It would seem from the *modus operandi* of the Mūlasangha that the influential and affluent laity played a significant role in what kind of religious activities were to be followed. An important aspect of their interference in the Sangha was to appoint clergymen to manage the religious establishments. Image worship became the central feature of these religious institutions. Settar has discussed that in order to survive and compete with the other religions of the time, the language of the discussion and debates became increasingly militant.[29]

The micro-level study of Shravana Belgola is interesting from various angles. Its history reveals clearly the changes in the interconnections between the spiritual values of the Jaina faith which were held high by the monks or clergy and the religious life and practices of the Jaina laity that changed over time in the given social context. The important role of the temples and monasteries in bringing about a change in religious practice has much to do with the generous donations that were received from the wealthy laity. It is thus our submission that the *tīrtha* here developed as a religious practice to enable laity to participate in the perpetuation of the spiritual values of their faith for which Shravana Belgola had already become very famous.

Keeping in mind the changing religious practices that were affecting Jainism and also the fact that there were different points of view emerging in the organization of the various Jaina Sanghas, the large corpus of the Jaina literary tradition during the early medieval and medieval times began to preach on the values of upholding the principle of renunciation. Keeping in line with the earlier Jaina teaching it encouraged young men and women to renounce life and become nuns and monks as the most important way to achieve salvation and this was considered to be the more direct path. On the other hand, those who were unable to take this path had the option of living as a householder in accordance with the basic principles of Jaina ethics. In case a layperson could lead an ideal life properly it would ultimately lead to a life of renunciation. This was surely a more circuitous path and often full of temptations and hurdles. We will now briefly reflect on some of these stories to emphasize the point that the tension between complete renunciation and the householders life was sought to solved by glorifying the former at an ideational level so that in the larger interests of the Jaina faith and the growing ritual did not undermine and erode the essential ethos of this philosophy. By taking some select examples from these stories, it will be our endeavour to look at the multidimensional responses of society towards this major essential concept of Jainism. In other words, we will detail how the resolute ideas of renunciation affected society and, in turn, how individuals in society responded to it.

An interesting story is that of the monk Ardrakumara[30] who faced several difficulties during the course of his pledge to take to renunciation and in the process also caused pain to his loved ones whom he ultimately abandoned. He got activated to take this decision after seeing an image of the Jina. As a young man he had renounced the world but had to break his vows to marry. He, however, could not forget that he had once been a monk and when a son was born to him he decided again to take to renunciation. The story goes on to inform us that since he and his wife had been married even in their previous birth, it was very difficult for him to take this decision but he did so nonetheless rationalizing that now his wife had their son to keep her company. The story thus explores the complexities of pain and sorrow in taking the decision to renounce as well as the difficulties of keeping the family intact. In this story all concerned, including the monk, go through a period of pain and sorrow at the decision taken to renounce the world.

Several stories of this sort narrating the difficulties faced by individuals in taking to renunciation occur in the Jaina anthologies but they vary in terms of how each of the members are afflicted by it. In another story of renunciation, that of the monk Vajrasvāmin,[31] we are informed how right from the beginning as a young man he was inclined towards becoming a monk. Despite this, he, however, reluctantly marries and then abandons his pregnant wife and renounces the world. The interesting aspect of this story is that the son born to this monk also wishes to follow in the footsteps of his father and become a monk. He then convinces his mother to let him go but she suffers a lot of pain in the process. The story emphasizes on this pain but equally informs its readers that the young lad had taken the right decision to renounce the world. In this narrative the father and son fulfil their ambitions to become monks but the wife/mother is full of sorrow but is generally benign in her attitude. This is not the case in all the stories where the women are affected in this way.

The story of the monk Sukośāla[32] ends with the anger of the women that is rather graphically depicted. In this story a king renounces the world to become a monk. Like the others, in this case too, his wife originally suffers from grief at this decision of his but this gradually turns to anger and hostility. We are informed in the story that she desperately tries to keep her son from becoming a monk but he too follows in the footsteps of his father. Unable to stop her son, full of grief and anger the mother dies. This story then moves on to the next life of the wife/mother when she becomes a tigress. As such her anger continues in this life and she uses her present form as tigress to devour the monk who had once been her son. Here, there is the emotion of anger that is being amplified since in her earlier plight as a wife and mother she was helpless when her husband and child left her to become monks. The tension in this case is not based on moral ambiguities but simply on pure human emotions that are difficult to explain. In another story of anger and abandonment, that of Celana,[33] the tenacious and unpredictable nature of human relations continue to yield fruit in the next life in terms of taking revenge. In this case the wife left behind when her husband became a monk, dies and becomes a demi-goddess tormenting her former husband who is now a monk. In this story, however, there is another aspect, namely, the image of a female devotee who emerges in the story to help the monk. Thus, complex emotions and, at the same time, exemplary piety both come to the forefront in this narrative.

These stories were used as a medium to convey to people the difficulties faced by families when men and, particularly male children, resorted to renunciation as the most desired goal of the Jaina faith. The ultimate aim of course was that, however, difficult the situation and, however, painful the separation and still further, however, difficult the ability to control anger, the end result was success of the ideal of renunciation. In this context it is important to point out that there were other stories which tell us about monks who had renounced the world but yet, continued to interact with it. These set of stories do not totally deny the world but try to explain it in positive light but within the context of the ideal of renunciation. In this context the story of Amarasimha is most fascinating. He lives and works in society but technically he is withdrawn from it or rather, detached from it in a form of renunciation.[34] Basically, in this story the monk lives an exemplary life like doing good deeds, like putting an end to blood sacrifice, bringing about an end of the plague—all to show the greatness of the Jaina faith. The practice of non-violence in the world is particularly stressed upon as a virtue that both the laity and the monks must possess. This is even stressed for the kings to adopt in the story of Abhayasimha, which is a dialogue between King Kumārapāla of Gujarat and the monk Hemachandra.[35]

The necessity of narrating some of the stories located in the real world of on going life and its happenings was that the monks had to preach the pristine teachings to the laity in an atmosphere which was continuously expanding and changing. The ideal of renunciation had to be particularly stressed among a Jaina laity that was, from the early medieval times, increasingly being drawn to image and temple worship. The aim of this chapter has thus been on highlighting the changes that took place at Shravana Belgola during the early medieval times wherein we had concluded that the spiritual life got merged and intrinsically entwined with religious practice. The idea of pilgrimage as it had emerged had been closely connected with the spiritual beliefs of the Jainas to perform austere penance so that the liberation of the soul could take place. Its later practice, on the other hand, dwelt more on the worship of images of god and the rituals that accompanied them. The latter cannot also be understood unless we give due emphasis to the role of the influential laity who worked hand in hand with the spiritual orders for the expansion of these places of pilgrimage. The literary endeavours, on the other hand, which we focused on in the latter half of the chapter were necessary reminders for both the laity and monks that the ultimate goal of renunciation could not be sidelined in any way. Stories were the best means on communicating that the pristine ideals of Jainism lay in renunciation.

In the end we reiterate that there are a variety of reasons that enable pilgrimage centres to develop. Some have to do with the larger cultural idiom in which Jainism developed. Others can be related to the social functions that the idea of pilgrimage performs. The most significant, however, has to do with the symbolism of ritual attached to it in the given ideology. In the case of Jainism this particularly evolved in it during the early medieval times. This is also the period during which most of the stories discussed above were systematized and popularized. Thus, in an overall sense both pilgrimage and literature mirror society in religious tradition. Therefore, we have argued that since there is socio-economic and cultural change from time to time, the idea and practice of pilgrimage continually got reinforced. Further, so that the essence of Jainism in its ideal of renunciation did not get diluted, the literary traditions were kept alive to propagate these ideals to the people at large. Studies on pilgrimage help us to see how they originate and thrive in given local situations during specific periods while, the literary traditions keep alive the sub-continental linkages within the religion—each reinforcing the other to keep the seminal message of the founder intact and further fortify the old memory of their sanctity.

NOTES

1. Quoted in Shah (2007: 140).
2. Sastry (1989: 38-9).
3. Majumdar (1968: 16; 408; 419).
4. Sastry (1989: 41; 23-37).
5. Hanumantha Rao (1993: 171-90) discusses its rapid development in Andhra during this period.
6. It has been pointed out by K.M. Shrimali (1988: 26-7) that one of the best ways to research into the history of *tīrthas* and sacred complexes is to undertake micro studies of specific sites and temples. This would enable an in depth study of their material setting and their role in society and economy.
7. Several of these stories have been put together as an anthology in Granoff (1998).
8. Basham (1954: 287-93).
9. Jain (1947: 22).
10. Hanumantha Rao (1993: 124). See also Stevenson (1915: 67).
11. Hanumantha Rao (1993: 146).
12. It is well known that brahmanical literature mentions more than 400 *tīrthas* in early medieval times and that the *Mahābhārata* and the Purāṇas contain 40,000 verses on *tīrthas* and legends connected with them. For details see: Kane (1973: 581-2, 730-825)
13. Nandi (1986: 117-18).

14. Details of various aspects of pilgrimage in Jainism discussed in Jain (1977: 127-8).
15. Nandi (1986: 160 ff).
16. Deo (1956: 397).
17. Nandi (1986: 107).
18. Nandi (1986: 107).
19. Premi (1956: 352).
20. Nandi (1973: 33-8, 65-6, 72-5).
21. Settar (1986).
22. Settar (1986: 5).
23. Settar (1986: 7).
24. Settar (1986: 5).
25. Settar (1986: 7).
26. Settar (1986: See Appendix I).
27. Settar (1986: 17).
28. Settar (1986: 18).
29. The post-twelfth century CE period had been discussed by Settar (1986: 23-30, 31-71) in a section entitled 'Emergence of Monuments: Shift in Spiritual Outlook' and in a separate chapter entitled: 'Age of Great Material and Religious Prosperity'. The ideas in the above paragraph have been summarized from these writings.
30. Granoff (1998: 21-37).
31. Granoff (1998: 38-48).
32. Granoff (1998: 49-56).
33. Granoff (1998: 57-61).
34. Granoff (1998: 76-83).
35. Garnoff (1998: 84-94).

CHAPTER 9

Nanakramguda: Inhabitants from Village to a Megapolis*

Continuity and integration mark the social landscape at a pan-Deccan level. This can best be seen when one analyses historical changes of a place or small locality. In this chapter I shall take one example to illustrate the diversity and vibrancy of historical evolution through the way people in a small locality remembers its past and clings to symbols and cultural practices and, at the same time, the several ways in which identities of belonging to a place remain intact. The focus is on looking closely at the historical memory of the inhabitants of an erstwhile village in the environs of the city of Hyderabad that is today booming as part of the special economic zones created to house multi-national companies. Both the particularity of space and the specificity of time have to be galvanized to enable us to lay bare how cognitive space of its people is articulated, which must necessarily be understood in its local environment. In elaborating these ideas we have accepted a definition that 'Cognitive space uses the analogy of location in two, three or higher dimensional space to describe and categorize thoughts, memories and ideas. Each individual has his/her cognitive space, resulting in a unique categorization of their ideas. The dimensions of this cognitive space depend on information, training and finally on a person's awareness. All this depends globally on the cultural setting'.[1]

*This chapter is partially based on an earlier paper that was orally presented under the title: 'Time, Space and Cognitive Space at Nanakaramguda' at the International Seminar on 'Culture and Cognition in Reconstructing the Past' Sub-Theme: Concept of Time and Space Dept. of History, University of Hyderabad, 17-20 December 2015. The Proceedings of the Conference are being prepared for publication.

The past is about social life through time. The textual traditions in every society indicate how there are always a few who embody the larger community's vision of space and time.[2] However, culture has to be understood in its broadest sense to engulf small communities and their day to day tasks, which we can learn about through the varied archaeological data that is found primarily locally. Culture as a way of life does not remain static and this has to be also reflected upon in terms of how people develop their ideas around their belief systems to understand the workings of the Universe. It changes in Time's interaction with Space and therefore, the necessity to look at the development of both these concepts through the prism of a particular locality. A substantial part of the ideas about time and the lived in space, its boundaries, etc., discussed in this chapter, are embedded in historical memory rather than in the written word. This, to use Bernard Lewis' words, is 'its inherited historiography' which 'may be described as the collective memory of a community or nation or other entity—what it, or its rulers and leaders, poets, and sages, choose to remember as significant, both as reality and symbol.'[3] Such collective memory of a society permits it to keep its boundaries vague and therefore, space remains inclusive over time. On the other hand, as trained historians we wish to define territories in several ways, especially political, and thereby, naturally tend to exclude. It would thus not be an exaggeration to state that most modern historians of ancient India are trained to study this so-called 'collective memory' encapsulated in the memory of people with suspicion, if not outright antagonism. This is because they are trained to believe that history, as opposed to memory, should be placed on a high pedestal as a mode of critical thinking, which maintains a safe distance (certainly in conceptual terms, as well as in terms of time and place) from the 'documentary evidence' it uses to write itself. In this sense the writing of local history cannot do without this collective memory which, the modern historian must negotiate with and not dismiss the cognitive capacity of this memory to identify the myriad fragments of evidence couched and nested in an alternative world view.

Empirical work[4] for this research was part of our initial project

(2012-13)[5] to document archaeological data and historical vestiges in terms of extant monuments, ordinary houses and the like in the hitherto rural settlements around the city of Hyderabad.[6] This was done alongside documenting heritage that is commonly called intangible so that the social and cultural aspects of life could also be reflected upon through collecting oral narratives.[7] It was noted that experiences of the community could not be extricated from their material setting. All this, as mentioned above, had to be done at the micro-level. In the case of the former it must be stated at the outset that we had to contend with only fragments of historical evidence while in the latter, one had to be forewarned of exaggerations and perceptions rooted only in personal memory.[8] Still our intention to weave a historical imagery of various localities was firmly linked to the tenacious ways with which these communities preserved, changed and renewed themselves to create a definitive cognitive space for recollecting their past and link it to the present.

Attempts to document began with a basic understanding that the usual archaeological and archival sources would provide us enough data that we could build on. It was a disappointment that no such official source material could be accessed. Neither archaeological reports, nor official Gazetteers[9] reported on these settlements in any significant way. The monumental Syed Ali Asgar Bilgrami's study on *Landmarks of the Deccan* [1927] meant to be 'A Comprehensive Guide to the Archaeological Remains of the City and Suburbs of Hyderabad', as its subtitle suggested, revealed nothing on these settlements extending its scope only to documenting major monuments of the Qutub Shahi period in what he called the 'suburbs' of Hyderabad. These were a few monuments in the Toli Chowki, Shaikpet and Dargah areas, which were found listed in this work. Based on oral memory, Lalita Gir etched out her reminiscences of living in the Shaikpet and Toli Chowki areas in the 1950-60s, which she defined as still very rural and marked by huge areas of natural landscape.[10] Fragmentary pieces of information[11] were collected from information printed or narrated on the two Sri Ranganath Swamy temples at Nanakaramguda and Gopanpalli[12] that were both sites of huge yearly gatherings (*yātras*) and are considered to be at least 400 year old monuments. Similarly, the Haji Mastan Dargah at Masjid Banda and the Fakhruddin Gutta Dargah at Puppalaguda become the focal point of the communities at the time of their respective annual urs. Only two of the places under the purview of our project's study provided immense historical data—at Patancheru[13] in the form of sculptural evidence that went back to the Chalukyan times, while at Dargah, firmly datable historical monuments that went back to the Qutub Shahi period. Other than these striking historical remains, most of the other villages under study for this project revealed data only on small shrines, burial areas and locally significant structures. Except on the campus of the University of Hyderabad, no systematic excavations[14] had been conducted in these villages by the various Government Departments of Archaeology.[15]

It was hoped that the Hyderabad Urban Development Authority that was active in the late nineties would have incorporated some of the old structures between Patancheru and Dargah. On studying the G.O.[16] notifying these heritage buildings and precincts it was noticed that most of the 137 buildings notified pertained to the major architectural monuments of the Qutub Shahi period in the areas around Mehedipatnam, Golconda, Shaikpet, Dargah and Patancheru and a few on the Himayat Sagar Road, Banjara Hills and Jubilee Hills.[17] It is interesting, however, that the Precincts (natural rock formations) that were notified[18] included two important ones that pertain immediately to the hinterland of the village settlements under study. The first included the 'Rock formations on hillocks around Durgam Cheruvu' situated behind Jubilee Hills and the second were those that cover the Raidurg and Madhapur localities and identified as Survey Nos. 44, 46, 63, 64 and 83. Another, much closer to the focus area of study was what is called the 'Rock Park' that referred to the Hillock behind Dargah Hussain Shah Wali Cheruvu accessible from the Old Bombay Road and Khajaguda Road in then Ranga Reddy District identified as Survey No. 246 of the Manikonda Jagir. And finally, the most significant one and actually located in a part of the University of Hyderabad was what is called the 'Mushroom Rock' identified as Survey No. 25 in Gachibowli, then located in the Serilingampalli Mandal of Ranga Reddy District. The Government's intention in issuing this G.O.

was to put into effect the Expert Committee's recommendations on 'Heritage Conservation' so that 'Heritage Buildings, Precincts, areas, Artefacts, Structures of Historical, Aesthetical, Architectural or Cultural value' could be conserved as per regulation 13 of the HUDA's zoning regulations.[19] It would not be out of place here to also mention that significant water bodies in many of these villages had also been listed as those that were to be saved, namely, Patancheru Cheruvu, Nanakramguda Kunta, Nalagandla Cheruvu, Manikonda Jagir Kunta, Gopi Cheruvu in Lingampally, Nalla Cheruvu in Tellapur among others.[20]

Given the absence of smaller structures from not only the heritage lists but also an absence of any recorded accounts of the history of these villages, the challenge before us was to retrieve a past in terms of its continuity and its reinvention in different ways. Against the background of the above-discussed historiographical and archaeological absences, in many ways our endeavour became the first to begin to write a sort of 'History' of these 'rural' settlements. Each was couched in its own sense of the past, central to their survival and identity but only articulated through their seasonal festivals and rites of passage and their memory of family or village histories. The close relationship with nature was evident in the initial survey of the landscape that we did. This has also been reported by one of the Newsletters of the Society to Save Rocks,[21] that the communities had safely guarded the rocks by making most of their shrines deep inside the rocks or, at their base. For generations then these natural formations have remained protected. For instance, in the case of Gopanpally, the old Ranganath Swamy temple was located in a niche under huge boulders, almost like a cave and surrounded on all sides by sheet rock and boulders. We found another temple under a natural Rock on the Fakhruddin Gutta hill at Puppalaguda called the Padmanabha Swamy Temple. Similarly, all the small shrines visited, even after the Emaar properties have taken away the land around the Nanakramguda village, were at the base of rocks and structures have been built using the rocky backdrop. Apart from this visible connection between human urge for the sacred and the necessity to protect the natural environment, our journey with the inhabitants during the year [2012-13] through the oral narratives, festival celebrations and earlier means of livelihood, revealed how dependant the people were on their environment. It is against this background that to document the cognitive space of these villages began based on memory and orality but, very much within the gambit of the current material existence of these communities. We now move on to elaborate on our findings at one of the places, namely, Nanakramguda.

> Talking about place, where we belong, is a constant subject for many of us. We want to know if it is possible to live on the earth peacefully. Is it possible to sustain life? Can we embrace an ethos of sustainability that is not solely about the appropriate care of world's resources, but is also about the creation of meaning—*the making of lives that we feel are worth living*. (Emphasis added) [bell hooks][22]

bell hooks has eloquently encapsulated a foundational human concern, namely, the necessity to understand one's place. This of course, not only refers to the physical space, but also to the economic, social and cultural spaces we move in and out of in our daily lives. Over time, these become an intrinsic part of our history and identity, to which we may feel at times, a very close affinity or, at other times, a distance, that is difficult to exactly pinpoint. We cite this quotation as it captures for us the intersecting terrain of time, place and social relations that our sojourn at Nanakramguda evoked during the short trips that we made to it during the one year of 2012-13. It clearly brought to the fore one extremely poignant emotion that of a sense of belonging to this 'Place'. Its present is being so shaken by tremendous economic changes that almost on a daily basis the 'Other' enters into the lives of its inhabitants. In fact, we argue in this paper that it is precisely because 'Otherness' has become so common in the habitation area we call Nanakramguda, that the sense of owning the place and its past has become central to their lives. Clinging to various elements of the tradition has made it possible for them to define a broad range of relationships in order to better understand the original 'Self', which has become the particular ethos of this historical point in time during the early twenty-first century. We see this as one historical point in a long series of similar antecedent historical points that needs to be documented as it marks for us the human condition and tenacity of a community to define itself through their memory against overwhelming odds. 'Cognition' thus occupies an important space in the retrieval of the past. Perhaps, this retrieval provides them a legitimacy that otherwise is being eroded by powers that are beyond the ken and control of the communities themselves. 'History' thus emerges from the ashes through the voices of people and their memory.

Located (Map 6.1, p. 195) at the first exit on the newly constructed Outer Ring Road and sandwiched between it and the recently designated Financial District of Gachibowli, Nanakramguda is today administratively located in the Serilingampally mandal of Ranga Reddy district at lat. 17'.41° N and long 78'.35° E. Compared to the slow pace of change inside the University Campus, Nanakramguda's changing profile is deeply impacted by the real estate business that is booming in this village after the establishment of the campuses of the Indian School of Business, the Software giants Wipro, Infosys and Microsoft among others and most pertinently, the landscaped high end housing complex called Boulder Hills alongside the Golf Course that are both part of the Emaar properties. Nanakramguda was an erstwhile agrarian settlement and was part of the large Manikonda Jagir during the period of Nizam's rule. Once properties were acquired for setting up the above mentioned economic and academic zones, many of the inhabitants, either wilfully sold their lands or, were coaxed to do so. As a result of this the northern perimeter of the village that was earlier an integral part of the sacred space that the villagers visited from time to time, became land that is now alien to them. The core of the *basti* (lived in space) with the simple and tiled-roofed housing of the inhabitants is intact in places and at others, it has been transformed to huge double storied modern constructions depending on which social strata or particular individuals it belonged to who may have made instant money on selling their lands. An unruly character of the village, the bifurcation of its shrines, the sudden emergence of new shops built by the so-called 'outsiders' now leaves us with the impression of an apparently confused 'Place'. Furthermore, the disappearing toddy trees and rock formations which were an integral part of the landscape around which this settlement was nested in for several hundred years is now to be seen in bits and pieces.

How can a 'Place' be historically constructed? As discussed above we could have done so on the basis of written records that already demarcate historical periods, events, personalities or monuments. Instead, we have culled together this account using the following sources emanating from documentation of art-historical data on temples, shrines, etc., oral narratives, lifestyles and festivals through video documentation of the continuing traditions of the inhabitants. Each of these sources represent a distinct methodological avenue that enabled us to shift from the purely academic concerns of a scientific documentation of only monuments to a more lively and vivacious capturing of their shifting social and cultural boundaries in a space that is literally slipping away from under their feet. Yet, we were able to create a cognitive space that portrays a brief history and the state of the cultural heritage at Nanakramguda village through the memory of its inhabitants.

Local informants tell us that the entry to Nanakramguda in the old days was restricted to from the side of Khajaguda, a village on the east side of what is today called the Outer Ring Road. Behind the well-known sixteenth century Sri Ranganath Swamy temple, which stands tall on the western extremity of the village, was a wall that prevented villagers from Gowlidoddhi and Gopanpally to enter directly. There were small pathways that lay to the north of Nanakramguda in what is today called the Emaar properties that were used by people to visit the sacred shrines bordering this part of the village. An extant old wall is visible outside the modern Sri Ranganath Swamy temple but is difficult to verify if this was the old boundary wall of the village. Today, on the other side of this wall is what is now designated as the 'Wipro Lake'. On the old revenue map this water body is named as the Medubai Kunta, an important source of water for the fields around it owned by residents of Nanakramguda. In the diagonally opposite direction on the other extremity of the village, just abutting the Outer Ring Road, is a water body designated merely as 'Pond' on the Google map. We were informed this was the important Patel Kunta, used then, as today, for the buffaloes of the village and other purposes. Other minor water bodies, interspersed with local vegetation were found in all directions especially in the north, as this is the zone where a large number of rock-formations have been found and, as is well known, these rocks protect underground water for long periods of time.

The sanctity of the natural life giving entities is often associated with the sacred and religious. Our plotting[23] of the extant historical structures showed a close proximity between the two. The Sri Ranganath Swamy temple is often seen as the only vestige of the historical past at Nanakramguda. It is located at a distance from the core of the village and surrounded by large open spaces. We learn that this temple is more than 350 years old but has always been in the hands of outsiders, most recently, is private property of the Pittie family Trust. The main deity in this temple (Figure 9.1) is Swami Mahavishnu Adisheshya[24] with three of his wives—Sridevi, Bhudevi and Niladevi—seen seated at his feet. An important and interesting facet of this religious ensemble is the existence of another female deity that is worshipped that clearly has indigenous

Source: Reproduced from brochure in Hindi produced by the Shri Ranganath Mandir, Rangabag Trust.

Figure 9.1: Vishnu Idol worshipped inside the Sri Ranganath Swamy Temple, Nanakramguda origins (Figure 9.2). In the local belief she is designated as another wife of Vishnu but is also referred to as his devotee, namely, Goda Devi. Often, local goddesses are integrated into classical traditions so as to be accepted by the local communities and this case is no different.

Interestingly, to make the local beliefs integral to this temple complex we have a Shiva Linga shrine outside the main temple, in close proximity to the ancient well that is regularly worshipped by the villagers till date. The main front entrance of the new Ranganatha Swamy temple under worship is surrounded by ruins of a much older temple. An old well, some *mandapas* and other structures of this temple (Figure 9.3) are still visible but there is little information on whether this was also a Vishnu temple or, one that belonged to

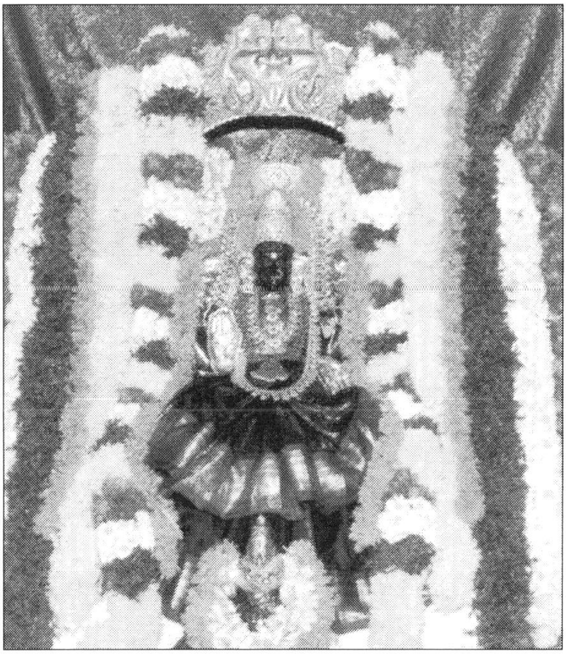

Source: Reproduced from brochure in Hindi produced by the Shri Ranganath Mandir, Rangabag Trust.

Figure 9.2: Goda Devi, Local Goddess near the Vishnu Idol, Sri Ranganath Swamy Temple, Nanakramguda

Source: Photo taken by the author.

Figure 9.3: An old well and a mandapa at Sri Ranganath Swamy Temple, Nanakramguda

a different sectarian affiliation. This encouraged us to move closer to the inner core of the settlement while continuing with our mapping project[25] (Map 9.1). A roadside shrine was located on the way to the inner habitation of the village as a typical Pochamma (local goddess) shrine. Nobody removes it from the wayside and occasionally, signs of worship are noticed around it. A significant result of this exercise was that some of the oldest shrines, now built over with all the symbols of more classical forms of temple construction, were those associated with the mother goddess. This is visible on the main street of Nanakramguda where now stands what is called the Mysamma (local goddess) temple. But this is not the only temple dedicated to her. A small shrine, without any construction over it was located at the innermost core of the Nanakramguda settlement (Figure 9.4). This, we were informed by more than one person, was the village deity called Gandi Maisamma around whom at the time of Navaratri and Ugadi worship was regularly done. Thus, this shrine without a constructed space turned out to be the most critical deity of the village and is worshipped even today in a rather traditional way, especially by the youth. We

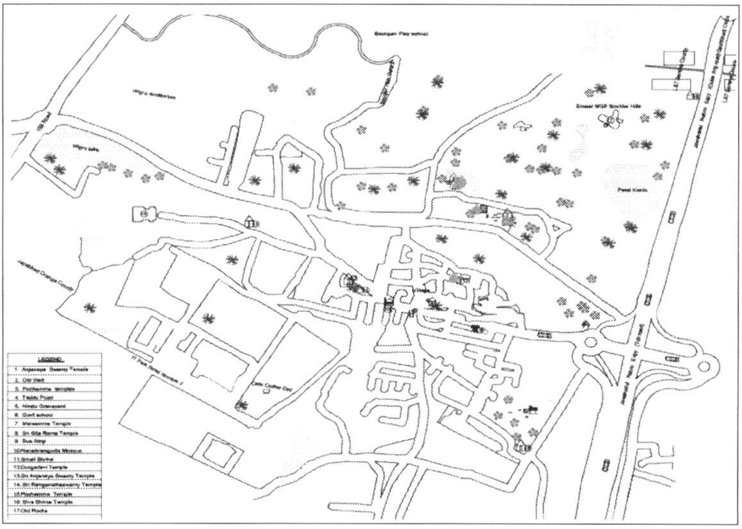

Source: Map prepared by the author.

Map 9.1: Components of Built-in and Natural Heritage at Nanakramguda

Source: Photo taken by the author.

Figure 9.4: Original Myasamma Shrine guardian of the village, Nanakramguda were able to record the existence of other shrines and temples at the inner core of Nanakramguda. The Rama and Sree Hanuman temple is a significant one around which the Sri Ramnavami celebrations were held. Similarly, close to the main street of the village an old Dargah, looked after by the Muslim community of the village, was documented.

The mapping of shrines did not end with the inner core of the Nanakramguda settlement. It was extremely significant during this process to note that the residents of the *basti* were eager to take us to those areas outside their habitation into, what is now called the Emaar properties, to emphasize their close religious attachment to these lands. In fact, our documentation shows how at least three critical clusters of shrines were found on these properties that continued to be worshipped even though the entry of the villagers to them had now got severely restricted and, in fact legally banned. Near what is now called the Golf Course were found the Hanuman and other shrines that nested in the midst of huge rocks (Figure 9.5).

Source: Photo taken by the author.

Figure 9.5: Hanuman Temple and other Shrines, near Golf Course, Nanakramguda

The Hanuman Temple, at the time of Sankranti is taken over by the followers of the Ayyappa and they live around it and other shrines for a number of days. Similarly, the Lodha Khatris have their Seetha Kalimata shrines (Figure 9.6) that are visited by them at regular intervals. In fact, we are informed that each family has one such shrine to placate the mother goddess. Further away, clearly inaccessible to the villagers were other small shrines in the Emaar properties which we plotted on the map. Interestingly, they lie in close proximity to another water body and in the midst of a natural environment marked by a rocky landscape.

The primary objective, however, was to record oral narratives of the various communities about the village, the lifestyle of their ancestors as well as their symbolic cultural traditions in the hope that this would enable us bring to visibility the historical textures of life in an agrarian settlement that did not boast of any literary records. In the genre of doing oral history it is well known that 'memory is the core of oral history from which meaning can be extracted and preserved.'[26] We address in this part of the chapter

Source: Photo taken by the author.

Figure 9.6: Kalimata Shrines, near Golf Course, Nanakramguda the social and cultural force of narratives that reflects on a sense of belonging while, carefully also telling us about 'Otherness'. It is well recognized today that oral history, unlike the traditional understanding of history as a discipline, 'deals exclusively with the living'. It is a cognitive space that is powerful but one that has been looked upon with suspicion by professional historians. For this reason one is forewarned that 'collective memory can preserve or distort a community's past.'[27] The extent to which the continuity with the past was possible given the fast changing environment, did impact the way these narratives emerged before us. Therefore, we have drawn only on those parts of these oral narrations that to some extent dispassionately talk about their social environment and their professions. By confining ourselves to these specific issues one has tried to avoid the pitfall of exaggerated claims to hoary antiquity and an unabashed admiration for the past. In this sense we have drawn on Nicole Boivin's [2010] understanding of material culture as a distinct way of life that can also be made connectable to thoughts, emotions and social relations.

Given the primarily economic subsistence pattern of the village of Nanakramguda which was agriculture and related activity, we began with meeting hitherto farming communities. This landowning Kapu-Reddy community was the one that had been most immediately affected with the onslaught of land acquisitions that Nanakramguda has faced since the last decade or so. This is encapsulated in what Shekar Reddy told us [Video link 6. Reddy_ Shekar_Cultivation on CD with author].

> I am born into an agricultural family and brought up in this village. I belong to Reddy community and my major occupation is agriculture (cultivation). Generally we used to farm crops like maize and paddy. The major source of water was Chittak Kunta (water reservoir) and it used to be filled during the rainy season. The other source of water was manmade wells. Right now we do not have any well or water bodies for water as they all have disappeared in recent years. During the development of IT parks we have lost everything like lands, water sources for cultivation. Since this has happened we are not doing any cultivation.

Anjji Reddy also informed us of the litigation that was still going on with the Government as the compensation that they had to get for their lands. The amount given was so small that they had no option but to go to the courts. The lore of plenty before the present is part of their narration in that we were told that about 100 acres of land was cultivated and at least eighty buffaloes were owned by them.

One would imagine from the above that the Kapus and Reddys formed the majority of the village. This was not the case. Instead, Shekar Reddy went on to explain to us the social structure of the village. He said: 'In our village Reddy population is almost 25 per cent, Lodhas 50 per cent and other communities are 25 per cent.' That the Lodhas were the large majority of the village population is corroborated with what Narasimha, an employee of our University, narrated to us in the Documentary Film we have made on this village. The Lodhas were known by their title 'Singh' and were migrants to the Nanakramguda from Uttar Pradesh. They style themselves as Lodha Khatris who were brought to the region under the Nizam's rule as guards needed by the then state apparatus. A huge wall in the shape of a rampart marks the entry into their current location of habitation reminiscent of old walled structures used in buildings from about the sixteenth century. Fateh Singh, [Video link 5. Lodha_R Fathe Singh on CD with the author] an elder of this community narrated: 'Our forefathers have migrated from Uttar Pradesh during the Nizam's period. Some of our community members were specially invited for security reasons as gaurds and the rest of the people used to do cultivation. We got land for cultivation during the Nizam's period. However, we lost all the lands now because of IT parks and other developments'.

The Lodha Khatris are fluent Hindi speakers and look different from the other inhabitants of the village and have a lifestyle that marks them out. Today, with their earlier profession having disappeared, it was interesting for us to observe that they have become the sole makers of big and small Ganesh idols. In a visit to their locality in late August of 2012 we saw their homes as well as open areas around them full of huge Ganesh idols, all ready to be sold for the then forthcoming Ganesh Chaturthi festival.

Thanks to two of our employees at the University of Hyderabad,

Narasimha and Balaram, we were able to get an incisive insight into the life of the Madigas or leather working community in this locality before modernization of agriculture came about. Their graphic description of the tasks that the Madigas did in the village has been captured in the documentary film. Narasimha's historical narration about the value of the Madigas to the community is best encapsulated in his own words:

> Madigas and many other communities were invited by Mr. Nanak Ram,[28] who built the Ranganatha Swamy temple. We used to do different works in the village but mainly we worked in two areas; one was footwear manufacturing and other was making leather threads (ropes). In those days these leather threads were mainly used for lifting water tubs from wells to pour water into vessels. Nowadays people are not using leather threads and many other natural cultivation methods in agriculture have been adopted because of technological development. During those days our community was very limited in terms of numbers but nowadays the numbers are increasing and traditional profession has changed and so we began to shift to other jobs.

In Narasimha's recollection he presented the case that since there was no work for many of the so-called 'working-class' communities, most of them migrated from Puppalaguda to Nanakramguda in search of work. Among the most significant work they did was to make leather 'pipes' that were critical to the farming communities as they were needed to carry water to the fields. Apart from this they made sandals for the Patels of the village and were the ones responsible for playing the traditional *dappu* (Figure 9.7) to wake-up the village community daily at 5.00 a.m. as also playing it on several ceremonial occasions.

Both Narasimha and Balaram narrated with great detail the way theirs were the communities responsible for the collection of wood (*katala*-sticks) from around the barren landscape around their villages to be made into bundles and then sold in the village. For a whole day's work, Balaram informed us that his mother would get Rs. 1.25 while he would get 75 paisa. As residents of Gowlidoddhi, they would come to Nanakramguda to sell these bundles as well as cow dung cakes that all the villagers needed for cooking. In Narasimha's narration we are told that they had to take these bundles to the Tahasildar's office in Nampally.

Source: Above Photograph from www.madigadandora.blogspot.in

Figure 9.7: *Dapu* playing by the Madiga community—a traditional task for them

Like the Madigas, other professional groups in the village too have been impacted by the changes taking place around them in the last decade or so. Among the array of other communities in the village the ones that we were able to interview are the Chakalis or Dhobis, the Kummaris or potters and the Gowds or Toddy Tappers. It was noticed that all of them related to their profession's past in positive ways but were helpless when seeing its current state deteriorate. Below are some poignant examples that reflect the overall social change sweeping Nanakramguda.

Kummaris

My name is Ramesh and my father's name is Narasimha and we belong to Kummari (Potter) community. We are not practicing our traditional occupation. We do not show interest in this profession as it needs a special skill that has to be practiced. Pottery making is an art. The same profession is carried on by my relatives (other family specially my father's brothers) who live in contiguous villages. My ancestors were very much active in the profession and there was huge demand for pots then. Some of them were also into agriculture but nowadays many families are shifting to other professions.' [Video link 1. Potter_Ramesh_1in CD with the author]

Chakalis

My name is Mallesh, my caste is Chakali (dhobi). We have been practicing this profession from past eighty years. Our family liked the profession during the earlier days but these days it's become very challenging for us and I left this traditional profession and entered into tailoring as well. In olden days there were five to six natural water bodies and now many of these water bodies are disappearing and some are still there but fully polluted because of the IT and Financial district buildings coming up and using our water resources in a different way. Since it is polluted we cannot even use that water for washing and we are getting skin diseases if we use this polluted water to wash clothes. Government had allotted separate land for the dhobis long back but we are still awaiting a proper response from the Government.' [Video link 4. Dhobi_ Mallesh_2 in CD with the author]

Yadagiri

My name is Yadagiri, I am continuing the same work of being a Dhobi. As per my knowledge my father and fore fathers were also in the same profession. We liked the profession during earlier days but nowadays it has become very challenging for us to leave this traditional profession and enter into other jobs, since we are not very educated. The other challenge is that we are not getting proper water for washing clothes as we have lost many natural water bodies and still others are polluted. The best thing from past to present is that nowadays we are getting good money for our Dhobi work when compared to earlier days. Perhaps, this is due to more people coming and residing in our midst. [Video link 3. Dhobi_ Yadagiri-1 in CD with the author]

Toddy Tapper

My name is Sattayya Goud and I belong to the Gouda (Toddy Tapper) community. We continue to practice the same profession that, as per my knowledge, my forefather's generation inherited from long back. There were many toddy plants around the village and I remember that earlier there were almost forty people who were dependant on this profession and our business was very active and good. For the past ten to fifteen years we are facing a problem because of the continuous changes in around the village. This is because the IT and other commercial developments have led to the removal many of the toddy trees (plants) and there are very few trees now left only near the ORR side. Despite this still four to five people are continuing the same profession. This is because we are not educated and we cannot join any other professions. These days people are not able to make good money in this profession because of the coming of foreign liquor shops that are now being patronized by people. [Video link 7. Toddy_Sattayya in CD with the author]

Ramesh's narration on the craft of pottery making is a perspective of the younger generation among the Kummaris. Just outside their house we noticed a Kiln (Figure 9.8), which the earlier generation of their community had used for making pots. Now we are told in the narration by his father, Narasimha [Video link 1. Potter_ Ramesh_1in CD with the author] that many of their relatives still continue the profession and are inhabitants of Khajaguda and Madhavpur. Residents of Nanakramguda have to now buy such pots from outside the village. In contrast, both the Dhobis indicate how their profession has had a different trajectory in the village. Both Mallesh and Yadgiri have continued with their traditional profession though the former has diversified to become a tailor as well. Both were perturbed by the basic source of their income being affected due to the pollution of water bodies that earlier they had used for washing clothes. Since control over them is now lost, they seem to be losing a hold over their traditional profession though Yadgiri does point out that with the influx of new population needing his services, his livelihood was better than in the

Source: Photo taken by the author.

Figure 9.8: Abandoned Kiln, Nanakramguda

past. Finally, Sattayya, the toddy tapper gave us an account of his profession that today is under threat simply because the toddy trees on which it is based are also fast disappearing. There is pathos, helplessness and grit in his statement throwing before us a tenaciousness that is only seen to be believed. The material existence of many of the communities is thus being impacted in different ways. It is clear that traditional professions that were rooted in a different landscape and economic activity are now withering away. However, it is through them that the community simultaneously remembers its past.

While mapping the old shrines on the northern periphery of the village we noted that access to these very critical parts of the community's sacred space had been wrested away from them. Yet, in different ways they continue to lay claims on this space, not by forcible occupation but, by emphasizing on emotional, deeply spiritual and symbolic relevance to their very existence, which then enables them to negotiate with the new owners to permit a short period of sojourn in areas that they are legally banned from. A few examples from the oral narratives about these snatched away shrines explicates this issue and consciously lays bare before us the tenacity and centrality of ideological formations that defy impositions. At the time of Sankranti the Hanuman and other shrines are taken over by the followers of the Ayyappa and they live around these shrines for a number of days. [Video link 8. Mr. Raju Singh_ Ayyappa on CD with the author] Raju Singh our informant told us:

> We, Ayyappa devotees, used to stay here near these shrines every year during Ayyappa Mala (November to February). Here the main deity is Lord Hanuman and there are some other shrines like those of Lord Shiva. Around the temple there are many beautiful boulders. This is a very old temple and we use to have regular Puja here but on every Saturday we will do a special Puja.

Similarly, the Lodha Khatris cling to their Seetha Kalimata shrines that are visited by them at regular intervals but especially around Ugadi and Navaratri time. Each family has one such shrine to placate the mother goddess. In our initial survey on the Emaar properties Ramesh of the Kummari *basti* took us to see these shrines because they are understood to have great antiquity as well as significance for the well being of the village. [Video link 10. Ramesh_ seethakalimatha on CD] The complicated relationship of the old and new is witnessed in this narration as below:

My name is Ramesh and Sri Seetha Kalimatha temple and other shrines are very old ones. Generally the Lodha Community used to visit and celebrate weeklong Utasavalu during Ugadi festival time. Tonsure (*keshakadanam*) is a common practice during the celebrations for all the age groups and especially for children. At present, because of restrictions from Emmaar and other developments near the temple we are facing many problems for regular celebrations.

This complicated relationship gets aggravated when an entire shrine is uprooted and its re-establishment has to be done (Figure 9.9). This was narrated to us with great indignation on Shivratri day celebrations wherein a new Shiva shrine was being relocated from its original location in what is now called the Emaar Properties to the Outer Ring Road near the L & T apartment complexes.

Source: Photo taken by the author.

Figure 9.9: Uprooted and now re-located Shiva Linga Shrine, Nanakramguda

Innumerable shrines and locations devoted to the worship of Lord Shiva were found adjoining other main temples clearly indicating the importance of this deity for local sensibilities

Some of the annual festivals have been studied and recorded by us through the one year (2012-13) of data collection. Like elsewhere, in this locality too, the Bonalu and Battukamma festivals have a special significance especially for women. They are closely related to fertility rites and therefore, are celebrated with earnestness and dedicated belief. Something integral to the community are the Ugadi festivities, clearly linked to the beginning of the New Year. We recorded the weeklong celebrations around Ugadi near the Seetha Kalimatha shrines. The traditional Shivaratri and Sri Ramanvami celebrations have different sections of the village devotees throng to these temples and both these were recorded; the former at Gowlidodhi and the latter at Nanakramguda.

Clearly, the format of their celebrations has changed incorporating new objects and material. One cannot conclude that there is something unique about the attachment of the people of Nanakramguda to these festivals. Rather, it is their particular persistence and reinvention in some cases that draws our attention. In an environment that is swaying the social and cultural ethos with modern gadgets and the television revolution we end with Ashoka Achary's simple observation [Video link 15. Gandi Mysamma on CD with the author] about the festivities on Ugadi day at the Gandi Maisamma shrine. This, as mentioned above, is seen as the deity that led to the establishment and protection of Nanakramguda. It is worth noting what he says:

> I was born and brought up in the village (Nanakramguda). We have been celebrating Gandi Mysamma Utsavalu from my childhood and still we are continuing the same. The only difference from past to present is that the youth is very much involved now a days in these celebrations. Earlier we used to have celebrations but they were not so active. We celebrated weeklong celebrations every year during Ugadi festival time.

It keeps us pondering as to why the youth is getting more attracted to securing this deity and its reinvention. There is indeed a cognitive space that they are clinging to that will, in turn, define their sense of 'belonging' to the place. In fact, at the beginning of the data collection in 2012 we found the shrine of Gandi Mysamma to be very simple and with a bare minimum of image and ritual items but, as we ended our work in the village in May 2013 we noticed a huge painting of Goddess Kali, a more Sanskritized manifestation of the goddess, came to occupy the same space. So here we are not seeing a mere clinging to the past and the place. But rather, the reinvention of the past in modern terms that will appeal to a new set of settlers to Nanakramguda that at this historical point in time enables them to accommodate new circumstances that have been thrown before them as its inhabitants. The symbolism of the past is thus being asserted but in visually understandable ways to a larger community so that it is not lost forever.

All of the above respondents referred to the past through terms like 'old days', 'long back', 'earlier days', 'the past', 'ancestors', 'tradition', 'earlier generations' and the like, which clearly indicates that there was no specific time period that they were referring to. In one case we have the use of the phrase 'the past eighty years' and in another the 'period of Nizam's rule'. Secondly, in all of the above narrations, the past is almost always linked to the present and very much rooted to what has materially happened to the community in contrast to what they have inherited. Further, these narrations present before us layers of new migrants entering the village from time to time beginning with the service working classes who came here looking for work, and those that later entered through state intervention or personal acquisitions of land and property. This meeting of peoples and cultures is somewhat typical of the Telangana region that we alluded to at the beginning. Nonetheless, each of them has begun to own the place called Nanakramguda. Yet, boundaries remain, as notions of the personal and group identity are intact even today despite many of them having moved out of their traditional occupations. So there is no 'original' inhabitant and no permanent 'outsider' except the ones who live totally outside the boundaries of what is defined as the settlement called Nanakramguda. However, how has the movement of peoples after the IT revolution impacted this definition of the 'Self'? We were able to assess this in the way the inhabitants of the inner core of the Nanakramguda *basti* linked their selfhood to the cultural symbols and festivals that had been part of their continuing tradition. All of these are couched in the minds—cognitive space—of the people carried forward from generation to generation. This clearly distinguishes them from the new settlers for whom such rites of passage, religious symbols, old wayside shrines and cultural practices around seasonal festivals were but remnants of a superstitious past that could be done away with. At best, the new settlers look at these annual recurrences as exotic and colourful symbols that have to be tolerated with a sense of resignation. For this set of 'migrants' and professionals, the development of the twenty first century is about the present and the future and not the past.

The journey of Nanakramguda has passed through the vicissitudes of time that we have only partially been able to capture—glimpses, that try to understand economic levels of subsistence that have always needed improvements, to the way the social and religious landscape of the settlement has evolved. Generally, it is assumed and imagined and, often feared, that the present fast track changes would destroy the past totally. But if this happens so will the identity of people be gone forever. However, our conversations with the inhabitants have revealed that this is something that they do not wish to let go off. As the first year of our documentation in the village ended in 2013, the *Hindu* carried a short piece on Nanakramguda entitled 'Hamlet unchanged: Welcome to Nanakramguda'. Sandeep Kumar the reporter writes: 'Despite the real estate boom and influx of corporate structures, life in this village, hardly 4 km from Tolichowki, *is much the same. Residents still wake up at the crack of dawn and streets turn deserted at dusk*, except for the occasional cab and motorcyclist passing by. *People here still lead life at their own terms*, of course sans proper infrastructure.[29] [Emphasis added]

The reflections in the above journalistic piece are about the unequal access to resources and facilities that the inner core of the settlement has whereas it is surrounded by opulence of an unimaginable kind. While these conditions of materiality are important and deserve our attention, it is the tenacity of thoughts, emotions and social relations—all embedded in the cognitive space of people emanating out of these, that permit us to still access the cultural past of a community. We collect the voices of 'history' and make these voices preserve the community's past in ways that enriches our understanding of the present. We began with notions of time and space as articulated in contemporary understanding of memory. We also suggested above that when looking at the past of a small locality the absence of the written word in the form of texts impeded that retrieval. This study enabled me to question my own methods of doing conventional historical research that is heavily dependent on the written word and the archive. Through the cognitive space of orality and memory the social and cultural landscape of the locality was retrieved along with its flexible notions of space and time to understand long term historical perceptions. Erasure has its place but not for people who understand their past, not in an alien land of the past, but as a living present that is firmly sustained through sensibilities and cognition that live on in the intangible realm.

NOTES

1. This is a dictionary meaning drawn from http://dictionary.sensagent.com/cognitive%20space/en-en/ accessed 17 November 2015.
2. Discussed at length in Parasher Sen (2009: 183-207).
3. Lewis (1987: 11-12).
4. Parasher Sen (2018) gives an overview of this project work that continued till 2016.
5. I acknowledge the financial support received from the University of Hyderabad's UPE II programme funded by the UGC that sanctioned me a project, which was an initial pilot study on this theme in 2012-13.
6. Kapur (2004: 50). See also Venkatsubramanian (2001: 5).
7. As defined by the UNESCO at http://www.unesco.org/culture/ich/index.php?lg=en&pg=00002 accessed 2 February 2012.
8. Thapar (2004: 216) stresses the need for us to engage with the past in ways that incorporate *various concerns and perceptions while keeping the rigors and methods of historical research intact.* [Emphasis added]
9. Those for the Medak and Ranga Reddy districts were consulted but little or no information on the villages under study around the University of

Hyderabad could be accessed. This chapter is focusing on only one of the villages under study, namely, Nanakramguda. On the whole twelve villages were studied in the UPE-II project under phase 2, 2014-16 and the archaeological data that these other villages threw up was different from that being discussed currently for Nanakramguda.

10. Gir in Bawa (2001: 20).
11. A printed brochure in Hindi with photos produced by the Shri Ranganath Mandir, Rangabag Trust, for Nanakramguda for instance, acted as a source of information.
12. Primarily based on oral conversations with caretakers of the shrine.
13. Parasher Sen with Himabindu (2006: 5-27).
14. Reddy (2008: 1-3) Chenna Reddy the then Director of the former Department of Archaeology and Museums, Government of Andhra Pradesh informed reporters about megalithic remains at the Kothaguda Botanical Gardens as reported to a news outlet.
15. Bawa (2001: 46-7).These excavations were conducted by the Commissioner, Archaeology and Museums, of the then Government of Andhra Pradesh, and written about. See also Rao (2010: 102-11).
16. *Hyderabad Urban Development Authority*, (1998) (Henceforth HUDA) 'March 1998 List of Heritage Buildings and Heritage Precincts (Rocks) in Hyderabad City' Vide G.O. Ms. No. 102 M.A. dated 23 March 1998, pp. 1-23.
17. HUDA (1998: 3-8).
18. HUDA (1998: 9) Annexure II.
19. HUDA (1998: 1).
20. HUDA in Bawa (2000: 58-9) No. 3195/PR/H/2000 dated 4 May 2000.
21. *Society to Save Rocks*, Hyderabad website http://www.saverocks.org/Geology.html accessed 31 January 2012.
22. bell hooks (2009: 1).
23. As part of this project under UPE-II we have procured old Revenue Maps of select villages wherever available and have used the data given therein on lakes, green patches etc. to plot historically important shrines, monuments by converting them into digital maps.
24. Acknowledgement: Photograph courtesy a printed brochure in Hindi printed by the Shri Ranganath Mandir, Rangabag Trust.
25. All maps for the research were made for the first time under this project.
26. Ritche (2003: 19).
27. Ritche (2003: 12).
28. The Documentary Film has captured snippets of how the village got its name. While an ancestor of this name emerges in the context of the

building of the Sri Ranganath Swamy shrine this name is reiterated in Narasimha's narration as Motilal Seth's ancestor. Balaram, on the other hand, an outsider to the village and a resident of Gowlidodhi narrates that his ancestors informed him that originally Nanakramguda was called 'Namakharamguda' alluding to the bullying tactics of the Lodhas who resided here and would apparently threaten and rob people and even trespass into their homes.

29. *The Hindu,* Hyderabad edition, 2 April 2013 Online accessed on 13 May 2013 at http://www.thehindu.com/news/cities/Hyderabad/hamlet-un-changed-welcome-to-nanakramguda/article4573961.ece

Bibliography

Alcock, Susan (2002), *Archaeologies of the Greek Past: Landscape, Monuments and Memories*, Cambridge University Press, Cambridge.

Allchin, B. & R. (1982), *Rise of Civilization in India and Pakistan*, Cambridge University Press (rpt. 1996, paperback edition).

Anand, Mulk Raj (1965), 'Conversation in Nagarjunakonda', *Marg*, Pathway, A Magazine of the Arts, vol. 18, no. 2, March, pp. 4-8.

Annual Report, Andhra Pradesh Department of Archaeology and Museums, 1978-9; 1984-5, Hyderabad.

Annual Report, Archaeological Survey of India, 1908-9, New Delhi.

Annual Report of Indian Epigraphy, 1960-2; 1964, Mysore.

Annual Reports, State Department of Archaeology and Museums, Government of Andhra Pradesh (1974-5), Hyderabad.

Avadhani, R. (2011), 'Discovery of Remains Throw Light on Vedic Religion', *The Hindu*, 28 February http://www.hindu.com/2011/02/28/stories/2011022863950600.htm (last accessed 8 October 2011) Online edition.

Bawa, V.K., ed. (2001), 'Excavations at a Megalithic Burial Site: A Menhir at Lingampalli, RR District, AP', reported by Commissioner of Archaeology, Government of Andhra Pradesh in *Huda-Intach Heritage Annual.*

Banerjee, N.R. (1965), *The Iron Age in India*, Munshiram Manoharlal, Delhi.

Basham, A.L. (1954), *The Wonder that was India*, Sidgwick and Jackson, London.

Begley, Vimla (1981), 'From Iron Age to Early Historical in South Indian Archaeology', in J. Jacobson, ed., *Studies in the Archaeology of India and Pakistan,* AIIS, Oxford and IBH, New Delhi, pp. 299-301.

—— (1996) *Ancient Port of Arikamedu: New Excavations and Researches 1989-92*, vol. 1, Pondicherry.

bell hooks (2009), *Belonging: A Culture of Place*, Routledge Taylor and Francis, New York.

Bhardwaj, H.C. (1979), *Aspects of Ancient Indian Technology*, Motilal Banarsidass, Delhi.

Bilgrami, Syed Ali Asgar (1927), *Landmarks of the Deccan: 'A Comprehensive*

Guide to the Archaeological Remains of the City and Suburbs of Hyderabad, The Government Central Press, Hyderabad: Deccan.

Boussac, Marie Francoise and Jean-Francois Salles, eds. (1995), *Athens Aden Arikamedu: Essays on Interrelations between India, Arabia and the Eastern Mediterranean*, Manohar, New Delhi.

Braudel, Fernand (1980), trans. Sarah Mathews, *On History*, University of Chicago Press, Chicago.

Burgess, Jas (1883), *Report on the Buddhist Cave Temples and Their Inscriptions*, Trübner & Co., London.

Census of India, Medak District, Government of Andhra Pradesh, 1997, rpt.

Chakravarti, Dilip K. (1985), 'The Issues of the Indian Iron Age', in S.B. Deo and K. Paddayya, eds., *Recent Advances in Indian Archaeology*, Deccan College, Poona.

Champakalakshmi, R. (1975-6), 'Archaeology and Tamil Literary Tradition', *Puratattva*, vol. 8, pp. 110-22.

—— (1986), 'Urbanization in South India: The Role of Ideology and Polity', Presidential Address, Section I, *Proceedings of the Indian History Congress* 47th Session, Srinagar, pp. 1-35.

Chapekar, B.N. (1969), *Report on the Excavation at Ter (1958)*, Deccan College, Poona.

Chatterjee, Anjana (1976), 'Socio Economic Conditions in Early Andhra 200 BC-300 AD', unpublished Ph.D. thesis, Jawaharlal Nehru University, New Delhi.

Chattopadhyaya, B.D. (1987), 'Transition to the Early Historical Phase in the Deccan: A Note', in B.M. Pande and B.D. Chattopadhyaya, eds, *History and Archaeology*, vol. II, Agam Kala Prakashan, New Delhi, pp. 727-9.

Chattopadhyaya, Sudhakar (1974), *Some Early Dynasties of South India*, Motilal Banarsidass, Delhi.

Childe, V.G. (1955), *Man Makes Himself*, Mentor Books, London (2nd edn.).

—— (1957), 'Civilization, Cities and Towns', *Antiquity*, vol. 31, March, pp. 97-120.

—— (1978) [rpt.], *What Happened in History*, Penguin, Harmondsworth.

Cohen, Ronald (1978), 'State Origins: A Reappraisal', in H.J.M.Claessen and Peter Skalnik, eds., *The Early State: Theories and Hypotheses*, Mouton, The Hague, pp. 31-75.

—— (1981), 'Evolution, Fission and the Early State', in H.J.M. Claessen and Peter Skalnik, eds., *The Study of the Slate*, Mouton, The Hague, pp. 81-115.

Collingwood, R.G. (1946), *The Idea of Prehistory*, Clarendon Press, Oxford.

Claessen, H.J.M. and Peter Skalnik, eds. (1978), *The Early State: Theories and Hypotheses*, Mouton, The Hague.

Cummings, Ralph W. (1973-4), *Historic Relics of ICRISAT Centre—A Report*, ICRISAT, Hyderabad.

Das, Jithendra (2008), 'Historical Site Discovered at Kondapur', *The Hindu*, 1 December, http://www.hindu.com/2008/01/12/stories/2008011254960500.htm (last accessed 8 October 2011). Online Edition.

De Certeau, Michel (1988), *The Writing of History*, Columbia University Press. New York.

Deo, S.B. (1956), *History of JainaMonachism from Inscriptions and Literature*, Deccan College, Dissertation Series 17, Poona.

—— (1985), 'Megaliths: Their Culture, Ecology, Economy and Technology', in S.B. Deo and K. Paddayya (eds.), *Recent Advances in Indian Archaeology*, Deccan College, Poona.

—— (1985), 'Historical Archaeology: Review and Perspective', in K.N. Dikshit, ed., *Archaeological Perspective on India since Independence*, Books and Books, New Delhi.

Deo, S.B. and K. Paddayya, eds. (1985) *Recent Advances in Indian Archaeology*, Deccan College, Poona.

Devahuti, D., ed. (1979), *Problems of Indian Historiography*, D.K. Publications, Delhi.

Davis, Natalie Zemon (1983), *The Return of Martin Guerre*, Harvard University Press, Cambridge, Mass.

Dhavalikar, M.K. (1985), 'Cultural Ecology of Chalcolithic Maharashtra', in S.B. Deo and K. Paddyya, eds., *Recent Advances in Indian Archaeology*, Deccan College, Poona.

—— (1973), 'Development and Decline of the Deccan Chalcolithic', in D.P. Agarwal and A. Ghosh, eds., *Radio Carbon and Indian Archaeology*, Tata Institute of Fundamental Research, Bombay, pp. 138-47.

Deshpande, M.N. (1963), 'Classical Influence of Indian Terracotta Art', in *Huitieme Congress International d'Arcahaeologie Classique*, E. de Boccard Conference Publication, Paris.

Dikshit, M.G. (1952), *Beads from Kondapur*, Archaeological Series No. 16, Government of Andhra Pradesh, Hyderabad.

—— (1949), *Etched Beads in India*, Monograph Series 4, Deccan College, Poona.

Epigraphia Indica (1973), vol. II, Delhi.

Erdosy, Gregory (1988), *Urbanization in Early Historic India*, BAR International Series, 430.

Fogelin, Lars (2005), 'Recent Research at the Buddhist Monastery of Thotlakonda', in C. Jarrige and V. Lefevre, eds., *South Asian Archaeology*, 2001, vol. 2, 2 vols., Editions Recherche Sur les Civilizations—ADPF, Paris, pp. 483-9.

—— (2011), *Archaeology of Early Buddhism*, Dev Books, New Delhi.

Francis, N.J. (2005), 'The Institutional Base of Early Buddhist Art at Amaravati', *Journal of Deccan Studies*, vol. III, no. 3: 1, January-July, pp. 47-89.

Frere, Mary (1989) *Old Deccan Days, or Hindoo Fairy Legends Current in Southern India Collected from Oral Tradition* [with an introduction and notes Bartle Frere], 4th edn., revd., Asian Educational Services, New Delhi, Madras. First published 1889.

Fussman, Gerrad (1987), 'Central and Provincial Administration in Ancient India: The Problem of the Mauryan Empire', *Indian Historical Review*, vol. XIV, nos. 1-2, pp. 64-7.

Gairola, K.C. (1955), 'The Administrative Structure of the Sātavāhana Empire', *Arts and Letters*, vol. XXIX, no. 2, pp. 42-6.

Granoff, Phyllis (1998) (Selected, Translated and with an Introduction), *The Forest of Thieves and the Magic Garden*, An Anthology of Medieval Jain Stories, Penguin Classics.

Ginzburg, Carlo (1980), *The Cheese and the Worms: The Cosmos of a Sixteenth Century Miller*, Johns Hopkins University Press, Baltimore.

Gir, Lalita (2001), 'Memories of Sheikhpet and Tolichowki in the Early 1960's, in V.K. Bawa, ed., *Huda-Intach Heritage Annual*. The Indian National Trust for Art and Cultural Heritage (INTACH), Hyderabad.

Gopalachari, K. (1941), *Early History of the Andhra Country*, University of Madras, Madras.

Green, Sally (1981), Introduction in V.G. Childe, *Man Makes Himself*, First Illustrated edition, Moonraker Press, Bradford-on-Avon, Wiltshire.

Gupta, Harsh K., Aloka Parasher Sen and D. Balasubramaniam, eds. (2000), *Deccan Heritage*, Indian National Science Academy, Universities Press, Hyderabad.

Gupta, P.L. (1990), 'Coins from Archaeological Excavations in Deccan', paper presented at Colloquium on South Indian Archaeology, Birla Archaeological and Cultural Research Institute, Hyderabad, 19-21 January.

—— (1963), *The Amaravati Hoard of Silver Punch-Marked Coins*, Andhra Pradesh Government Museum Series No. 6, Hyderabad.

Gupta, Sunil (2005), 'A Historiographical Survey of Studies on Indo-Roman Sea Trade and Indian Ocean Trade', *Indian Historical Review*, vol. 32, no.1, pp. 140-64.

Gurukkal, Rajan (1989), 'Forms of Production and Forces of Change in Ancient Tamil Country', *Studies in History* (New Series), vol. 5, no. 2, pp. 159-75.

—— (1998), 'Characterizing Ancient Society: The Case of South India', Presidential Address, Ancient India Section, Indian History Congress, Punjabi University, Patiala, 59th Session.

Hart III, G.L. (1976), 'Ancient Tamil Literature: Its Scholarly Past and Future', in B. Stein, ed., *Essays on South India*, Vikas Publishing House, New Delhi.

Hiebert, Paul G. (1975-6), 'A Brief History of Patancheru or Poṭṭaḷakere, Andhra Pradesh', *Journal of the Andhra Historical Research Society*, XXXVI (II-IV), pp. 1-12.

Heitzman, James (1997), *Gifts of Power: Lordship in an Early Indian State*, Oxford University Press, Delhi.

—— (1984), 'Early Buddhism, Trade and Empire', in K.A.R. Kennedy and Gregory L. Possehl (ed.), *Studies in Archaeology and Plaeoanthroplogy of South Asia*, American Institute of Indian Studies, New Delhi.

Hodder, Ian (1986), *Reading the Past: Current Approaches to Interpretation in Archaeology*. Cambridge University Press, Cambridge.

Hussain, Khwaja (1985), 'Local History', Presidential Address, *Proceedings of Andhra Pradesh History Congress*, IX Session, Kurnool.

Hyderabad Metropolitan Development Authority (2009), 'Declaration of Heritage Precincts in Hyderabad Metropolitan Development Authority Area—Final Notification', Department of Municipal Administration and Urban Development.

—— (1998), 'March 1998, List of Heritage Buildings and Heritage Precincts (Rocks) in Hyderabad City'.

—— (2000), 'Notification: Save Lakes for a Better Future', in V.K. Bawa (ed.), *Huda-Intach Heritage Annual*. The Indian National Trust for Art and Cultural Heritage (INTACH), Hyderabad.

Indian Archaeology: A Review (1954-60); (1962-79), Archaeological Survey of India, New Delhi.

Jain, J.C. (1947), *Life in Ancient India as Depicted in the Jain Canon*, New Bombay Book Company, Bombay.

Jain, J.P. (1977), *Religion and Culture of the Jains*, Bharatiya Jnanpitha, New Delhi.

Kane, P.V. (1973), *History of Dharmasastra*, vol. IV, Bhandarkar Oriental Research Institute, Poona.

Kapur, Kirti (2004), 'Department of Art, Culture and Language: An Analysis', Department of the National Capital Territory, Centre for Civil Society, New Delhi.

King, Anna (1984), 'Some Archaeological Problem regarding Gangetic Cultures in Early Historical India', in Kenneth A.R. Kennedy and Gregory L. Possehl, eds., *Studies in Archaeology and Palaeoanthropology of South Asia*, American Institute of Indian Studies, New Delhi.

Khazanov, A.M. (1978), 'Some Theoretical Problems of the Study of the Early State', in H.J.M. Claessen and Peter Skalnik, eds., *The Early State: Theories and Hypotheses*, Mouton, The Hague, pp. 77-92.

Kumar, Sandeep (2013), 'Hamlet Unchanged: Welcome to Nanakramguda' *The Hindu,* Hyderabad edition, 2 April. Online accessed on 13 May 2013.

Krishnasastry, V.V. (1978), 'Archaeological Discoveries in Andhra Pradesh', in B.K. Gururaja Rao, ed., *A Decade of Archaeological Studies in South India,* Karnataka University Press, Dharwar, pp. 1-6.

—— (1981), 'Recent Archaeological Discoveries of the Sātavāhana Period in Andhra Pradesh', in P. Sitapati, ed. (1981), *Sātavāhana Seminar Souvenir,* Special Issue, Hyderabad.

—— (1983), *Proto and Early Historical Cultures of Andhra Pradesh,* Archaeological Series 58, Government of Andhra Pradesh, Hyderabad.

—— (1990), 'Recent Trends in Archaeology of Andhra Pradesh', Presidential Address, Section V, Indian History Congress, Calcutta, 51st Session.

Lewis, Bernard (1987), *History: Remembered, Recovered, Invented,* Touchstone Edition (Princeton University Press, 1st pub. 1975).

Lüders, H. (1973), 'A List of Brahmi Inscriptions from the Earliest Times to about AD 400', Appendix to *Epigraphia Indica,* vol. X, Delhi.

Lynton, Nandani (1984), 'The Use of Ethno-archaeology in Interpreting South Asian Prehistory', in K.A.R. Kennedy and G.L. Possehl, eds., *Studies in the Archaeology and Paleoanthropology of South Asia,* American Institute of Indian Studies, New Delhi.

Maheshwari, G. (2010), 'Excavation Work at Kondapur, Medak District Andhra Pradesh', http://archaeologyexcavations.blogspot.com/2010/08/excavation-work-at-kondapur-district.html (last accessed on 8 October 2011).

—— (2011), *The Hindu,* 28 February, http://www.hindu.com/2011/02/28/stories/ 2011022863950600.htm (last accessed on 28 October 2011), 5 August. Online edition.

Majumdar, R.C., ed. (1968), *The Age of Imperial Unity,* 4th edn., Bharatiya Vidya Bhavan, Bombay.

Maloney, Clarence (1976), 'Archaeology in South India: Accomplishments and Prospects', in Burton Stein, ed., *Essays on South India,* Vikas Publishing House, New Delhi, pp. 1-40.

Margabandhu, C. (1985), *Archaeology of the Sātavāhana Kshatrapa Times,* Sundeeep Prakashan, New Delhi.

—— (2005), 'Roman Influence on the Art of Clay Modelling of the Satavahanas: A Study in Cultural Fusion', *Indian Historical Review,* vol. 32, no. 1, pp. 165-88.

Mcdams, Robert (1966), *Evolution of Urban Society: Early Mesopotamia and Pre-Hispanic Mexico,* Aldine, Chicago.

Mitra, Debala (1969), 'Foreign Elements in Indian Population in S.K. De, U.N. Ghoshal, A.D. Pusalker and R.C. Hazra, eds, *The Cultural Heritage of India*, vol. II, Ramakrshna Mission Institute of Culture, Calcutta, pp. 610-26.

—— (1980 [rpt.]), *Buddhist Monuments,* Sahitya Samsad, Calcutta.

Morrison, Kathleen D. (1995), 'Trade, Urbanism, and Agricultural Expansion: Buddhist Monastic Institutions and the State in the Early Historic Western Deccan', *World Archaeology*, vol. 27, no. 2, pp. 208-21.

—— (2002), 'South Asia: Introduction', in Kathleen Morrison and Laura L. Junker, eds., *Forager-Traders in South and Southeast Asia, Long Term Histories*, Cambridge University Press, Cambridge.

Murthy, M.L.K. (1979), 'Ekistic and Subsistence Patterns in Prehistoric Archaeology of Andhra Pradesh', *Andhra Pradesh Journal of Archaeology,* vol. I, no. 1, pp. 13-19.

Murthy, Narasimha A.V. (2000), 'Early Historic Cultures of Karnataka', in G. Kamalakar, ed., *South Indian Archaeology*, Bharatiya Kala Prakashan, New Delhi.

Murthy, S.S. Ramachandra (1985), *A Study of Telugu Place Names*, Agam Kala Prakashan, New Delhi.

Murthy, Y. Balarama (1981 [rpt.]), *Andhrula Sankshipta Charitra* (Telugu), Visalaandhra Publishing House, Vijayawada.

Nagaraju, S.N. (1981), *Buddhist Architecture, of Western India, c. 250 BC-AD 300*, Agam Kala Prakashan, Delhi.

Nandi, R.N. (1973), *Religious Institutions and Cults in the Deccan (c. AD 600-1000)*, Motilal Banarsidass, Delhi.

—— (1986), *The Social Roots of Religion in Ancient India*, New Bagchi and Co., Calcutta.

Paddayya, K. (2005), 'Colonel Colin Mackenzie and the Discovery of the Amaravati Site', *Journal of Deccan Studies*, vol. 3, no. 1, pp. 28-31.

—— (2019), *Neolithic Ashmounds of the Deccan: Their Place in the Archaeology of Peninsular India*, Aryan Books International, New Delhi.

Prasad, P.R.K. (1993), 'Sada Coins in Coastal Andhra', in A.V. Narasimha Murthy (ed.), *Studies in South Indian Coins,* 3, New Era Publications, Madras, pp. 53-62.

—— (1999), 'Pre-Sātavāhana Phase at Amaravati-Dharanikota', in Ajay Mitra Sastri (ed.), *The Age of the Sātavāhanas*, vol. II, Aryan Books International, Delhi, pp. 327-40.

Prasad, N.R. (1993), *Recent Buddhist Discoveries in Visakhapatnam District Andhra Pradesh: Relic Caskets at Bavikonda*, State Department of Archaeology and Museums, Hyderabad.

—— (1994), *Bavikonda: A Buddhist Site in North Coastal Andhra Pradesh*, State Department of Archaeology and Museums, Hyderabad.

Premi, N.R. (1956), *Jaina Sahitya Aura Itihasa*, Hindi Granth Karyalaya, Bombay.

Rao, M.S. Nagaraja [with contributions by K.R. Alur and Vishnu Mittre] (1971), *Protohistoric Cultures of the Tungabhadra Valley: A Report on Hallur Excavations*, Published by the author, Dharwar.

Rao, M. Malleswara (2008), 'Historical Site Discovered at Kondapur', *The Hindu*, 12 January, http://www.hindu.com/2008/01/12/stories/ 2008011254 960500.htm (last accessed on 8 October 2011), Online edition.

Ramaswamy, N.S. (1974), *Amarāvatī: The Art and History of the Stūpa and the Temple*, Government of Andhra Pradesh, Hyderabad.

Rao, B.K. Gururaja (1972), *The Megalithic Culture of South India*, Prasaranga University of Mysore, Mysore.

Rao, B.S.L. Hanumantha (1993), *Religion in Andhra* (a Survey of Religious Developments in Andhra from early times up to AD 1325), 2nd edn., Archaeological Series No. 69, Department of Archaeology and Museums, Government of Andhra Pradesh, Hyderabad, 1st edn., 1973.

Rao, K.P. (2010), 'Gacchi Bowli: A Preliminary Report', *Puratattva*, Bulletin of the Indian Archaeology Society, no. 40, pp. 102-11.

Rao, J. Varaprasad (2001), *Prehistoric Environment and Archaeology of the Krishna Tungabhadra Doab*, Bharatiya Kala Prakashan, New Delhi.

Rao, M. Rama (1961), *Sātavāhana Coins in the Andhra Pradesh Government Museum*, Government of Andhra Pradesh, Hyderabad.

Rapson, E.J. (1908), *Coins of the Andhra Dynasty, the Western Kshatrapas, the Traikutaka Dynasty and the 'Bodhi' Dynasty*, Longman and Company, London.

Ray, Amita (1983), *Life and Art in Early Andhradesa*, Agam Kala Prakashan, Delhi.

Ray, H.P. (1986), *Monastery and Guild: Commerce under the Sātavāhanas*, Oxford University Press, Delhi.

—— (1995), 'A Resurvey of "Roman" Contacts with the East', in Marie Francoise Boussac and Jean-Francois Salles, eds., *Athens, Aden, Arikamedu: Essays on the Interrelations between India, Arabia and the Eastern Mediterranean*, Manohar, New Delhi, pp. 97-114.

Raychaudhuri, H.C. (1982 [rpt.]), 'The Geography of the Deccan', in G. Yazadani (ed.), *The Early History of the Deccan*, pts. I-IV, Oxford University Press, New Delhi, pp. 3-15.

Rea, Alexander (1894), *South Indian Buddhist Antiquities*, Government Press, Madras.

Reddy, Chenna P. (2008), 'Hyderabad's History could date back to 500 BC',

Thaindian News, 10 September 2008, pp. 1-3 accessed online on 12 November 2015.

Reddy, D.R. and P.S.N. Reddy (1984), *Uninscribed Coins in Andhra*, Numismatic Society of Hyderabad, Hyderabad

—— (1993a), *Kotalingala Coinage of Sātavāhanas and Other Local Rulers: A Profile*, Numismatic Society of Hyderabad, Hyderabad.

—— (1993b), *Coins of the Megha Vahana Dynasty of Coastal Andhra*, Numismatic Society of Hyderabad, Hyderabad.

Reddy, E. Siva Nagi et al. (2008), *Buddhist Archaeology in Andhra Pradesh*, Department of Archaeology and Museums, Government of Andhra Pradesh, Hyderabad.

Review Essay (1994) on Jacque Le Goff's 'History and Memory', in *History and Theory*, vol. 33, no. 1.

Ritche, Donald (2003), *Doing Oral History: A Practical Guide*, Oxford University Press, New York.

Romanis, F. De and A. Tchernia (1997), *Crossings: Early Mediterranean Contacts with India*, Manohar, New Delhi.

Rouse, Irving (1972), 'Settlement Patterns in Archaeology', in Ruth Tringham (with Peter Ucko and G.W. Dimbleby, eds., *Man, Settlement and Urbanism*, Proceedings of a meeting of the Research Seminar in Archaeology and Related Subjects held of the Institute of Archaeology, London University, Duckworth, London.

Roy, Anamika (1994), *Amaravati Stūpa*, 2 vols, Agam Kala Prakashan, Delhi.

Sarkar, H. (1986), 'Growth of Cities in Andhradesa 200 BC-AD 200', Presidential Address, *Proceedings of the Andhra Pradesh History Congress*, 10th Session, Guntur.

—— (1987), 'Emergence of Urban Centres in Early Historical Andhradesa', in B.M. Pande and B.D. Chattopadhyaya (eds), *Archaeology and History: Essays in Memory of Shri A. Ghosh*, vol. II, Agam Kala Prakashan, New Delhi, pp. 630-45.

Sarkar, H. and M.D. Khare (1966), 'Kesarapalli 1962', *Ancient India*, no. 22, pp. 37-74.

Sarma, I.K. (1971), 'Nagarjunakonda Tavvakallo Dorikina Nanem Accuhmukka', *Bharati* (in Telugu), January, pp. 3-15.

—— (1975a), 'Amaravati Stupamu: Neti Puravastru Parisodhanalu', *Bharati* (in Telugu), August, pp.15-21.

—— (1975b), 'Some Inscriptions from Amaravati Excavations and the Chronology of Mahāstūpa', *Studies in Indian Epigraphy*, vol. I, pp. 60-74.

—— (1980), *Coinage of the Sātavāhanas Empire*, Agam Kala Prakashan, New Delhi.

—— (1985), 'Early Sculptures and Epigraphs from South-East India: New

Evidence from Amaravati', in Frederick M. Asher and G.S. Gai, eds., *Indian Epigraphy: Its Bearing on the History of Art,* Oxford and IBH: American Institute of Indian Studies, New Delhi, pp. 15-25.

—— (1988), *Studies in Early Buddhist Monuments and Brāhmī Inscriptions of Andhradeśa,* Dattsons Publishers, Nagpur.

—— (1994), 'Some Early Telugu Inscriptions', *Epigraphia Andhrica,* vol. IV.

—— (1999), 'New Evidence on the Early Sātavāhana Coinage Culture and Commerce', in Ajay Mitra Sastri, ed., *The Age of the Sātavāhanas,* Aryan Books International, New Delhi, pp. 341-8.

Sarma, M. Radhakrishna (1972), *Temples of Telangana,* Munshiram Manoharlal, New Delhi.

——, ed. (with K.D. Abhyankar and S.G. Moghe) (1987), *History of Hyderabad District 1879-1950,* Bharatiya Itihasa Sankalana Samiti, Hyderabad.

Sarma, Nagabhushan M., M. Sastry Veerabhadra and C. Seshagiri Rao (eds.), 1995, *History and Culture of the Andhras,* Potti Sriramula Telugu University, Hyderabad.

Sastri, Ajay Mitra (1978). 'Satyabhadra, A Hitherto Unknown Ruler of Vidarbha', *Annals of the Bhandarkar Oriental Research Institute,* Diamond Jubilee number, pp. 963-7.

—— (1981), 'Pre-Satavahana and Satavahana Coinage of the Deccan', *Journal of the Numismatic Society of India,* vol. 43, no.1, pp. 1-16.

—— (1982), 'Pre-Sātavāhana and Sātavāhana Coinage of the Deccan', *Journal of the Numismatic Society of India,* vol. 44, pp. 2-6.

—— (1987),*Early History of the Deccan: Problems and Perspectives,* Sundeep Prakashan, New Delhi.

—— ed. (1999), *The Age of the Satavahanas,* Aryan Books International, Delhi.

Sastri, K.A.N. (1987 [rpt.]), *A History of South India: From Pre-Historic Times to the Fall of Vijayanagara,* Oxford University Press, Madras.

Sastry, P.V.P. (1978), 'Unknown Coins of Sātavāhana and their Predecessors', *Numismatic Digest,* vol. 2, no. 1, pp, 10-21.

—— (1979a), 'Coins of Simuka Sātavāhana Discovered', *Andhra Pradesh Journal of Archaeology,* vol. I, no. 1, pp. 133-9.

—— (1979b), 'Some More Coins from Kotalingala', *Numismatic Digest,* vol. 3: 1 and 2, pp. 17-28.

—— (1989), 'Political System in Early Coastal Andhra', in Devendra Handa, ed., *Ajaya Sri: Recent Studies in lndology,* 2 vols., Munshiram Manoharlal, Delhi.

—— (1992), *Vaddamanu Excavations and Explorations in the Krishna Valley* (1981-5), Birla Archaeological and Research Institute, Hyderabad.

—— (1994), *Satavahana Epoch: A New Light,* A Telugu Goshti Publication, Hyderabad.

Sastry, T.V.G., M. Kasturi Bai and J. Varaprasad Rao (1984), *Veerapuram: A Type Site for Cultural Study in the Krishna Valley,* Birla Archaeological and Research Institute, Hyderabad.

Sastry, T.V.G. (1989), 'Early History of Jainism' and 'An Earliest Jaina Site in the Krishna Valley', *Arhat Vacana,* vol. 1, nos. 3-4, June-September.

—— (2004), 'An Unwritten Chapter in the History of Early Deccan', in Aloka Parasher Sen, ed. (assisted by B. Subrahmanyam and E. Siva Nagi Reddy), *Kevala-Bodhi, Buddhist and Jaina History of the Deccan: The BSL Commemorative Volume,* Bharatiya Kala Prakashan, New Delhi, pp. 229-37.

Sateesh, P.V. (2001), 'Cultivating Diversity', *Sunday Magazine,* special issue on *Earthspaces, Hindu Folio,* 20 May 2001.

Schwartsberg, S. (1978), *A Historical Atlas of South Asia,* University of Chicago Press, Chicago.

Sen, Aloka Parasher (1987), 'Kondapur: A Forgotten City (Reflections on the Early History of Telangana)', *Proceedings of the Indian History Congress,* 48th Session, 1987, Goa University, Bambolin, Panjim, pp. 82-90.

—— (1991), 'Social Structure and Economy of Settlements in the Central Deccan (200 BC-200 AD)', in Indu Banga, ed., *The City in Indian History,* Manohar, New Delhi, pp. 19-45 (also in *Social Science Probings,* 1988, March-December, pp. 1-19).

—— (1992), 'Nature of Society and Civilization in Early Deccan', *Indian Economic and Social History Review,* vol. 29, no. 4, pp. 437-77.

—— (1993), *Social and Economic History of the Deccan: Some Interpretations,* Manohar, New Delhi (rpt. 2019).

——(1996), 'Small Localities and the Writing of Regional History', Presidential Address, Section I, Ancient Andhra History and Archaeology, Proceedings of the Andhra Pradesh History Congress, 20th Session, Guntur.

——(1999), 'Urban Settlements in the Deccan and Sātavāhana History', in Ajay Mitra Sastri, ed., *The Age of the Sātavāhanas,* vol. I, Harananda Publications, New Delhi, pp. 153-91.

—— (2002), 'Lajja Gauri—The Universe Within and In/Out?', *Religioni et Societa,* vol. 44, pp. 13-41.

—— ed. (2004) (assisted by B. Subramanyam and E. Siva Nagi Reddy), *Kevala-Bodhi, Buddhist and Jaina History of the Deccan: The BSL Commemorative Volume,* 2 vols., Bharatiya Kala Prakashan, New Delhi.

—— (2006), 'The Making of Digital Historical Atlas: Some Examples from South India', *International Journal of Technology Knowledge and Society,* vol. 2, no. 4, pp. 9-18.

—— (2006) (with R. Himabindu), 'Understanding Local History: Archaeological Remains at Patancheru', *Journal of Deccan Studies,* vol. IV, no. 2, July-December.

—— (2007), 'Localities Coins and the Transition to the Early State in the Deccan', *Studies in History*, vol. 23, no. 2, pp. 231-69.

—— (2007a), 'Names, Travelers and Inscriptions in Early Historic India', *Indian Historical Review*, vol. XXXIV, no. 1, January, pp. 47-90.

—— (2008), 'Urban Centres—Deccan', in Gautam Sengupta and Sharmi Chakraborty, eds., *Archaeology of Early Historic South Asia*, Pragati Publications, New Delhi.

—— (2009), 'Perceptions of Time, Cultural Boundaries and "Region" in Early Indian Texts', *Indian Historical Review*, vol. 36, pt. 2, pp. 183-207.

—— (2018), 'Documenting Heritage of Localities around Hyderabad—Issues and Challenges', *eSocial Science*, 26 July. http://www.esocialsciences.org/Articles/Online Journal.

Senart, E. (1905-6), 'The Inscriptions in Caves at Nasik', *Epigraphica Indica*, vol. VIII.

Seneviratne, Sudarshan (1980-1), 'Kalinga and Andhra: The Process of Secondary State-Formation', *Indian Historical Review*, vol. 7, nos. 1 and 2, pp, 54-69.

Service, Elman R. (1975), *Origins of State and Civilization: The Processes of Cultural Evolution*, W.W. Norton and Company, New York.

Settar, S. (1986), *Historical Experiments on Sepulchral Hill*, Institute of Indian Art History, Karnatak University, Dharwad.

Sharma, Dinesh C. (2006), 'Development of Disaster?' 13 February 2005 hosted by website Boloji.com, 27 May.

Shah, Viraj (2007), 'Medieval Jaina Pilgrimage Centres in Maharashtra', *Journal of Deccan Studies*, Special Issue on Jainism (Guest Editor: Aloka Parasher Sen), vol. V, no. 1, January-June.

Shimada, Akira (2005), 'The Political Setting of the Amaravati Stupa: Recent Studies', *Journal of Deccan Studies*, vol. 3, no. 1, pp. 33-46.

Shrimali, K.M. (1988), 'Religion, Ideology and Society', Presidential Address, Ancient India Section, *Indian History Congress*, 49th Session, Karnataka University, Dharwad [rpt.].

Singh, Thakur Raja Ram (1979), 'Prehistoric and Early Historic Remains in Andhra Pradesh', *The Andhra Pradesh Journal of Archaeology*, vol. I, no. 1, pp. 1-12.

—— (1987), 'The Pre-Sātavāhana Andhra Kings of Central Godavari Valley, The Andhra Kings of Asmaka, Mulaka', paper presented at the UGC Seminar on Recent Archaeological Studies in Andhra Pradesh, Kakatiya University, Warangal, March.

—— (1995), 'The Pre-Sātavāhana Andhra Kings: A Fresh Study', *Journal of Archaeology*, Sātavāhana Special, vol. III, no. 2, 1995, pp. 1-37.

Singh, Upinder (2001), 'Amaravati: The Dismembering of the Mahacaitya (1797-1886)', *South Asian Studies*, vol. 17, no. 1, pp. 19-40.

Sircar, D.C. (1970), *Select Inscriptions Bearing on Indian Civilization*, vol. I, University of Calcutta, Calcutta.

Sivaramamurthy, C. (1942), *Amaravati Sculpture in the Madras Government Museum*, Government Press, Madras.

Sjoberg, G. (1957), *The Pre-Industrial City, Past and Present*, Glencoe, Illinois.

Skilling, Peter (2008), 'New Discoveries from South India: The Life of Buddha at Phanigiri, Andhra Pradesh', *Arts Asiatique*, vol. 63, pp. 96-118.

Soja, Edward W. (1989), *Post-Modern Geographies : The Reassertion of Space in Critical Social Theory*, Verso, New York.

Springborg, Patricia (1992), *Western Republicanism and the Oriental Prince*, Polity Press, Cambridge.

Stephens, W.B. (1977), *Teaching Local History*, Manchester University Press, Manchester.

Stevenson, S. (1915), *The Heart of Jainism*, Oxford University Press, Oxford.

Subbarao, B. (1958), *The Personality of India*, Faculty of Arts, University of Baroda, Baroda.

—— (2011), Regions and Regionalism in India, Critical Quest, rpt., New Social Sciences Library, New Delhi.

Subramanyam, B. (1997), *Pre- and Proto-historic Cultures of the Krishna Tungabhadra Valley*, Oxford and IBH Publishing Company, New Delhi.

Subrahmanyam, B. and E. Siva Nagi Reddy (2004), 'Recent Discoveries from Deccan', in Aloka Parasher Sen (ed.), *Kevala-Bodhi: Buddhist and Jaina History of the Deccan (The BSL Commemorative Volume)*, Bharatiya Kala Prakashan, New Delhi, vol. 2, pp. 365-8.

Subramanyam, B.J. Vijaya Kumar, G.V. Ramakrishna Rao, K.S.B. Kesava, (2008), *Phanigiri, A Buddhist Site in Andhra Pradesh (An Interim Report 2001-2007)*, Department of Archaeology and Museums, Government of Andhra Pradesh, Hyderabad.

Subramanyam, B.R. (1963), 'Appearance and Spread of Iron in India: An Appraisal of Archaeological Data', *Journal of the Oriental Institute*, vol. XIII, no. 1, pp. 351-3.

Subrahmanyam, R. (1965), *Nagarjunakonda, 1954-60*, vol. I, Memoirs of the Archaeological Survey of India, No. 75, Archaeological Survey of India, New Delhi.

—— (1968), *The Guntupalli Brahmi Inscriptions of Kharavela*, Andhra Pradesh Epigraphical Series 3, Hyderabad.

Sundara, A. (1984), 'Archaeology and National Integration', Presidential

Address, Section V, Indian History Congress, Annamalainagar, 45th Session.

Taylor, Griffith (ed.), *Geography in the Twentieth Century*, Metheun, London, 1953.

Taylor, Peter J. (2005), *Ecology, Interpretation Engagement*, University of Chicago Press, Chicago.

Thakur, V.K. (1981), *Urbanisation in Ancient India*, Abhinav Publications, New Delhi.

Thapar, Romila (1966), *A History of India*, vol. I, Penguin, London.

—— (1984), 'Interpretation of Ancient Indian History', in *Ancient Indian Social History: Some Interpretations*, Orient Longman, Delhi (rpt.).

—— (1987), *The Mauryas Revisited: S.G. Deuskar Lectures on Indian History*, Centre for Studies in Social Sciences, Calcutta.

—— (1997), 'Early Mediterranean Contact with India: An Overview', in F. De Romanis and A. Tchernia, *Crossings: Early Mediterranean Contacts with India*, Manohar, New Delhi.

—— (2004), *Somanath: The Many Voices of History*, Viking, Penguin Books, New Delhi.

Tiwari, A. (1980), 'Uninscribed Punch Marked Coins from Eran-Vidisa', *Numismatic Digest*, vol. 4, no. 1, pp. 4-10.

Tringham, Ruth (1980), 'The Concept of "Civilization" in European Archaeology', in I.A. Sabloff and C.C. Lamberg-Karlovsky, eds., *The Rise and Fall of Civilizations*, Cummings, California, pp. 410-84.

Todorov, Tzvetan (1986) (tr. Loulou Mack), 'Race, Writing and Culture', in Henry Louis Gates Jr. (ed.), *'Race', Writing and Difference*, The University of Chigao Press, Chicago.

Venkataramanayya, N. (1975-6), *Journal of the Andhra Historical Research Society*, Government of Andhra Pradesh, vol. 36, pt. II-IV.

Venkatsubramanian, K. (2001), *Report of the Steering Committee for Art and Culture, for the Formulation of the Tenth Five Year Plan (2002-7)*, Planning Commission, Government of India, New Delhi.

Wheeler, M. (1947-8), 'Brahmagiri and Chandravalli 1947: Megalithic and Other Cultures in the Chitaldurg District, Mysore State', *Ancient India*, no. 4, pp. 180-310.

White, Hayden (2005), 'Introduction: Historical Fiction, Fictional History, and Historical Reality', *Rethinking History*, vol. 9, nos. 2 and 3, June-September, pp. 147-57.

Yazdani, G. (1941), 'Excavations of Kondapur, An Andhra Town *c.* 200 BC-200 AD', *Annals of the Bhandarkar Oriental Research Institute*, vol. 13, nos. 3-4, pp. 171-85.

—— (1940-1), 'Kondapur Excavations', in *Annual Report,* Archaeology Department of H.E. the Nizam's Dominions, Hyderabad.
—— ed. (1982 [rpt.]), *The Early History of the Deccan*, I-IV, Oxford University Press, New Delhi.

WEBSITES

APDAM State Department of Archaeology and Museums, Government of Andhra Pradesh, Hyderabad http://museums.ap.nic.in/phanigiri.htm (last accessed 30 September 2011).
Archaeology Excavations Blogspot 'Excavation Work at Kondapur Medak District Andhra Pradesh', 5 August 2010 http://archaeology excavations. blogspot.com/2010/08/excavation-work-at-kondapur-district.html (last accessed on 8 October 2011).
Archaeological Survey of India, New Delhi http://asi.nic.in/asi_museums_kondapur.asp (last accessed on 8 October 2011).
Digital Historical Atlas for South India now accessible at the French Institute of Pondicherry Historical Atlas of South India Website: http://www.ifpindia.org/histatalas (last accessed 1 January 2010).
Taylor, Peter J., *Ecology, Interpretation Engagement*, University of Chicago Press, London, 2005.http://books.google.co.in/books google e-book select pages accessed 11 January 2014 pages displayed by permission of University of Chicago Press.
Skilling, Peter (2008), 'New Discoveries from South India: The Life of the Buddha at Phanigiri, Andhra Pradesh', *Arts Asiatiques*, vol. 63, pp. 96-118. doi: https://doi.org/10.3406/arasi.2008.1664 https://www.persee.fr/doc/arasi_0004-3958_2008_num_63_1_1664
Society of Save Rocks, Hyderabad website http://www.saverocks.org/Geology.html (last accessed on 31 January 2012).
The Hindu, Hyderabad edition, 2 April 2013 Online accessed on 13 May 2013 athttp://www.thehindu.com/news/cities/Hyderabad/hamlet-un-changed-welcome-to-nanakramguda/article4573961.ece
UNESCO at http://www.unesco.org/culture/ich/index.php?lg=en&pg=00002 accessed 2 February 2012.

Index

Made in the USA
Las Vegas, NV
23 October 2024

07ab089d-969e-41e6-9e20-a11b7273bdd9R01